2017-2020
The Rules in Practice

Bryan Willis

2017-2020
The Rules in Practice

Bryan Willis

FERNHURST
BOOKS

This edition published in 2016 by Fernhurst Books Limited
62 Brandon Parade, Holly Walk, Leamington Spa, Warwickshire, CV32 4JE
Tel: +44 (0) 1926 337488 | www.fernhurstbooks.com

First published in 1985 by Fernhurst Books
Subsequently published in 1989, 1993, 1997, 2001 & 2005 by Fernhurst Books and in 2009 & 2013 by Wiley Nautical,
an imprint of John Wiley & Sons Ltd

A catalogue record for this book is available from the British Library
ISBN 978-1-909911-52-9

Front cover photograph © Ocean Images

Design & typeset by PPL & Rachel Atkins
Illustrations by PPL
Printed in Italy by Printer Trento

MIX
Paper from
responsible sources
FSC® C015829

Contents

Introduction

This book is primarily for competitive sailors who race in dinghies and keelboats. The Racing Rules of Sailing apply to all forms of sailboat racing, though there are some variations for sailboards, kiteboards, match racing, team racing, radio-controlled boat racing, etc. I have aimed to examine about one hundred situations that are a regular feature of both championship and club racing. Unlike most other books on the racing rules, I look at these situations from the point of view of you, the helmsman. Placing you in each of the boats involved in turn, I explain your rights and your obligations. Being confident about this knowledge means you can avoid breaking a rule and having to take a penalty, and can concentrate on exploiting the situation to gain boat lengths over your immediate rivals.

It is a popular misconception that to be good at boat-to-boat tactics you need to know the rules. The rules, the rule numbers, the case law – all that can be sorted out before the start of the hearing if there is a protest. What you need to know out there on the water are your rights and your obligations; what you are allowed to do, and what you must and mustn't do. You need to know that automatically and subconsciously, so that you can concentrate on manoeuvring and sailing fast, to exploit the situation to the full. It is just as satisfying to come away from a mark in the lead having approached it in second place as it is to spend twenty minutes overhauling your rival with superior boat speed. Conversely, there is no satisfaction in sailing faster than everyone else on a leg if you throw away your position through being uncertain about your rights and obligations when you come to round the mark.

The book should also be useful in the preparation of a protest, or the defence should you be protested. Each situation shows the critical questions that have to be considered and that will determine the 'facts found' and, therefore, the result of the hearing.

Because almost all the rules of racing apply to the boats rather than to the people sailing them, most books on the rules, and indeed the rules themselves, use the pronoun 'she'. Since I aim to look at situations from the point of view of you, the helmsman, I use the pronoun 'you'; and for the helmsman of the other boat 'he' and 'him'.* However, bear in mind that it is what the boat does that matters. The intentions of the people sailing the boats are irrelevant (provided that they are not malicious). Even most hails are irrelevant. What each boat actually does is usually all that counts.

This ninth edition has been updated to comply with the changes that come into effect on 1st January 2017 published by World Sailing (formerly known as the International Sailing Federation).

My sincere thanks to Marianne Middelthon from Norway for her help and advice in updating the book. Her selfless dedication to the sport has become legendary.

*Publisher's note: or 'she' is implied throughout.

The Rule Changes

Every four years the rules are updated. In 1997 there was a major revision of rules and terminology. The old 'Yacht Racing Rules' became the new simplified 'Racing Rules of Sailing'. A leeward boat was no longer allowed to 'luff as she pleases' and everyone became required to try to avoid collisions. Every four years since 1997 a few new rules that change the way the game is played have been introduced, plus numerous small changes for improvement in clarity. The most significant changes from the 2013-2016 rules are included in this chapter.

If you are new to racing and this is your first book on the rules, you really don't need to read this section because comparing what the rules were, to what they are now, will be of little interest. Move on to the real-life situations, or put the book with your kit ready to refer to it if there is an incident you are unsure about. This section is for sailors who have been racing a while.

As usual there are many small changes aimed at making the rules easier to understand or less ambiguous. There are also some changes that affect the way we play the game of sailing, but you may be pleased that there are far fewer significant changes this time, compared with 4 years ago.

The International Sailing Federation, which changed its name from the 'International Yacht Racing Union' not so many years ago, has changed its name again, and is now known as 'World Sailing'.

A 'U' flag has been added to the Preparatory Signals, It looks like this:

It means 'Rule 30.3 is in effect' so you can expect to see it, sometimes, displayed on the starting vessel as the preparatory signal four minutes before a start.

Rule 30.3 (the 'U-flag rule') is a new rule: 'If flag U has been displayed, no part of a boat's hull, crew or equipment shall be in the triangle formed by the ends of the starting line and the first mark during the last minute before her starting signal. If a boat breaks this rule and is identified, she shall be disqualified without a hearing, but not if the race is restarted or resailed.'

So it is slightly less severe than 'the Black flag rule' which does not permit a boat breaking that rule to sail in a restarted or resailed race. The 'Black flag rule' (which used to be rule 30.3) is now rule 30.4.

Race officers now have the following choices for 'preparatory signals' to be displayed at four minutes before the start, to warn what will happen to boats that are in the triangle formed by the starting line and the windward mark (or, in the case of the I flag, not completely on the pre-course side of the starting line or its extensions) at any time in the final minute before the starting signal:

 P flag: no penalty - boats can return any way they like to the pre-start side before starting.

 I flag: boats must sail back across an extension (i.e. not across the line itself) to the pre-start side before starting.

 Z flag: boats get a 20% scoring penalty (even if the race is restarted or resailed, in which case they are permitted to take part). They still must come back to the pre-start side and start.

 Z+I flags: boats must sail back across an extension (i.e. not across the line itself) to the pre-start side before starting, and in addition they get a 20% penalty.

 U flag: boats breaking this rule are disqualified. However they can sail in the race if it is restarted or resailed.

 Black flag: boats breaking this rule are disqualified even if the race is restarted or resailed.

There is a new rule (rule 6) requiring competitors and support persons not to be involved in betting or corrupt practices.

There is a new rule (rule 7) requiring competitors and 'support persons' to comply with 'Regulation 35, Disciplinary, Appeals and Review Code'. To include coaches (and parents) in these obligations is an important change.

There are some long-anticipated rule changes to rule 69 (which is about cheating and bringing the sport into disrepute) which include a new requirement for competitors, owners and 'support persons' not to commit an act of misconduct, which, strangely, was missing from previous editions of the rules. ('Support persons' are defined as anyone who provides support to a competitor e.g. parent, coach, manager, etc.).

A new rule has been added to Rule 18.2 (Giving Mark-Room):

(d) Rules 18.2(b) and (c) cease to apply when the boat entitled to mark-room has been given that mark-room, or if she passes head to wind or leaves the zone. This clarifies the situation where the outside boat has given mark-room to the inside boat and the question arises as to when only the 'normal' rules apply. An outside leeward boat might want to luff. Once mark-room has been given then the outside boat's obligation to give mark-room has been satisfied. The inside keep-clear boat loses 'protection' once she has been given room. Basically if the inside boat is able to respond without risk of hitting the mark, then she must respond.

Rule 18.3 (Tacking in the Zone) has been rewritten; the rule now applies only at a port-hand mark. (It was confusing trying to apply it at a starboard-hand mark.) So now, approaching a port-hand windward mark, if you are tacking below or ahead of a starboard-tack boat, and as you go through head-to-wind and any part of your boat is inside the zone, then even though

you become the right-of-way boat (clear ahead or to leeward), if the starboard tacker is forced to sail above close-hauled to avoid you, you break this rule, or, if she was clear astern and then chooses to go below you, you must give her mark-room.

Rule 19.1 (Room to pass an obstruction) has been changed so as to remove the conflict that occurred when three boats all overlapped with each other approach a mark with the windward boat on the inside. Rule 19 used to require the windward (inside) boat to give room to the middle boat to keep clear of the outside (leeward) boat (an obstruction) but rule 18 required the middle boat to give room to the inside boat (to pass the mark). The new rule 19 (requiring the windward of three boats to give room to the middle boat) no longer applies at a mark, so it is clear that each of overlapping boats must give mark-room to the boat (or boats) inside her.

Rule 22.3: Dinghies hovering in a good place on the start line have developed a technique where they back the sail on the leeward side when heading above close-hauled on starboard tack. The sail unstalls, forcing the boat not just to move astern but also to windward. The boat ahead always did and still does lose her right-of-way status if she is moving astern by backing her sail. What has changed is that if she moves towards a boat to windward of her (i.e. on her windward side) she now loses her right-of-way status (as leeward boat) if this sideways momentum is caused by backing a sail. These activities of course are relevant only to light dinghies where position on the starting line is everything, and speed can be built up very quickly. Heavier boats don't hover! They approach the line with speed, maybe starting some distance from the favoured end, and gaining over the boats hovering at the favoured end who have to build speed. Rule 22.3 now reads: 'A boat moving astern, or sideways to windward, through the water by backing a sail shall keep clear of one that is not'.

Rule 49.2: If you sail a keelboat with lifelines, you might want them to be sloppy so that your crew can get more of their weight outboard. Class rules for boats with lifelines usually include a requirement with respect to how much deflection is permitted, but for boats that have no applicable rule, there is a new requirement that lifelines must be taut.

Rule 55 is about disposal of trash into the water. The rule makes it clear that no trash should be put in the water at any time while afloat. However, it now also includes the ability for a protest committee to give a penalty less than disqualification for a breach of the rule.

'Support persons' (e.g. coaches, parents, etc.) are now subject to the same rules governing behaviour as are competitors and boat owners. A breach of good manners or sportsmanship, unethical behaviour or 'conduct that may bring the sport into disrepute' are dealt with under a re-worded rule 69. Anyone (a sailor, a measurer, even a spectator) can submit a report to the protest committee claiming a breach, and the protest committee may then decide whether it is appropriate to open a hearing under rule 69. In such a hearing, support persons may be penalized if it is found that they have broken rule 69.

A measurer or measurement committee at a championship finding that a boat doesn't meet the class rules, used to have to report the anomaly to the race committee, which would then decide whether or not to lodge a protest. Now the 'technical committee' can itself lodge a protest. **(Rule 60.4)**

Sometimes a member of a protest committee has what might be perceived as a conflict of interest. He or she must declare it before the start of the hearing and if both parties agree, or the committee rules it is insignificant (after considering the views of the parties, the level of the conflict, the level of the event, the importance to each party, and the overall perception of fairness) the person can remain. At major events the person with a conflict of interest cannot be a member of a protest committee. Nationality alone would not normally be considered a conflict of interest. **(Rule 63.4)**

When a boat is penalized under a class rule and the protest committee decides that the boat also broke the same rule in earlier races in the same event, the penalty may now be imposed for all such races. No further protest is necessary. **(Rule 64.3(c))**

There is a new rule dealing with the appointment of a technical committee by the organizing authority or the race committee to be responsible for equipment inspection and event measurement. **(Rule 92)**

A boat having been found to have broken Rule 2 (Fair Sailing) used to have a mandatory score of 'DNE' (do not discard, meaning the boat had to count the disqualification in her overall score). Now the protest committee may impose either a DSQ or a DNE.

A change to the introduction to Part 2 means that now a boat that damages another boat while not racing may be penalized, giving some comfort to those who found it unfair that their boat had been damaged (and maybe could not even race) but there was no penalty on the other boat.

Rule 40: When Y-flag is displayed ashore, personal buoyancy must be worn at all time afloat.

There is a page on the World Sailing website for relevant documents referred to in the rulebook: www.sailing.org/ racingrules/documents.

1. The Basics

There are certain obligations that you have all the time, so I will state them here and not repeat them in the rest of the book.

You must sail fairly. Sailboat racing is the greatest sport. Generally, we don't have umpires or judges or referees; we police ourselves. Cheats can spoil any sport, and currently our sport is almost free of cheats (unlike some other sports). We all need to work to keep it that way. So the rules require that as a sailor you conduct yourself in a sportsmanlike manner at all times, and don't bring the sport into disrepute. This principle applies as much to club racing as it does to championships. Trying to gain an advantage by deliberately breaking a rule or lying at a protest hearing is cheating and the penalties for cheating can be severe. In recent years, competitors found guilty of cheating have been disqualified from entire championships and some have been banned by their national authorities or by World Sailing from taking part in competitive sailing for a year or more. **(Basic Principle 'Sportsmanship and the Rules', Rule 2 & Rule 69 'Allegations of Gross Misconduct')**

You must help anyone you see in danger. If you lose a position while acting as the hero, you will be entitled to redress. **(Rule 1.1 'Helping Those in Danger', Rule 60.1(b) 'Right to ... Request Redress', Rule 62.1(c) 'Redress')**

When you break a rule of Part 2 ('When Boats Meet'), and the other party is aggrieved, you must promptly sail clear and do your penalty turns. To continue to race without taking a penalty knowing you have broken a rule, hoping that the other boat will not lodge a protest, or hoping you might outwit the protestor in the protest room, is a breach of the Basic Principle 'Sportsmanship and the Rules'. Even when you have right of way or the right to room, you must try to avoid contact. If you have broken a rule and there is serious damage, then the alternative penalty option (e.g. 'doing turns') is not open to you and you must retire. **(Rule 14 'Avoiding Contact', Rule 44.1 'Taking a Penalty')**

Whether or not you may display advertising on your hull or sails will usually depend on what your class association has decided at its AGM. If you go to an open regatta, the organizers might require you to put event sponsor advertising (which they will supply) on the forward part of your hull. You may advertise (if it's not offensive) as much as you like on clothing. **(Rule 80 'Advertising' and the World Sailing Regulation 20, Advertising Code)**

I emphasize that these principles apply all the time, and to every situation described in this book.

If you are involved in an incident during a race and you believe another boat (or boats) broke a rule, and you want to protest if he doesn't take a penalty, then you must hail 'protest' at the first reasonable opportunity. No other word will do; it must be 'protest' and it must be hailed immediately after the incident. In addition, if your hull is 6 metres long or more, you need to display a protest flag and keep it displayed until the end of the race. **(Rule 61.1(a))**

There are a few terms and definitions that you need to know before we start. (See also page 94.)

World Sailing
World Sailing is the international governing body that publishes the racing rules and, for guidance on their interpretation, publishes cases and calls that have been decided and submitted by national authorities.

National authority
Every sailing nation has a national body to administer sailing on waters within its jurisdiction. In Great Britain this is the Royal Yachting Association, in the United States it is US Sailing, in Australia it is Australian Sailing, in New Zealand it is Yachting New Zealand, and so on.

Organizing authority
The body that decides to hold an event and arranges the venue. The organizing authority might be a club, a class association or a national authority, or a combination of

1

these. At least one of its constituents must be affiliated to the national authority. Sailing clubs are the organizing authorities for their club racing. They might be affiliated to their national authorities through state or district organizations that are in turn affiliated to the national authority. An international class association usually joins with a club to form the organizing authority to run a world championship, or, with the approval of the national authority, the class association may organize the event themselves. The organizing authority must appoint a race committee. At a principal event (such as an open regatta or a national championship) it may also appoint a protest committee or, at an international event, an international jury.

Race committee

The race committee, appointed by the organizing authority, is responsible for producing sailing instructions, organizing the racing and publishing the results. When no protest committee or jury has been appointed, the race committee must form or appoint a protest committee when one is needed.

Protest committee

A protest committee is appointed by the organizing authority for an event, or on an 'ad hoc' basis by the race committee, to hear protests and requests for redress. The term 'protest committee' is sometimes used to describe an international jury when it hears protests and requests for redress. A protest committee may also be required to go afloat during dinghy regattas to encourage rule compliance and implement the 'yellow flag protest system' for penalizing boats breaking rule 42 'Propulsion' (Appendix P).

International jury

Appointed by the organizing authority, its membership is made up of people of different nationalities, the majority of whom must be international judges (certified by World Sailing). Provided that it conducts itself in accordance with the procedures described in Appendix N, its decisions are not open to appeal.

Appeal authority

Each national authority normally appoints a committee to hear appeals by competitors (and race committees) against decisions of protest committees (but not international juries). For example, in the United Kingdom, the Royal Yachting Association's Racing Rules Group hears appeals; in the United States of America, appeals are decided by District Appeals Committees, and some are subsequently referred to the US Sailing's Appeal Committee. There is no higher appeal authority than the one provided by the national authority having jurisdiction over the event. World Sailing does not hear appeals.

Obstruction

'An object that a boat could not pass without changing course substantially, if she were sailing directly towards it and one of her hull lengths from it. An object that can be safely passed on only one side and an area so designated by the sailing instructions are also *obstructions*. However, a boat *racing* is not an *obstruction* to other boats unless they are required to *keep clear* of her, or, if rule 23 applies, avoid her. A vessel under way, including a boat *racing*, is never a continuing *obstruction*.' The committee boat, a rescue boat, a capsized dinghy, the shore, perceived underwater dangers or shallows, and a boat on starboard tack on a collision course in relation to a port-tack boat are all obstructions. In the case of the committee boat it will also be a mark when it is specified as being at one end of the starting or finishing line, but you should remember that the rules about marks and obstructions do not apply at starting marks surrounded by navigable water from the time boats are approaching them to start and until they have passed them. A half-metre diameter inflatable buoy is not an obstruction whether or not it is a mark, however, other rules may prevent you from being pushed onto such buoys.

Zone

'The area around a *mark* within a distance of three hull lengths of the boat nearer to it. A boat is in the *zone* when any part of her hull is in the *zone*.'

Keeping clear (see diagram opposite)

'A boat *keeps clear* of a right-of-way boat if the right-of-way boat can sail her (current straight line) course with no need to take avoiding actions and, when the boats are *overlapped*, if the right-of-way boat can also change course in both directions without immediately making contact.' In dinghies in a Force 2 on flat water, 'keeping clear' can be synonymous with 'avoiding a collision' (for example, in a 'port and starboard' encounter on a beat in which the port-tack boat ducks under the stern of the starboard-tack boat), but were they to be large keelboats in a Force 6 and a heavy sea, an

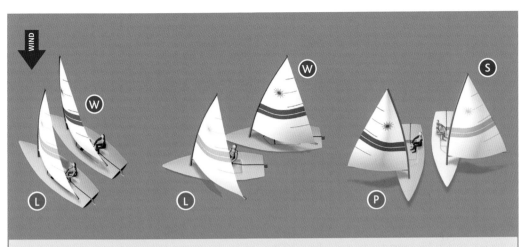

Keeping clear: In all of these situations L and S cannot change course in either direction without immediately making contact with the keep-clear boat, so the keep-clear boat (W or P) is not keeping clear.

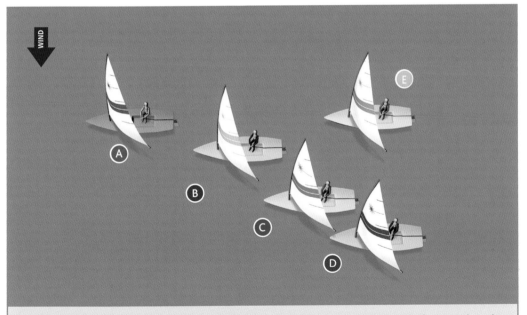

Overlap, clear ahead, clear astern: A is clear ahead of all the other boats, and of course the other boats are all clear astern of A. B and C are overlapped. C and D are overlapped. C and E are overlapped, and D and E are overlapped. D and B are also overlapped because C is between them, but B and E are not overlapped because there is no intervening boat. The bits of the boat that count for overlaps are 'hull and equipment in normal position', so a bowsprit would count if it is in its normal position at the time.

obligation on you to 'keep clear' might mean leaving a hull length or more between you and the right-of-way boat. Furthermore, when you are the keep-clear boat, you must not intimidate the right-of-way boat such that he thinks there is going to be a collision and is forced to take avoiding action. So even in fairly light conditions it's as well to look under the boom and give him a smile, so he knows you are paying attention, before diving under his stern and missing him by a millimetre.

Hailing

A hail is a meaningful word or string of words capable of being heard in the prevailing conditions by the occupants of the boat to which it is addressed. (This is not a defined term – but it's a useful definition, supported by appeal cases.) You are never actually required to make a hail, but when you want to protest you have to hail 'Protest' at the first reasonable opportunity; and when you're approaching an obstruction close-hauled and need a boat to give you room to tack, he is not required to take any action until you hail.

When the other boat hails you, you don't always have to respond. You should remember the situations when you must respond to a hail from the other boat:

■ When he hails for room to tack because he's approaching an obstruction.

■ When, after you have hailed for room to tack because you are close-hauled and need room to tack at an obstruction, he replies 'You tack'.

Some other hails might help to establish something, such as the right to room at a mark, or warn a port-tack boat of your presence ('Starboard!') but these hails in themselves place no obligation on anyone to do anything, so they have no real relevance.

When a hail from you means the other boat must respond, there is an obligation on you not to make the hail unless the conditions exist for you to make the hail. For example, when you are close-hauled and have a reasonable belief that you are approaching shallow water and cannot tack without the possibility of colliding with a boat astern or to windward, you may of course hail for room to tack, but you have no right to hail merely for tactical reasons.

Layline

The course on which your boat, sailing close-hauled on starboard tack, can fetch a windward mark which is to be rounded to port is the starboard tack layline for that mark, and the most windward line on which you would approach the mark on port tack is the port tack layline. High performance boats with powerful asymmetric spinnakers or gennakers go much faster down-wind by reaching and gybing, so a leeward mark also has laylines which are the proper courses for the boats approaching on each tack.

Tidal streams distort laylines; a stream going with the wind makes the angle between the windward mark port and starboard laylines wider, and the leeward mark laylines narrower. As the wind gets lighter, the angle between the leeward mark laylines for high performance boats with asymmetric spinnakers or gennakers gets dramatically wider.

A cross-course tidal stream swings the laylines towards the tide. 'Layline' is not a term used in the rulebook, but the term 'proper course' is, and laylines are the extremes of proper courses, so need to be understood. And of course an understanding of the importance of laylines is essential for all tacticians.

Luffing rights

This term is not used in the rulebook either, but sailors often use it, and so I use it in this book. You have 'luffing rights' when you have the right to sail higher than your proper course, forcing a boat to windward of you to change course to keep clear. Provided you didn't establish the overlap to leeward of the windward boat, from astern and within two of your hull lengths, as a leeward boat you have luffing rights, and may luff right up to head to wind, but you must give the windward boat room to keep clear. **(Rules 11 & 16)**

Before the starting signal there is no 'proper course' so any leeward boat may luff up to head to wind no matter how the overlap was established (provided the windward boat can keep clear). But at the moment the starting signal is made, any leeward boat that established the overlap from clear astern within two hull lengths must bear away to close-hauled (if the first leg is a beat) unless as a result of sailing above close-hauled she promptly sails astern of the other boat (which allows her to tack out of the windward boat's wind shadow). **(Rules 11, 16 & 17)**

Proper course (see diagram below)
A proper course is 'a course a boat would sail to *finish* as soon as possible in the absence of the other boats referred to in the rule using the term. A boat has no *proper course* before her starting signal.' You're never required to sail a proper course, but there are some situations in which you mustn't sail above or beyond your proper course, so you need to know what a proper course is.

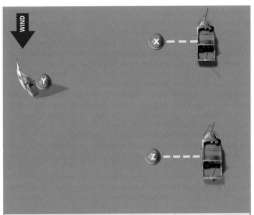

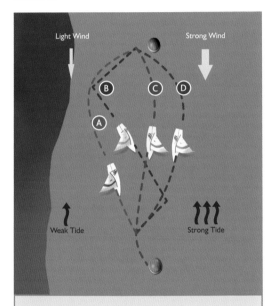

Proper course
When your proper course is being questioned, provided that you can establish a logical reason for it, and you sail it with some consistency, it is your decision as to what is your proper course. Any of these could be a 'proper course'. A has elected to sail in the weakest tide. B sails fastest downwind by broad reaching and gybing, C is sailing the rhumb line, while D chooses the windier side of the course. If 'playing the waves' makes a boat go faster, then the wiggly course she sails is her proper course. **(Rule: Definition Proper Course & World Sailing Case 14)**

Sailing the course
For this triangular course the sailing instructions read 'Course: mark X, round to port; mark Y round to port; mark Z round to port, finish'. In this case it's OK to leave mark Y to starboard (or to make contact with it) on the way from the start to mark X, because mark Y is not a mark that 'begins, bounds or ends' the first leg. **(Rules 28.1 & 31)**

Sailing instructions
The race committee must produce sailing instructions and make them available to you in time for you to read them before the race or series. They contain two types of information:

■ The intentions of the race committee; these instructions contain the word 'will'. For example, 'All marks will be large orange spheres'.

■ The obligations of boats and individual competitors; these instruction contain the word 'shall'. For example, 'All marks shall be rounded to port'.

The two types of instructions are mixed together because they are ordered chronologically.

It is imperative that you read the sailing instructions carefully before a race or series. I doubt if there is a champion who has not at some time lost an important race or series through failing to read or remember some particular sailing instruction.

1

The penalty for not complying with a sailing instruction describing a boat's obligation is disqualification from a race (unless some other penalty is specified), but the penalty can usually be applied only after a hearing.

No such penalty can be applied to the race committee when it does not carry out its own intentions specified in the sailing instructions, or it fails to comply with a rule which governs its conduct (Parts 3 and 7 of the Rules). What penalty could be imposed without adversely affecting innocent competitors? (The committee could be hung, drawn and quartered, but who would run the next race?) The race committee is invariably trying to do a good job of running the races but from time to time, it makes a mistake. If the committee makes an improper action or omission that affects your finishing position in the race or series, and if this is through no fault of your own, then you can ask for 'redress'. A good race committee, realizing its erroneous action has affected a boat's finishing position, will itself initiate a redress hearing. Chapter 18 deals with redress hearings. One of the most common errors is to write confusing or ambiguous sailing instructions about the course, resulting in some boats sailing one course and some sailing another.

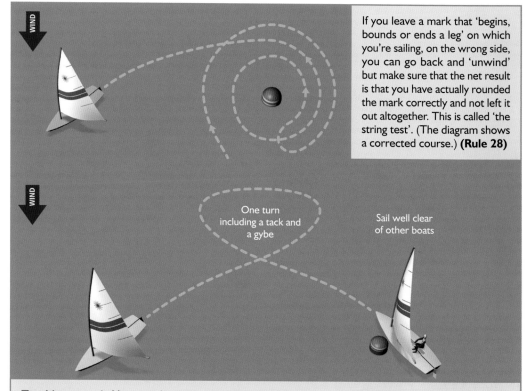

If you leave a mark that 'begins, bounds or ends a leg' on which you're sailing, on the wrong side, you can go back and 'unwind' but make sure that the net result is that you have actually rounded the mark correctly and not left it out altogether. This is called 'the string test'. (The diagram shows a corrected course.) **(Rule 28)**

One turn including a tack and a gybe

Sail well clear of other boats

Touching a mark: You mustn't touch a starting mark after the preparatory signal, or a mark that 'begins, bounds or ends' the leg on which you're sailing, or a finishing mark before you have finished and cleared the line and marks. However, if you do, you may exonerate yourself by getting well clear of all other boats as soon as possible and promptly completing a turn including a tack and a gybe. **(Rules 31, 44.1 & 44.2)**

2. Before the Preparatory Signal

Before going afloat you usually have to enter, register or 'sign on' and may be required to show your boat's measurement certificate. These requirements will be described in the sailing instructions.

To the water! Although the 'when boats meet' rules apply in the same way before as they do after the preparatory signal, there is no penalty for breaking a rule of Part 2 When Boats Meet unless you interfere with a boat that is racing. **(Rule 23.1)**

If you break a rule of Part 2 (the 'when boats meet' rules) before the preparatory signal, you do not need to retire or take a penalty (but you or your insurance company might have to pay for the damage if there is any).

The rules or sailing instructions (including all of Part 4 of the rules) requiring you to do something 'whilst racing' don't apply before the preparatory signal either, because you're not 'racing' till the preparatory signal.

However, you can be disqualified (after a protest and a hearing) for breaking some other sailing instruction, even if you're not racing when the breach occurs. **(Definition Racing)**

If your boat is damaged in a collision and it wasn't your fault, it is useful to be able to present to your insurance company a protest form showing that the hearing found the other boat to have broken a racing rule. So it's worth remembering that you can protest another boat for breaking a rule of Part 2 (the 'when boats meet' rules) before the preparatory signal or after the finish, and if the other boat does not accept that he broke a rule, the protest committee must hear the protest if it is valid, even though, if the protest is upheld, no penalty is applied to the other boat. You must hail 'Protest', display a protest flag if your boat is more then 6 metres long, and lodge the written protest within the time limit. The protest committee decides which boat broke which rule; it cannot decide who is responsible for the costs of repair or proportional responsibility; that is a matter for agreement by you and the other owner, or by your respective insurance companies, or, failing agreement, by a court of law or an arbitrator. Nevertheless, the protest decision with respect to which boat broke a rule can be used to support a claim for damages.

The standard signalling system for starting a race is a series of visual signals (usually flags) each accompanied by a sound signal. The sequence begins with the 'warning signal' (usually your class flag) at five minutes before the start. One minute later is the 'preparatory signal' signalling the beginning of the four-minute 'preparatory period' in which boats are 'racing' (even though they are not going anywhere) and a boat breaking a rule of Part 2 must take an exonerating turns penalty. The visual signal is usually flag P (blue with a white square in the middle) which means there will be no 'starting penalty'. At one minute before the start, the preparatory flag is lowered, and at the start the class flag is lowered. When there are a lot of boats all eager to get a good start, the race committee can substitute flag P with flag I, flag Z, flag U or a black flag to bring into effect a penalty system during the final minute. **(Rules 26 & 30)**

The sailing instructions might vary the standard signalling system. For example, the Warning Signal might be 10 minutes before the start instead of the standard five.

You should be near the committee boat and watching it closely when the warning signal is made so that you can set your watch. This is especially important in a big fleet where you might start some distance from the committee boat when it is often impossible to see the visual starting signal or hear the 'gun' (and remember, the sound takes a while to travel the length of a long starting line).

3. In the Preparatory Period

This section covers the period from the preparatory signal to the time at which boats are approaching the line to start.

At the moment of the preparatory signal your boat must be afloat and off moorings and thereafter not be hauled out or 'made fast' (tied up) except to bail or reef or make repairs. However, you may anchor at any time, but you must recover your anchor if possible before proceeding. Your crew may stand on the bottom (in shallow water of course) to hold the boat. **(Rule 45)**

You are vulnerable in the preparatory period because no one is sailing any particular course so the risk of collision is great. However, if you break a rule of Part 2 (the 'when boats meet' rules) you can take a penalty (by getting well clear of other boats as soon as possible after the incident and then promptly sailing two circles including two tacks and gybes). So unless the breach is shortly before the starting signal, the penalty is a light one. **(Rules 44.1 & 44.2)**

If you hit a starting mark, you may exonerate yourself by getting well clear of other boats as soon as possible and then promptly take a One-Turn Penalty. **(Rules 44.1 & 44.2)**

If you are going to sail in championships or open regattas, you need to look out for the starting penalty signals and know what they mean because they may affect the way you plan your start (balancing the risk of being a premature starter and the reward of getting a cracking good start).

No penalty

The vast majority of races are started with no penalty system in force. The P flag is used as the preparatory signal. You are allowed to be on the course side of the starting line right up to the starting signal. If any part of your boat, crew or equipment is on the wrong side of the line at the moment of the starting signal, you simply have to get back completely behind the line to start properly (known as a 'dip start'). On a starting line with plenty of room, the cost of making a mistake (by crossing prematurely) is small.

The I Flag Rule
('return round an end' penalty system)

When flag I is displayed as the preparatory signal, the 'I Flag Rule' will come into effect when the flag is struck at the 'one minute signal' (one minute before the starting signal). This means that in the final minute, if any part of your boat is on the course side of the line, you must thereafter sail from the course side across one of the starting line's extensions before you can start. This is normally done by sailing around one of the ends of the line. The idea of the rule is that it stops boats milling around on the course side of the line in the final minute, and encourages boats not to cross the start line prematurely, especially in the middle of the starting line. If you sailed to the course side early in the last minute, you may be able to sail from there and across an extension of the line and still get a good start, but if you crossed just before the starting signal, with many boats or a big distance between you and an end, the penalty will be heavy. **(Rule 30.1)**

The Z Flag Rule
(20% penalty system)

When flag Z is displayed as the preparatory signal, and if any part of your boat is on the wrong side of the line in the final minute, your finishing position will have 20% of the number of boats entered for the race added on. You must still return to start properly or you will be scored OCS (meaning 'on the course side of the starting line at the start'). If there is a general recall, or the race is abandoned after the start and resailed, the 20% penalty is still applied. If you are over again in the next attempt at starting the race, you'll get another 20%. **(Rule 30.2)**

The U Flag Rule
(DSQ unless there is a re-start penalty system)

When flag U is displayed as the preparatory signal and in the final minute any part of your boat is on the wrong side of the line, you will be disqualified,

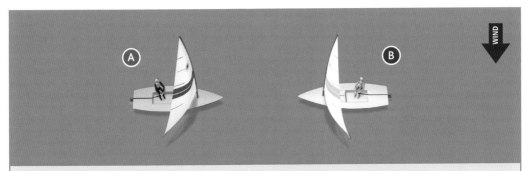

You are A:
- You're on port tack (because your sail is on the starboard side) so you're the keep-clear boat and you must keep clear. **(Rule 10)**
- If you change course so that you are no longer on a collision course, and B changes course back onto a collision course, you must change course again and make every effort to keep clear. **(Rule 10)**

You are B:
- You're the right-of-way boat.
- You may change course, but if you do you must give A room to keep clear, so you mustn't change course so close to A as to prevent him from keeping clear. At a protest hearing, if there is a collision and doubt whether in altering course close to A you failed to give him room, a protest committee is likely to find against you. **(Rule 16)**

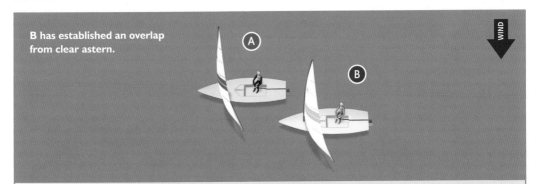

B has established an overlap from clear astern.

You are A:
- While there's no overlap, you may change course as you please; you have no obligations.
- When B gets his overlap to leeward, the situation changes and you must now keep clear of him.
- You need do nothing till there's an overlap, even if you are sitting 'hove-to'; but once he's established the overlap you must manoeuvre to keep clear (by luffing or drawing ahead or even tacking if need be). Bear in mind once he's given you a chance to keep clear, he's allowed to luff right up to head to wind. **(Rules 11 & 15)**

You are B:
- While you are clear astern you must keep clear. **(Rule 12)**
- You mustn't establish an overlap so close to A that if A luffed or bore away he would immediately make contact **(Rule 11, Definition Keep Clear)**
- Once the boats are overlapped, you become the right-of-way boat and may luff right up to head to wind. However, you must give A room to keep clear. Even if you don't luff, you can't come charging in while A is hove-to and not initially give him room to pull his sail in and get going. **(Rules 11, 15 & 16)**

unless the race is postponed or abandoned. If there is a general recall, or 'abandon and resail' you may start in the re-started race. **(Rule 30.3)**

The Black Flag Rule
(DSQ penalty system)

When a black flag is displayed as the preparatory signal and in the final minute any part of your boat is on the wrong side of the line, you will be disqualified, unless the race is postponed or abandoned before the starting signal. If there is a general recall you must not start in

the next attempt to get the race under way. Even if the race doesn't get started that day, you won't be eligible to start in it when it does get started. **(Rule 30.4)**

These 'starting penalty' systems can be brought into force for any start. The race committee simply uses the appropriate flag as the preparatory signal.

3

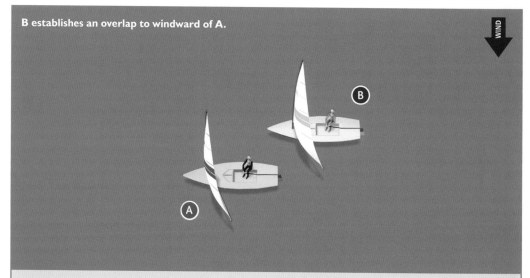

B establishes an overlap to windward of A.

WIND

You are A:
* Before the overlap you have no obligations, except that any change of course must be such that it gives B room to keep clear. **(Rules 12 & 16)**
* When B gets an overlap nothing changes; you may still change course if you wish but then you must give B room to keep clear. **(Rules 11 & 16)**
* You may continue to luff, up to head to wind, provided you give B room to keep clear. **(Rules 11 & 16)**
* However, if there is an obstruction (such as the committee boat or another sailboat which is not keeping clear) to windward of B which prevents B from responding, then you may not luff; indeed you may even have to bear away to give B room to pass the obstruction. **(Rule 19.2 (b))**

You are B:
* You must keep clear before and after you are overlapped. **(Rules 12 & 11)**

The general principle about windward and leeward situations in the preparatory period is that a leeward boat may luff up to head to wind provided she gives the windward boat room to keep clear. It doesn't matter how the overlap was established, or the relative positions fore-and-aft of the two boats. The windward boat must keep clear.

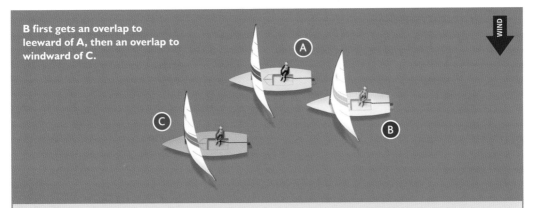

B first gets an overlap to leeward of A, then an overlap to windward of C.

WIND

You are A: When B first gets an overlap to leeward of you, because there is a possibility of his bow running into your boom, you must begin to manoeuvre to keep clear. If B luffs after he gets the overlap, you will have to luff too. If B is sailing higher than you are, you'll have to luff, but you don't have to begin to do anything until there is an overlap. **(Rule 11)**

You are B: When you're astern, you must keep clear. When you first get the overlap to leeward of

A, it must not be so close that if A luffs there will immediately be contact. You must give A room to keep clear. Provided you give A room when you change course you can luff to sail to windward of C. You must keep clear of C even if he luffs. **(Rules 12, 11 & Definition Keep Clear)**

You are C: You may luff if you wish, but if you do you must allow B and A room to keep clear. **(Rule 16)**

3

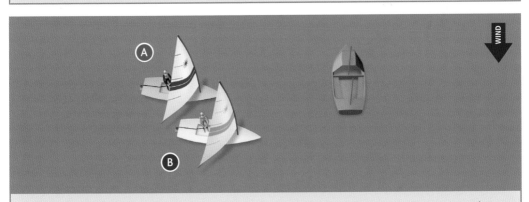

WIND

A and B are overlapped approaching an obstruction (which may or may not be a mark), before they are approaching the line to start.

You are A: You must keep clear, but if B decides to go under the committee boat, you have the right to room if you want to do the same.

You are B: You may choose to go either to windward or to leeward of the obstruction, in spite of any protestations from A. But if you decide to go to windward, you must change course in such a way that A is able to keep clear. If you go to leeward you must give A room to pass under the committee boat if he wants to. **(Rules 11, 16 & 19.2(b))**

3

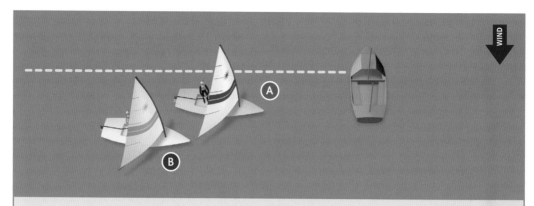

You are A: You have the right to room to pass under the committee boat even though it's a starting mark because you are not 'approaching the line to start'. You don't have to hail, but it's probably a good idea if you think you're not being given enough room. You can change your mind and tack if you want to.

You are B: It is too late now to decide to go to windward of the committee boat, so you must give room to A whether he asks for it or not. You need to give sufficient room for A to pass 'in a seamanlike way'. **(Rule 19.2(b))**

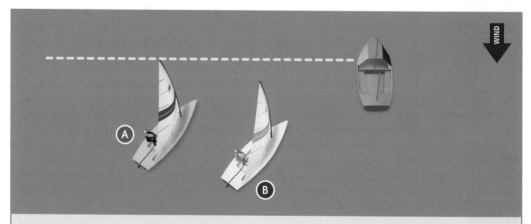

You are A: You are the keep-clear boat and if B luffs you must keep clear, but if B tacks you become the right-of-way boat while he's tacking and B must keep clear of you. **(Rules 11 & 13)**

You are B: You have no right to hail for room to tack (if you are approaching the starting line to start) because the committee boat is a starting mark and the rules don't give you the right to room to tack at a starting mark if it's surrounded by navigable water. You had better bear away before you get trapped. If there are any boats overlapped to leeward of you they must give you room to pass under the committee boat. **(Preamble Section C & Rule 19.2)**

4. The Start

This section covers the period from your approach to the starting line shortly before the starting signal, to when you have started and cleared the starting line.

The race committee must make the time between the preparatory signal and the starting signal exactly correct, and must make the correct visual signals at those times. It is allowed to fail to make the sound signal, but the visual signals must be on time. That is why it is important that you check the preparatory signal by watching the committee boat signals (or better still, listening to the time-keeper counting down to the preparatory signal, if you can get close enough); then you can rely on the starting signal being exactly four minutes later. **(Rule 26)**

When the race committee makes an individual recall signal (when there are premature starters), it must not only display the visual signal (flag X) but also make a sound signal (an additional bang or horn). If it doesn't, and you are really in doubt as to whether or not you were a premature starter, you may assume you have started correctly and sail on. If the race committee scores you as OCS (on the course side at the start) you will be entitled to redress. But it is doubtful you would get your finishing position reinstated, because in assessing what is 'fair to all boats', the protest committee will take into consideration that you had an advantage over the other boats at the start by being over the line.

If you are in no doubt that you are a premature starter, you must return to start properly, whether or not the race committee makes the correct signal. **(Rule 29.1, World Sailing Case 31)**

At the moment of the starting signal.

You are A: You may want to luff to close-hauled but you may not. B is keeping clear and to luff now would deprive him of room to keep clear. **(Rule 16.1)**

You are B: You are the keep-clear boat, but your course and speed are such that you will pass safely ahead of A who is not allowed to change course if that deprives you of room to keep clear. Mind you, if there is an incident and he didn't luff, you'll be likely to lose the protest!

4

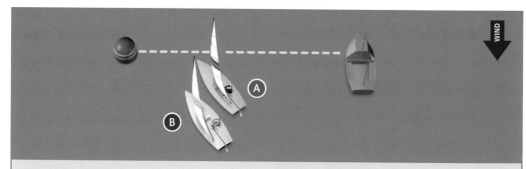

You are A: As windward boat you must keep clear. **(Rule 11)**

You are B: However you came to be overlapped, (you might have come from astern, or you might have tacked to leeward of A) you may luff (above close-

hauled if necessary) to get round the mark, but if you luff you must give A room to keep clear. If you established the overlap from clear astern, then you mustn't sail above your proper course, so once you have passed the mark you must bear away to close-hauled or below.

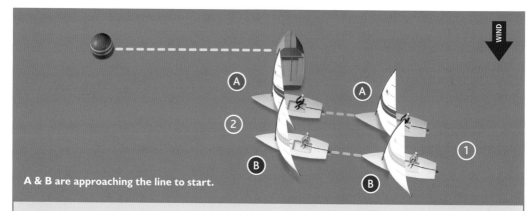

A & B are approaching the line to start.

You are A:
• As windward boat you must keep clear of B. If there are no other boats behind B, you could try to slow and tuck in behind B, but don't let your boom touch B.
• You have no right to room to go under the committee boat.
• Next time you want to start at the starboard end, don't get caught in this position!

You are B:
• Position 1: Before the starting signal, however the overlap was established, you may luff as high as you like, but if you change course you must give A room

to keep clear. If you luff slowly now, A has got room to keep clear by sailing the wrong side of the committee boat. **(Rules 11, 16 & Preamble Section C)**
• After the starting signal, if you established the overlap from clear astern, you must not luff higher than your 'proper course' (close-hauled or the course which takes you just astern of the committee boat). **(Rule 17)**
• Position 2: If you sail a straight course which allows A enough room to sail astern of the committee boat, then to luff when he cannot escape would not be giving him room. So if you want to shut him out, you need to luff at position 1. **(Rules 11, 16 & Preamble Section C)**

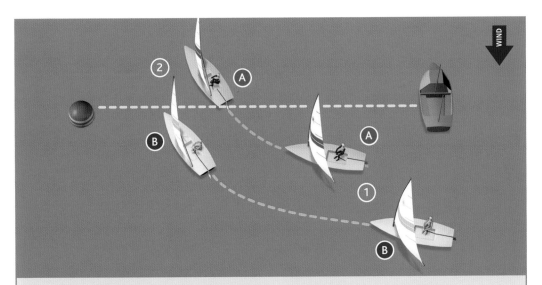

You are A: You may initially do as you please, but as soon as B gets his overlap to leeward you become the keep-clear boat, and if you are on a collision course, or B luffs onto a collision course, you will have to luff to keep clear even if this means you'll be OCS (on the course side at the start). **(Rule 11)**

You are B:
• Initially, being clear astern, you are the keep-clear boat and must keep clear. **(Rule 12)**
• When you first get the overlap you become the right-of-way boat, but you must not be so close to A that he can't keep clear. **(Rule 15)**
• Before the starting signal you may luff up to head to wind but you must give A room to keep clear **(Rule 16)**
• At the moment of the starting signal you must promptly bear away to a course no higher than close-hauled. **(Rule 17)**

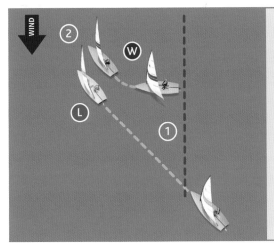

Whether or not L has luffing rights (the right to sail above his proper course) after the starting signal, depends on how the overlap was established.

Here the overlap was established at a distance more than two of L's hull lengths from W, so L has luffing rights. **(Rule 17)**

4

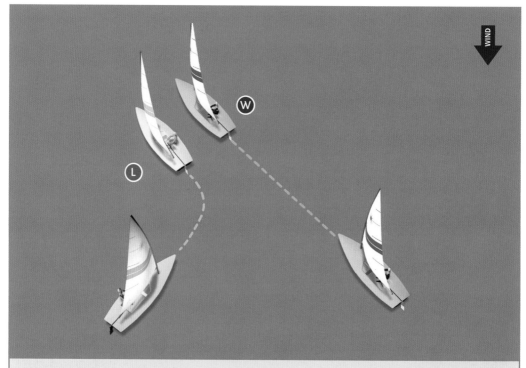

Here L tacked into the position to leeward of W. L has luffing rights and may luff as high as he likes but must give W room to keep clear. **(Rules 11, 15, 16 & 17)**

The diagram opposite shows a reaching start. Before the starting signal (when there is no proper course), all the leeward boats (B, D, F and H) may luff up to head to wind, if they can give room to the windward boats to keep clear. At the moment of the starting signal, a boat without luffing rights sailing higher than her proper course must bear away. Assuming that their proper courses are to the right of the picture, which of the leeward boats may luff (sail above their proper course) after the starting signal?

You are A or C or E or G: You must keep clear of the leeward boats under you; and you must keep clear of X coming down the starting line on starboard tack. **(Rules 11 & 10)**

You are B: You established your overlap from clear astern, but you were more than two lengths away from A at the time. You have luffing rights. You may sail higher than your proper course before or after the starting signal – right up to head to wind if A can keep clear. But you must not luff A into the path of X, coming down the start line on starboard tack; in fact you might have to bear away and give more room to A. **(Rules 11, 17 & 19.2(b))**

You are D: You established your overlap from clear astern, and you were within two hull lengths of C at the time. You are the only leeward boat not to have luffing rights. Before the starting signal (when there is no proper course) you may sail as high as you like, but at the starting signal you must bear away if necessary and then mustn't sail higher than your proper course during the existence of the overlap as long as the boats remain on the same tack (unless the gap between the two boats gets to be more than two hull lengths). **(Rules 11 & 17)**

You are F: E established the overlap to windward of you, so you have luffing rights. You may sail higher than your proper course after the starting signal – right up to head to wind if E can keep clear. **(Rule 11)**

You are H: You established your overlap by completing a tack to leeward of G. You have luffing rights. You may sail higher than your proper course after the starting signal – right up to head to wind if G can keep clear. **(Rule 11)**

You are X: You are not going to be very popular, but as you are on starboard tack you have right of way over all the other boats. 'Proper course' is not relevant when boats are on opposite tacks. **(Rule 10)**

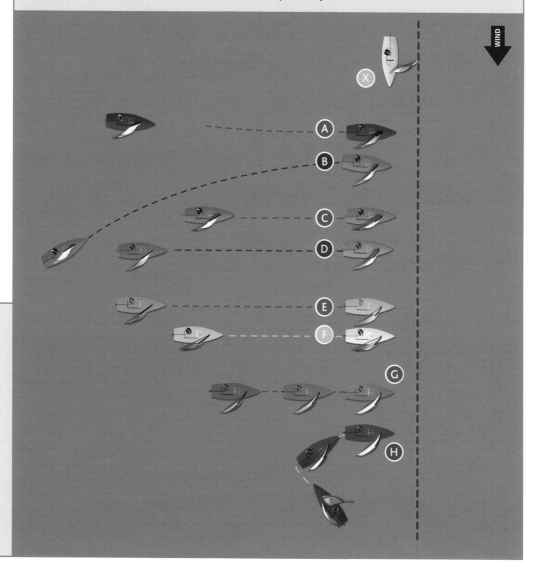

4

Starting limit marks

Most on-the-water starting lines are between a small buoy (the 'outer distance mark', or 'ODM') at the port end, and the mast of a committee boat at the starboard end. These must be described in the sailing instructions. Both the ODM and the committee boat are 'marks' because they have a 'required side' when boats start. The committee boat is also an obstruction, and an inside boat therefore has the right to room when everyone is milling about before the start, but not when boats are approaching the line to start. Then no one has the right to room at any starting mark (provided that it is 'surrounded by navigable water').

The most common starting limit mark is the 'inner limit mark' or 'inner distance mark' ('IDM'). Not just the description of the IDM but also the obligations of boats with respect to it must be written into the sailing instructions. You can ignore a sailing instruction like 'There will be an IDM, which will be a yellow mark with a pink flag laid near to the committee boat'.

IDMs cause a lot of problems. The most common reasons to use one are to help protect the committee boat, and to keep boats from sailing very close to the committee boat, blocking the race committee's view of the starting line.

Let's look at three examples of a limit mark sailing instruction.

1. 'A yellow mark with a pink flag will be laid near the committee boat. Boats shall not pass between this mark and the committee boat after the preparatory signal.'

Such a sailing instruction does not give the mark a required side (rather it specifies a prohibited area which by definition is an obstruction) so it could be argued that you have the right to room to avoid the 'obstruction', and you may hit the buoy without penalty (provided you don't cross the imaginary line between it and any part of the committee boat); and if you are forced into the 'prohibited area' by a boat breaking a rule you can escape penalty by protesting the boat that forced you to break the sailing instruction. (Rule 60.1(a) gives you the right to a hearing and Rule 64.1(a) exonerates you.)

2. The most sensible sailing instruction would be: 'A yellow mark with a pink flag will be laid near the committee boat. Boats approaching the line to start shall pass between this mark and the ODM' or 'boats shall pass this mark to starboard'. This would require you to pass the IDM on your starboard side when you are 'approaching the line to start from the pre-course side of the starting line'. Under this sailing instruction, the IDM is a mark because it has a required side, so there is no question of any right to room when you're approaching the line to start. If you get forced the wrong side by someone to leeward who has not broken a rule (for example, by luffing you gently the wrong side of the mark), then you'll just have to sail back and unwind, and pass it on the correct side.

3. In an attempt to really discourage boats from the

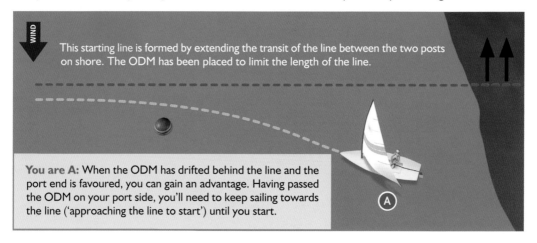

WIND

This starting line is formed by extending the transit of the line between the two posts on shore. The ODM has been placed to limit the length of the line.

You are A: When the ODM has drifted behind the line and the port end is favoured, you can gain an advantage. Having passed the ODM on your port side, you'll need to keep sailing towards the line ('approaching the line to start') until you start.

Ⓐ

area between the IDM and the committee boat, the race committee might write a sailing instruction like this: 'A yellow mark with a pink flag will be placed near the committee boat. When approaching the line to start, boats shall pass between this mark and the ODM and after the preparatory signal boats shall not pass between this mark and the committee boat'.

With this sailing instruction the IDM has a required side, so it is a mark. This means there's no right to room when approaching the line to start and if you get forced between the mark and the committee boat by a boat that didn't break a rule, then you'll have to retire. (I don't recommend such a draconian sailing instruction, but I often see them.)

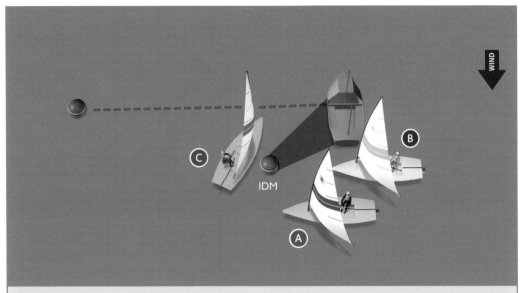

You are A:
• You may luff to shut out B, forcing him into the forbidden triangle (unless it has been described as an obstruction – in which case you must give him room). **(Rule 19.2(b) & Definition Obstruction)**

You are B:
• You must keep clear of A and you cannot claim room if the IDM has a required side in the sailing instructions. However, if the area between the mark and the committee boat is simply a prohibited area, then A must give you room (whether you ask for it or not, but it's best to hail). **(Rules: Preamble Section C, 19.2(b) & Definition Obstruction)**
• If you hit the mark but pass it on the correct (starboard) side, you can exonerate yourself by sailing clear and then take a One-Turn Penalty if your only breach was hitting the mark, or a Two-Turns

Penalty if you broke a 'when boats meet' rule (for example by not keeping clear of A). If you broke a 'when boats meet' rule and you hit the mark, a Two-Turns Penalty will exonerate you for both.
• If you are forced the wrong side of the mark, then whether or not you can successfully protest A, or exonerate yourself, all depends on the wording of the sailing instruction.

You are C:
• If this is the best end to start and the IDM is behind the line you can gain something here by starting right at the end of the line. But having passed the IDM on your starboard side, you must be careful if the sailing instruction prohibits you from sailing between the IDM and the committee boat; you'll need to keep out of the prohibited triangle so if there is too much time left before the starting signal, this approach is not a good idea.

5. The Gate Start

5

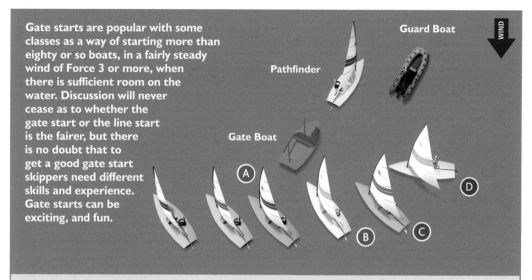

Gate starts are popular with some classes as a way of starting more than eighty or so boats, in a fairly steady wind of Force 3 or more, when there is sufficient room on the water. Discussion will never cease as to whether the gate start or the line start is the fairer, but there is no doubt that to get a good gate start skippers need different skills and experience. Gate starts can be exciting, and fun.

This is how a gate start works. A pathfinder is appointed. Usually it is one of the competing boats near the top of the fleet. Just before the starting signal he sets off on a port tack close-hauled course. A guard boat is sometimes used, to motor along on the pathfinder's starboard bow, to ensure other boats don't run into the pathfinder and ruin the proceedings.

A gate boat takes up a position astern of the pathfinder, exactly matching the pathfinder's speed and course. Boats then start on starboard tack behind the gate boat. Those that think they sail faster than the pathfinder, or think the left side of the beat is best, start early (near the beginning of the run). Those that think the pathfinder sails faster than they do, or think the right side of the beat is best, wait around where they expect the entourage to be, five minutes or so after the starting signal. Knowing the exact time is unimportant; the skill is in 'coming out of the gate' close-hauled at full speed by luffing from a reach to close-hauled, missing the starboard quarter of the gate boat by a few millimetres. The pathfinder is usually released after five minutes; he can tack any time after being released, gaining a few hull lengths by not having to sail behind the gate boat – a reward for being forced to start at the extreme right

side of the beat, and not being allowed to tack on any shifts for the first five minutes of the race.

You are A or B: This is really just the same situation as the starboard end of a fixed starting line. You have to keep clear of a boat to leeward, and you have right of way over a boat to windward. You must also keep clear of the gate boat.

You are C: If you can sail close-hauled without changing course, then you can ignore D. Or you can luff D to force him to luff alongside the gate boat, but you can't luff him into the gate boat, because if you luff you must give him room to keep clear. **(Rule 16.1)**

You are D: You will need to slow, not to go behind C as you would if this was a fixed-line start, but to be level with him, as are A and B. Remember, the gate boat is moving at the speed of the pathfinder. You must keep clear of the gate boat. If you touch the gate boat (or the guard boat or – heaven forbid – the pathfinder), you must retire (no chance of taking a Turns Penalty) unless you think it wasn't your fault. For example, if C forces you to collide with the gate boat by luffing you can hail 'Protest', sail on, and lodge a protest after the race.

6. On the Beat

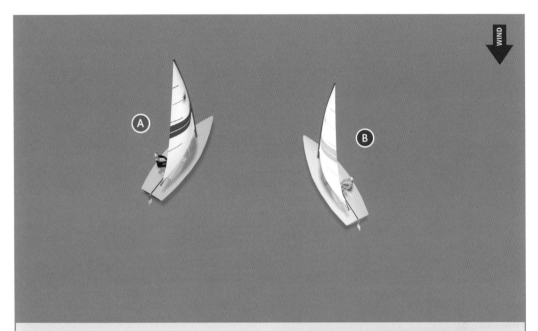

You are A:
• Your obligation is simple: to keep clear. **(Rule 10)**
• If you are going to bear away behind B, you must do it in such a way that B is not left in doubt that you are going to succeed. **(Rule 10)**
• If you decide to tack, you must complete the tack ahead or to leeward of B without B having to change course to keep clear until your tack is complete. If there is doubt about whether you tacked far enough from B, a protest hearing is likely to go against you. **(Rules 13 & 15)**

You are B:
• If you change course you must give room to A to keep clear. Furthermore, if A is keeping clear by ducking your stern you mustn't change course if as a result A would immediately need to change course to continue keeping clear. **(Rule 16.2)**
• You are not required to make a hail (like 'Starboard') but it is often a good idea to do so if

you think that A hasn't seen you because:
1. You must try to avoid contact, and if there is contact and there is damage or injury, you may be penalized. **(Rule 14)**
2. Even if there is no chance of damage, getting tangled up with a boat required to keep clear can cost many hull lengths and no redress can be claimed for places lost **(Rules 14, 16 & 62.1(b))**
• If you want to continue on starboard tack, and don't want A tacking into a position which forces you (from a tactical point of view) to tack, you may bear away and go behind A. You could shout 'Carry on', or 'Pass ahead of me' but nothing you shout puts any obligation on A that he doesn't already have. Although an early bear-away and/or a hail will often make A decide to carry on, if A is an experienced and skilled racing sailor and is determined to force you into a tactically disadvantageous position, it is not easy to prevent him.

6

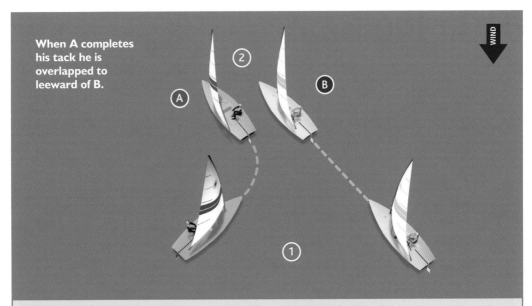

When A completes his tack he is overlapped to leeward of B.

WIND

You are A:
• As you approach on port tack, and while luffing to head to wind, your obligation is simple – to keep clear of B. **(Rule 10)**
• When you pass through head to wind and until you are close-hauled on the new tack you must continue to keep clear of B. **(Rule 13)**
• When your tack is complete, you become the right-of-way boat, but it is only at that instant that B has to begin to take any avoiding action, so you mustn't be in a position where it is impossible or difficult for B to keep clear. Remember that he doesn't have to anticipate that you are going to be there. If he is able to keep clear only by making an unseamanlike manoeuvre, then your tack was too close. **(Rule 15)**
• When your tack is complete, you become the right-of-way boat and you have luffing rights, but you cannot use them until you have given B room to keep clear (which requires both space and time). After giving B this opportunity, you may luff above close-hauled if you want to, but your luff must be such that B is able to keep clear. **(Rule 16)**

You are B:
• You must not change course if by so doing you prevent A from keeping clear, or force him to make an unseamanlike manoeuvre in order to keep clear. If there is a header (adverse wind shift) just as A is tacking, you may be prevented from fulfilling your wish to bear away for a few seconds. You may, of course, tack while A is tacking. **(Rule 16)**
• You may change course towards A as he approaches on port tack (whether or not there is a wind shift), forcing A to tack earlier, provided you give him room to keep clear. **(Rule 16)**
• You don't have to anticipate A becoming the right-of-way boat. Other than to avoid contact, you are not required to alter course to avoid him until his tack is complete.
• Once A's tack is complete and he is to leeward, you become the keep-clear boat, and you must keep clear even if he luffs. If he executed a good 'lee bow', and you will be affected by his back-wind, it's usually tactically sound to tack. **(Rule 11)**
• Remember that A has luffing rights: once he has given you the opportunity to keep clear he may luff.
• You are not prohibited from tacking, even if A has changed course to keep clear, provided that you give A room to keep clear.

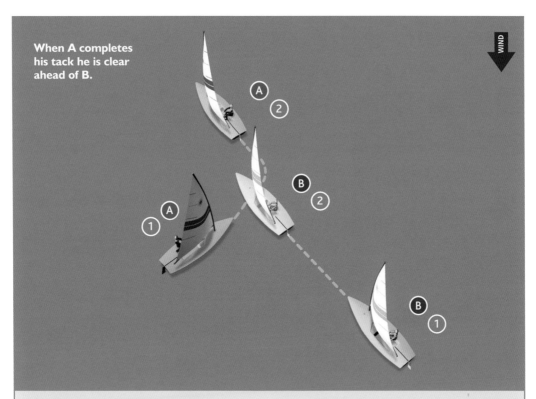

When A completes his tack he is clear ahead of B.

WIND

You are A:

• As you approach on port tack your obligation is simple – to keep clear of B. **(Rule 10)**

• While you are tacking (until you are close-hauled on the new tack) you must keep clear of B. **(Rule 13)**

• When your tack is complete you become the right-of-way boat, but it is only at that instant that B has to begin to take any avoiding action, so you mustn't be in a position where B doesn't have room to keep clear. Remember that he doesn't have to anticipate that you are going to be there. If he is able to keep clear only by making an unseamanlike manoeuvre, then your tack was too close. **(Rule 15)**

• When you complete your tack you may be sailing more slowly than B, and if B establishes an overlap to leeward of you, you become the keep-clear boat again, and you must keep clear. Only if B was able to luff or tack away after your tack was completed can you claim that you should be given a chance to fulfil your new obligation to keep clear. If your tack was so close that B had no chance to do anything but establish the overlap it would be your own action that got you into this situation. If there is doubt, a protest decision will probably go against you. **(Rule 11 & 15)**

You are B:

• You must not change course if by doing so you prevent A from keeping clear, or force him to make an unseamanlike manoeuvre in order to keep clear. If there is a lift (beneficial wind shift) just as A is passing ahead, you may be prevented from fulfilling your wish to luff for a few seconds. **(Rule 16)**

• Provided you don't deprive A of room to keep clear, you can tack away at any time. If you get an overlap to leeward of A, after his tack is complete, you may not sail above close-hauled unless you promptly sail astern of A (for example, to tack away). **(Rule 17)**

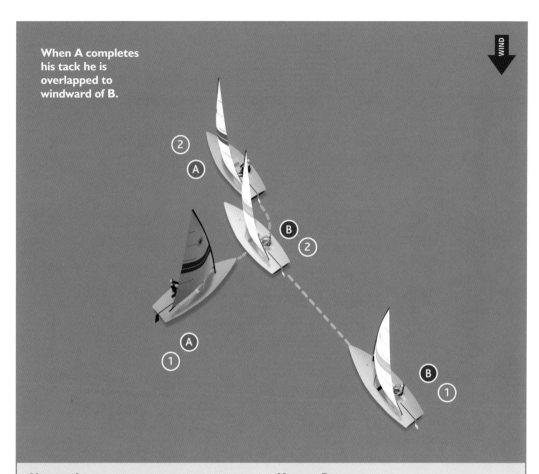

When A completes his tack he is overlapped to windward of B.

WIND

You are A:
• As you approach on port tack your obligation is simple – to keep clear of B. **(Rule 10)**
• While you are tacking (until you are close-hauled on the new tack) you must keep clear of B. **(Rule 13)**
• When your tack is complete, you are overlapped on B's windward bow putting B in your wind shadow. The manoeuvre is known as a 'slam dunk'. You are still the keep-clear boat. Furthermore, B has luffing rights and may luff above close-hauled, and you must keep clear. **(Rule 11)**
• At the completion of your tack you must not be so close to B that B cannot luff without immediately making contact with you. **(Rule 11 & Definition Keep Clear)**

You are B:
• You are the right-of-way boat throughout this manoeuvre, and unless you change course, you do not need to give A room to keep clear. If there is a lift (beneficial wind shift) just as A is passing ahead, you may be prevented from fulfilling your wish to luff for a few seconds. **(Rule 16)**
• At the completion of A's tack you are overlapped to leeward of A, so you have luffing rights, and may luff above close-hauled, but if you luff you must give A room to keep clear. **(Rule 16)**

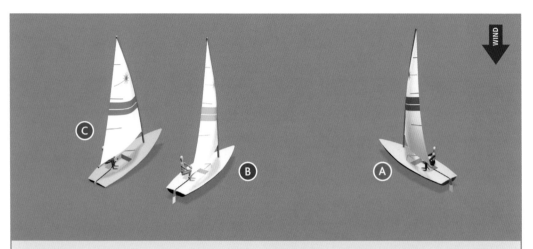

You are A:
- Your rights and obligations are exactly the same as those of boat B on page 33.

You are B:
- You must keep clear of A. **(Rule 10)**
- You have the right to choose either to go under A's stern or, as you need to change course substantially to avoid A, to tack, irrespective of any hail from C. **(Rule 20 & Definition Obstruction)**
- If you decide to go behind A, you must allow C room to pass under A's stern should he also choose to do so (though unless you are in a team race and C is an opponent, he'd probably rather tack). **(Rule 19.2(b))**
- If you decide to tack, you must hail C for room to tack ('Room to tack' is the best hail) and then tack as soon as you can do so without colliding with C. You need to hail early enough to allow C time to respond to your hail before you have a problem with A. This is especially important if there are boats to windward of C. **(Rule 20)**
- You must not hail C for room to tack, and then go behind A (unless C does not respond to the hail). **(Rule 20)**
- If you decide to hail for room to tack, and C does not respond, hail again more loudly. The pivotal issues in a protest in relation to this situation are often whether or not the hail was made and if it was, whether it was in time for C to respond; typically the helmsman of the leeward boat says he

hailed, and the helmsman of the hailed boat says he didn't hear a hail. The protest committee will be more inclined to find as fact that a hail was made if it has been repeated more loudly.
- If you can keep clear of A by making only a small (or no) change of course, then you do not have the right to hail and must pass under A, giving room to C if he chooses to go under A as well. **(Rules 19.2(b), 20, Definition Obstruction & World Sailing Case 3)**

You are C:
- Obviously you may tack if you want to.
- You must keep clear of A, and as windward boat, you must keep clear of B if he luffs. If B sails behind A, then if you wish to also go behind A you have the right to room to do that, and B must give you room (whether or not you ask for it). **(Rules 10, 11 & 19)**
- If B hails for room to tack, then you must either immediately tack, or hail 'You tack'. If you hail 'You tack' you take on the responsibility of giving B sufficient room to tack and keep clear of you. If you choose to tack, you don't have to carry out the tack any faster than is normal for you, but you must begin the manoeuvre immediately. If there are boats to windward of you preventing you from tacking, you must hail them for room to tack, and then tack when it is safe to do so. You are under no obligation to tack unless and until B hails for room. **(Rule 20)**

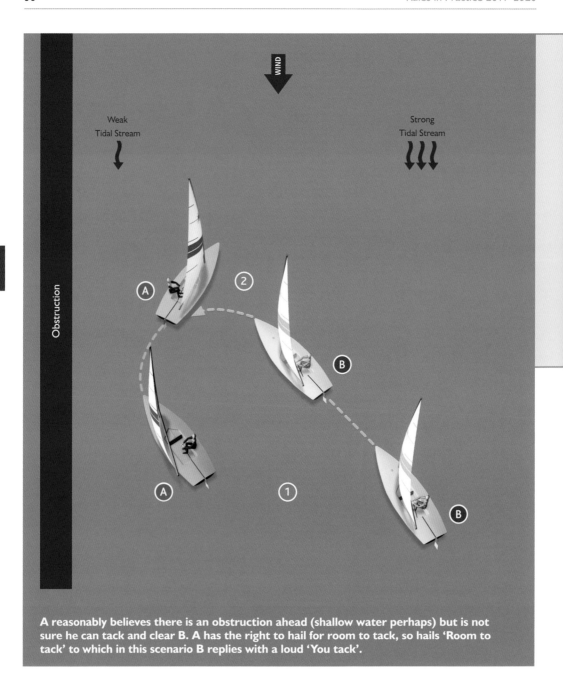

A reasonably believes there is an obstruction ahead (shallow water perhaps) but is not sure he can tack and clear B. A has the right to hail for room to tack, so hails 'Room to tack' to which in this scenario B replies with a loud 'You tack'.

You are A:

- You need to tack, but if you do, B will be (or might be) in the way, so you have the right to hail B for room to tack. **(Rule 20.1)**
- You are permitted to hail only if you really believe there is an obstruction ahead, but underwater weed or shallows count as an obstruction. **(Definition Obstruction)**
- Until you hail, B is under no obligation to do anything. **(Rule 20)**
- If there is a boat to windward or astern of B that would prevent him from tacking, you will need to hail in time for him to hail for room. He does not have the right to hail till you hail. **(Rule 20.3)**
- If he doesn't immediately respond to the first hail (by commencing a tack, or by hailing back to you 'You tack', or hailing to a boat that will be in his way) hail again more loudly.
- When he responds, either by tacking or hailing 'You tack', you must tack as soon as possible even if there is a lift (advantageous wind shift) and you'd like to change your mind and continue sailing near the shore out of an adverse tide. **(Rule 20.2(d))**

You are B:

- You must keep clear if A luffs to head to wind because you will be windward or astern. **(Rules 11 & 12)**
- Although you are under no obligation to do anything until A hails, if it's windy and noisy, you must be reasonably attentive to his need to hail.
- In response to his hail you must either tack as soon as possible or immediately hail back 'You tack' to A or 'Room to tack' to a boat that might obstruct you. **(Rule 20.2(c))**
- If you want to tack but cannot tack because of a boat to windward or astern, you must hail that boat for room to tack and tack as soon as possible. **(Rule 20.3)**
- If you hail 'You tack' you must keep clear of A while he tacks, and having completed his tack, you have to give him room to keep clear. **(Rule 20.2(c))**

6

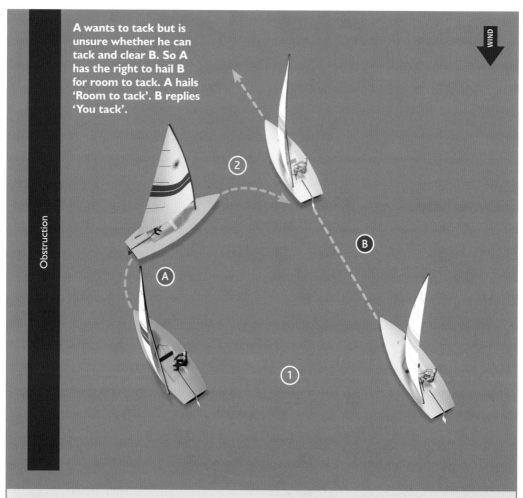

A wants to tack but is unsure whether he can tack and clear B. So A has the right to hail B for room to tack. A hails 'Room to tack'. B replies 'You tack'.

WIND

Obstruction

6

You are A:

• Having hailed for room to tack, you must tack immediately there is room, even if there is a lift (advantageous wind shift) and you'd like to continue sailing near the shore out of the adverse tidal stream. **(Rule 20.2(d))**

• When you have completed your tack you become the keep-clear boat and you must try to keep clear of B. If you can bear away under B's stern without difficulty (as you can in this diagram), then you must do so. You become required to keep clear only when your tack is complete, and if you then

cannot keep clear, or you manage to keep clear only by making an unseamanlike manoeuvre, then B has broken rule 20 and you should protest. **(Rules 10 & 20.2(c))**

You are B:

• When you hail 'You tack' you undertake to keep clear of A while he tacks, but having completed his tack, you also have to give him room to keep clear. In this diagram you have done so (just!); A can, without difficulty, bear away behind you, so no rule is broken. **(Rules 10 & 20.2(c))**

These hails of 'Room to tack' and 'You tack' (if the hailed boat decides not to tack), are the only hails that actually place an obligation on another boat to do something, so make sure they are loud and clear. You can say them in a common language (unlike the hail of 'protest' which must be in English, which simply reserves the right to lodge a protest). If there is no common language, the hailed boat can assume that these hails are being made because of the situation the boats are in with respect to an obstruction.

Remember, you are not permitted to make the hail unless the situation permits you to do so, and if a hail is made you must respond to it.

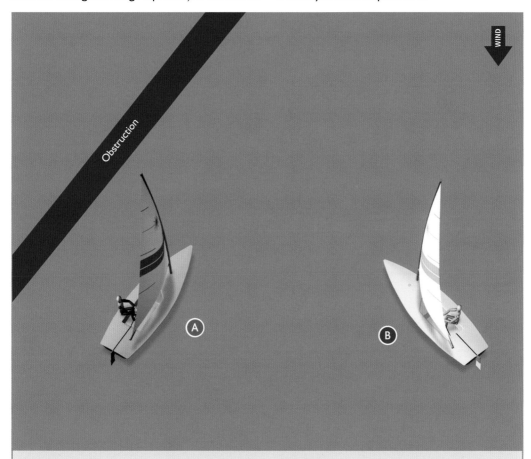

You are A:
• You are in big trouble. You don't have the right to room, and the obstruction prevents you from tacking. If you force B to change course, you must take a Two-Turns Penalty. **(Rules 10 & 44.1)**
• You should have thought of this possibility earlier when there was time to bear away under B!

You are B:
• You could be Mr Nice Guy and tack now, or you could sail on till you are forced to tack to avoid contact with A, in which case A will have broken rule 10 and must take a penalty. **(Rules 10 & 44.1)**

7. Rounding the Windward Mark

Rounding a port-hand windward mark

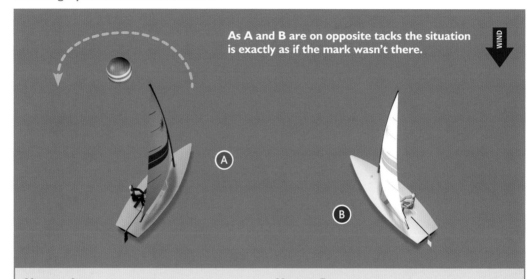

As A and B are on opposite tacks the situation is exactly as if the mark wasn't there.

WIND

You are A:
- You are the keep-clear boat. You have no right to mark-room while you are on opposite tacks. You must keep clear. **(Rules 10 & 18.1(a))**
- As you will see from the next few scenarios, it is risky to approach the mark so high on the layline if you are going to be on a collision course with a starboard-tack boat.

You are B:
- You are the right-of-way boat, but if you change course you must give room to A to keep clear. **(Rule 16)**

You are A:
- As you approach on port tack, you must keep clear. **(Rule 10)**
- While you are tacking you must keep clear. **(Rule 13)**
- You have passed head to wind outside the zone, completed your tack and you are overlapped inside B. You have tacked into this right-of-way position and B is

not required to anticipate your becoming the right-of-way boat. You must give B room to keep clear without having to change course till after your tack is complete. You are now the leeward boat with luffing rights. **(Rules 11 & 15)**
- Having given B room to keep clear without him having to anticipate your becoming the right-of-way boat, you may luff at any time (you may need to luff

above close-hauled to squeeze round the mark, but even without that need you can luff) or continue on a close-hauled course straight past the mark, or bear away round the mark, but if you luff beyond what you need to sail your course around the mark you must give B room to keep clear. **(Rules 11, 16 & 21)**

• If your only proper course is to gybe around the mark you must not sail higher than your proper course as you round the mark. **(Rule 18.4)**

• If after having given room to B to keep clear at the completion of your tack, you are below your layline, you may luff to head to wind if you need to. **(Rule 18.2(b) & 18.2(c))**

You are B:

• While A is approaching on port tack and while he's tacking you mustn't change course to prevent him from keeping clear. This doesn't stop you bearing away early to force him to tack earlier to avoid you, provided he can do it without difficulty. **(Rules 13 & 16)**

• If you are forced to change course to avoid A before he has completed his tack (without having changed course yourself towards A), he will have broken rule 13 and must take a turns penalty.

• When A completes his tack he becomes the right-of-way boat, and you must keep clear. Because he passed head to wind outside the zone, he has luffing rights and unless his only proper course is to gybe around the mark, he may luff at any time as high as he likes, or sail straight on. You must keep clear. **(Rules 11, 18.2(b) & 21)**

• If A passed head to wind within the zone, then A has no right to force you to sail above close-hauled. If he does you can protest but you must still keep clear if you can. **(Rules 18.3(a) & 11)**

7

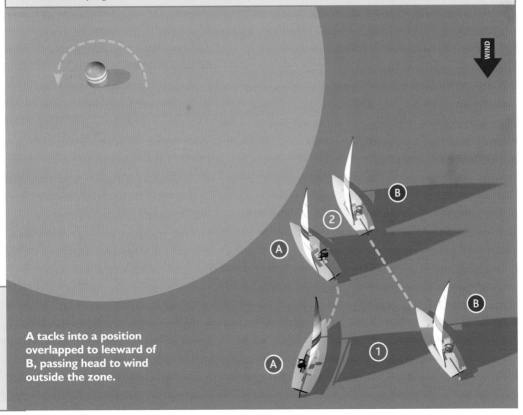

A tacks into a position overlapped to leeward of B, passing head to wind outside the zone.

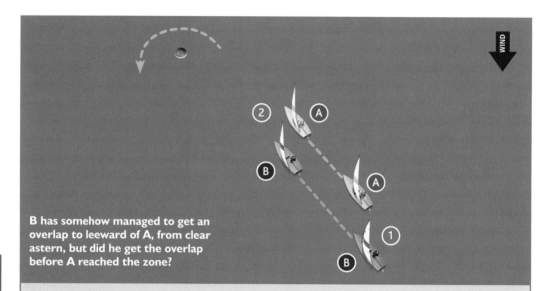

B has somehow managed to get an overlap to leeward of A, from clear astern, but did he get the overlap before A reached the zone?

7

You are A:
- If there is doubt as to whether the overlap was established before you reached the zone, then B does not have the right to round inside. It is a good idea to tell him so, and keep clear. **(Rules 18.2(e) & 11)**
- Because B got his overlap from clear astern, he has no luffing rights, but if the overlap is established before you reached the zone, then he may still sail his proper course around the mark, and you must keep clear. His proper course is a wide rounding if that's how he would round without your being there. Because B is right-of-way boat he is not constrained to the room he is entitled to by rule 18. You must keep clear. **(Rules 11)**

You are B:
- If the boats become overlapped, without doubt, before A reaches the zone, and are overlapped at the zone, you have the right to sail your proper course as you round the mark. This means you may sail the course you would have sailed in the absence of A, even if this means sailing above close-hauled to 'shoot' the mark. You may even head up a bit so that you don't get too far from the mark as you complete the rounding. A must give you mark-room, but more important, A must also keep clear of you. **(Rules 11 and 18.2(b))**
- If there is 'reasonable doubt' as to whether A had reached the zone when you established the overlap, you must presume that you are too late. If A is shouting to you that you established your overlap too late, you'd be wise to slow and keep clear by letting him round first. **(Rule 18.2(e))**

You are A:
- As you approach on port tack, you must keep clear. **(Rule 10)**
- While you are tacking you are the keep-clear boat and you must keep clear. **(Rule 13)**
- You have completed the tack well outside the zone, and you are overlapped inside B. You have tacked into this right-of-way position and B is not required

to anticipate you becoming the right-of-way boat. You must give B room to keep clear without having to change course till after your tack is complete. You are now the leeward boat with luffing rights. **(Rules 11 & 15)**
- Having given B room to keep clear without having had to anticipate, and having been overlapped at the zone, you have luffing rights and the right to round

inside. You may bear away round the mark, or continue on a close-hauled course, or luff at any time, but if you luff (other than to 'shoot' the mark) or bear away more sharply than necessary to sail your course around the mark, you must give B room to keep clear. **(Rules 11, 16 & Definition Mark-Room)**

• However, if your only proper course is to gybe around the mark, you must not sail higher than your proper course as you round the mark. **(Rule 18.4)**

• If there is 'reasonable doubt' as to whether you had reached the zone when you passed head to wind, you are safer not to thereafter force B to sail above close-hauled. **(Rule 18.3)**

You are B:

• While A is approaching on port tack and while he's tacking you mustn't change course to prevent him from keeping clear or make it difficult for him to keep clear, or force him to immediately alter course. This doesn't stop you bearing away early to force him to tack earlier to avoid you, provided he can keep clear without difficulty. **(Rules 13 & 16)**

• If you are forced to change course before A has completed his tack (without having changed course yourself towards A), A will have broken Rule 13.

• As A completes his tack, he becomes the right-of-way boat, and you must keep clear. He has luffing rights and unless his only proper course is to gybe around the mark, he may luff at any time or sail straight on. You must keep clear and give mark-room. **(Rules 11 & 18.2(a))**

• If there is doubt as to whether you have broken the overlap when you reached the zone, then A has the right to room. If A is shouting to you that he is overlapped at the zone, you'd be wise to keep clear and give mark-room. **(Rule 18.2(e))**

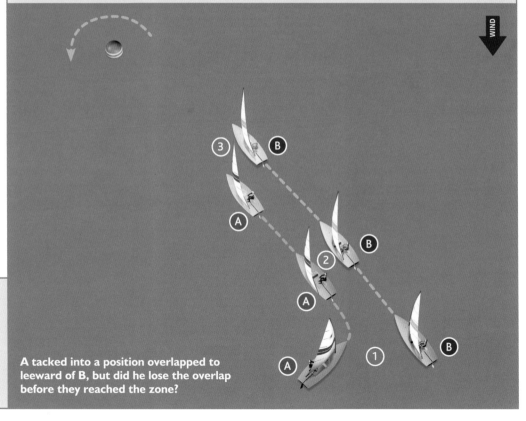

A tacked into a position overlapped to leeward of B, but did he lose the overlap before they reached the zone?

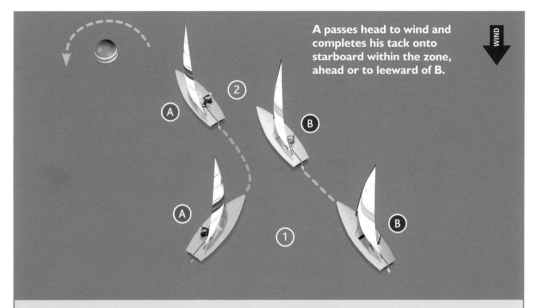

A passes head to wind and completes his tack onto starboard within the zone, ahead or to leeward of B.

WIND

7

You are A:
• As you approach on port tack, you must keep clear. **(Rule 10)**
• While you are tacking you must keep clear. **(Rule 13)**
• You have passed head to wind within the zone. You have tacked into this right-of-way position but B is not required to anticipate your having become the right-of-way boat. You must give B room to keep clear without having to change course till after your tack is complete. **(Rule 15)**
• Now you have another problem. Even after your tack is complete, you must not force B (who is probably sailing faster than you are) to luff above close-hauled in order to avoid you. **(Rule 18.3)**

You are B:
• While A is approaching on port tack and while he's tacking you mustn't change course to prevent him from keeping clear or make it difficult for him to keep clear. This doesn't stop you bearing away early to force him to tack earlier to avoid you, provided he can keep clear without difficulty. **(Rules 13 & 16)**
• If you are forced to change course before A has completed his tack (without having changed course yourself towards A), A will have broken Rule 13.
• If A completes his tack to leeward of you he becomes the right-of-way boat, but if you can avoid him only by sailing above close-hauled (which is almost inevitable in this diagram) then he has broken rule 18.3(a) and must take a penalty. However, as windward boat you must keep clear if you can. **(Rule 11)**

A passes head to wind inside the zone and completes his tack nearly overlapped, or overlapped to windward of B.

You are A:
• As you tack you must keep clear of B. You might need to slow, and pass behind B. **(Rule 13)**

• If at the moment you complete your tack B is overlapped to leeward, then B has luffing rights. You must continue to keep clear of B even if B luffs right up to head to wind. **(Rule 11)**
• If at the moment your tack is complete B is clear astern, and chooses to go between you and the mark, you must give mark-room to and keep clear

A passes head to wind inside the zone and completes the tack clear ahead of B.

You are A:
- As you tack you must keep clear of B. **(Rule 13)**
- If you complete your tack without forcing B to change course to avoid you, the next thing you have to worry about is that if B, with superior speed, can avoid you only by sailing above his close-hauled course, then you have broken a rule, and must take a penalty. **(Rule 18.3)**
- Furthermore, if B chooses to bear away and gets an overlap to leeward of you, you must give him mark-room. **(Rule 18.3)**
- Basically, for this manoeuvre to succeed, you must stay clear until you have left the mark astern. **(Rule 18.3)**

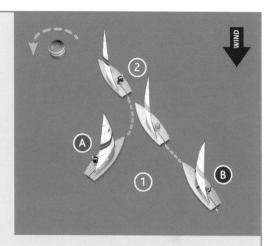

You are B:
- When A's tack is complete, you become the keep-clear boat, but if the only way you can avoid him is to luff above your close-hauled course, he has broken a rule and must take a penalty. **(Rule 18.3)**
- If you choose to bear away and get an overlap to leeward of A, A must give you mark-room and you may sail your proper course around the mark. **(Rule 18.3)**

of B, who is allowed to sail his proper course (the course he would have sailed had you not been there). **(Rule 18.3)**

You are B:
- If you were clear astern when A completed his tack, you may choose to go inside if you want to, and then sail your proper course (the course you would have sailed had A not been there) and if you need to luff above close-hauled to be able to round the mark as necessary to sail the course, you do not need to give room to A to keep clear. **(Rules 18.3, 21 & Definition Mark-Room)**
- If you were overlapped to leeward of A when A completed his tack, you have luffing rights and you may sail any course, but if you luff above the course necessary to round the mark, you must give A room to keep clear. However, if your only proper course is to gybe at the mark, you can sail your proper course but no higher. **(Rules 11, 16, 18.3, 18.4, 21 & Definition Mark-Room)**

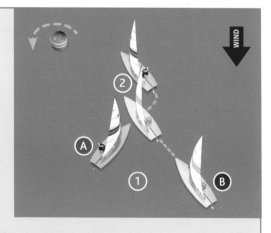

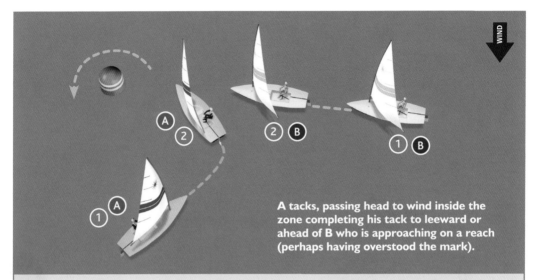

7

A tacks, passing head to wind inside the zone completing his tack to leeward or ahead of B who is approaching on a reach (perhaps having overstood the mark).

You are A:
• You must complete your tack without forcing B to change course to keep clear. **(Rule 13)**
• After you have completed your tack, you are the right-of-way boat but you mustn't be in a position that forces B to sail above his close-hauled course in order to keep clear of you - this applies as long as the boats are in the zone. **(Rule 18.3)**
• Even though you have luffing rights, you must not prevent B from passing the mark. **(Rule 18.3)**

• Once the boats have left the zone you may luff (you have luffing rights) but if you do you must give B room to keep clear. **(Rules 11, 16 & 18.1)**

You are B:
• You need do nothing till A's tack is complete, then you must keep clear, but if the only way you can keep clear is by sailing above close-hauled, then A must take a Two-Turns Penalty. **(Rule 18.3)**

Rounding a starboard-hand windward mark

A and B are on opposite tacks so the situation is exactly as if the mark wasn't there. (Rule 18.3 does not apply.)

You are A:
You are the keep-clear boat. You have no right to room at the mark. You must keep clear. **(Rule 10)**

You are B:
You hold right-of-way, but if you change course you must give A room to keep clear. **(Rule 16)**

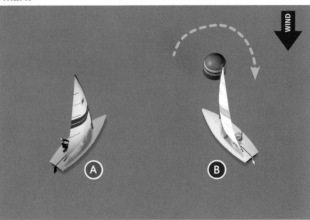

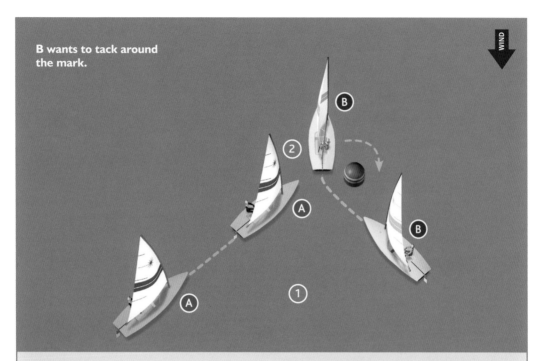

B wants to tack around the mark.

You are A:
• As you approach on port tack, you must keep clear. **(Rule 10)**
• At position 2, B has luffed to head to wind. He is still on starboard tack. You must keep clear. **(Rule 10)**
• If you keep clear by luffing, you must not end up so close alongside him that if he bears away around the mark he will immediately make contact - that would no be keeping clear and he'd then be exonerated for breaking rule 16. **(Rule 10 & Definition Keep Clear)**
• If you luff and tack, you must keep clear. **(Rule 13)**

You are B:
• As A approaches you must not change course so as to make it difficult for A to keep clear. In addition, because A is sailing a course to pass astern of you, you must not change course if as a result A has to immediately change course to continue keeping clear of you. **(Rules 16.1 & 16.2)**
• At position 2 you must not turn any more, because once you pass head to wind you become the keep-clear boat, and A is so close behind that he will be forced to change course. **(Rule 13)**
• If A ducks your stern before you pass head to wind, leaving the mark on the wrong side, you'll probably be able to tack but you will be the keep-clear boat while you're tacking, and you'll probably be the windward boat when you've completed your tack. In either case you must keep clear. **(Rules 13 & 11)**
• If A luffs to avoid you when you're head to wind, and gets overlapped on your port side, you may be able to tack if you don't over-rotate, and you will be right-of-way boat again when your tack is complete. You must give A room to keep clear, both as the tack is completed and if you bear away around the mark. **(Rule 16)**
• If A tacks, then immediately he is past head to wind you can complete your tack. **(Rule 13)**
• The best tactic in this scenario if you haven't room to complete a tack before A gets too close, is to slow down at position 1 to force A to tack, then tack.

7

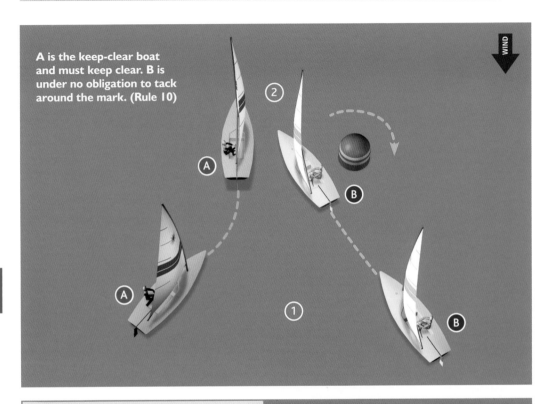

A is the keep-clear boat and must keep clear. B is under no obligation to tack around the mark. (Rule 10)

WIND

You are A:
You were keeping clear of B by passing ahead. B has altered course so he must give you room to keep clear. **(Rule 16)**

You are B:
As much as you may like to luff to tack around the mark, you cannot do this if the change of course doesn't give A room to keep clear. **(Rule 16)**

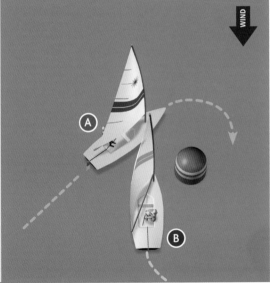

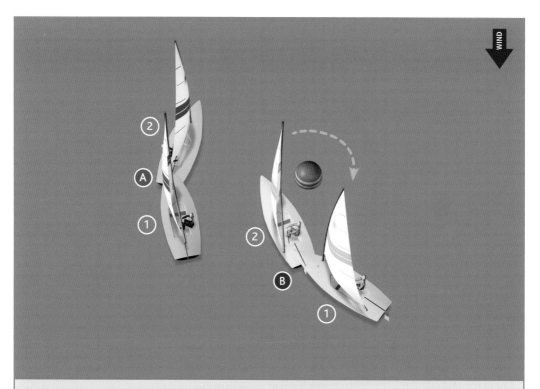

You are A:
* At position 1 when you begin to luff to tack, you are clear ahead and, therefore, the right-of-way boat.
* When you pass head to wind you must keep clear of B. Because B has luffed (while you were still right-of-way boat) you may be prevented from completing your tack. **(Rule 13)**
* Next time you approach the mark with an opponent close astern, try to be on the layline, rather than half a length to leeward.

You are B:
* As A luffs to head to wind, you may luff too. You don't have to anticipate that he is going to tack.
* When A passes head to wind you become the right-of-way boat, so if you change course after that, you must give him room to keep clear. In the diagram he does have room – he can turn back onto starboard tack. **(Rules 12, 10 & 16)**
* To prevent A from tacking in front of you, you need to luff till he reaches head to wind, and then sail straight. Tack when there's room.

When the windward mark is an obstruction

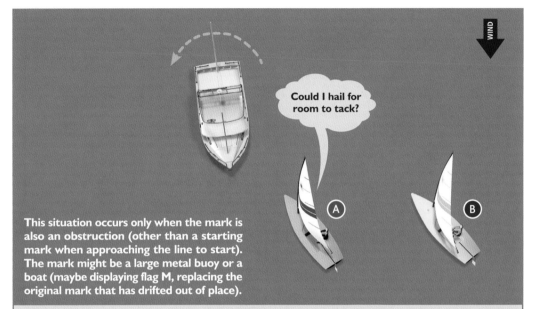

Could I hail for room to tack?

This situation occurs only when the mark is also an obstruction (other than a starting mark when approaching the line to start). The mark might be a large metal buoy or a boat (maybe displaying flag **M**, replacing the original mark that has drifted out of place).

You are A:
• Provided that you need to tack, and you are certain the other boat is not fetching the mark, you may hail to B for room to tack. 'Water' may be misunderstood; 'Room to tack' is best. **(Rule 20.1)**
• If B hails 'You tack' in response to your hail, and then ducks your stern or crosses safely ahead of you and fetches the mark, you have broken a rule (because you had no right to hail). If he is agrieved you must take a penalty, or he could protest you. If he responds to your hail by tacking, he might protest and claim in a protest hearng that he could have layed the mark, or that you could have easily sailed below the mark. **(Rule 20.1)**
• If you judge that B can get round the mark without passing head to wind the mark without passing head to wind, you are still the right-of-way boat provided you don't pass head to wind yourself. So even if you don't have luffing rights, you may go up to head to wind in order to 'shoot the mark', and B must keep clear. **(Rule 11 & Definition Proper Course)**
• For you to have the right to hail, you have to be close-hauled or above and on a course from which you must make a substantial change to avoid

the obstruction. If you were further to leeward, so that the obstruction was not in your path, then you would not have the right to hail; you would have to slow down and tack behind B or bear away and gybe. **(Definition Obstruction)**
• If you do hail for room to tack, you must tack as soon as there is room. You can't hail and then 'shoot the mark' by going head to wind and bearing away around the mark. **(Rule 20.2(d))**

You are B:
• As the windward boat you must keep clear if A luffs in an attempt to 'shoot the mark'. If he luffs as needed to shoot the mark he does not have to give you room to keep clear. **(Rules 11 & 21)**
• If A hails for room to tack, even if you are sure that you could get round the mark without tacking, you must respond to the hail (by tacking or hailing 'You tack'). You cannot just tell A that he has no right to hail for room to tack. **(Rule 20.2(b))**
• If A hails for room to tack, and you are not sure that you can get round the mark without tacking, then you must either tack or hail back 'You tack' and give room to A to tack. **(Rules 20.2(b) & (c))**

7

8. On the Reach

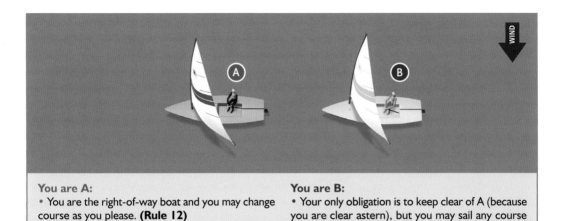

You are A:
• You are the right-of-way boat and you may change course as you please. **(Rule 12)**

You are B:
• Your only obligation is to keep clear of A (because you are clear astern), but you may sail any course you like. **(Rule 12)**

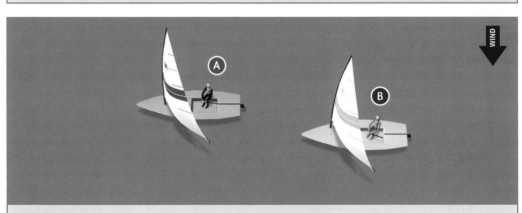

You are A:
• With B aiming to overtake you on your leeward side, you might be happy not to manoeuvre in case doing so discourages him, and he decides to take your wind on your windward side.
• On the other hand if you are approaching a port hand mark, you don't want him to get an inside overlap, so you may bear away to encourage him to stay to windward.
• While clear ahead, you remain the right-of-way boat and may luff or bear away as you please.

You are B:
• As you are clear astern you must keep clear, but you may luff or bear away as you please.

8

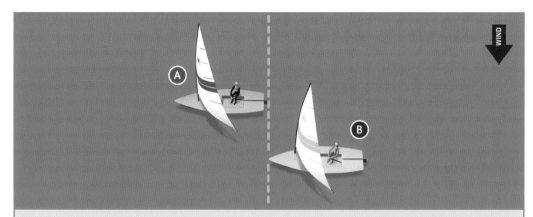

You are A:
- When B gets an overlap to leeward you become the keep-clear boat, but provided you keep clear, you may change course as you please. **(Rule 11)**
- If B sails a course you think is higher than his proper course, you may protest, but you must still keep clear. **(Rule 11)**

You are B:
- When you get your overlap to leeward of A, you will become the right-of-way boat, but A doesn't have to anticipate your getting the overlap, so you must initially give him room to keep clear. You mustn't get the overlap so close to his quarter, that if he luffed there would immediately be contact. **(Rule 15 & Definition Keep Clear)**
- Once you've got an overlap, although you don't have luffing rights, you may sail up to, but not above, your proper course. You must not sail above your proper course while the overlap exists and you are within two of your hull lengths of A. If there are other boats coming up behind, your proper course may be to luff. **(Rules 11 & 17)**
- If you luff (up to your proper course), you must give A room to keep clear. **(Rule 16)**

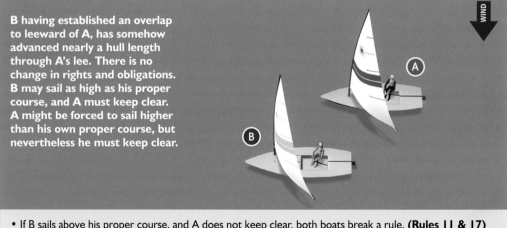

B having established an overlap to leeward of A, has somehow advanced nearly a hull length through A's lee. There is no change in rights and obligations. B may sail as high as his proper course, and A must keep clear. A might be forced to sail higher than his own proper course, but nevertheless he must keep clear.

- If B sails above his proper course, and A does not keep clear, both boats break a rule. **(Rules 11 & 17)**

The boats are in the same positions as they were in the previous diagram, but here the situation has arisen through A establishing an overlap from astern to windward of B. The boats' rights and obligations are quite different, because B has luffing rights.

You are A:
- You must keep clear of B. **(Rule 11)**
- Provided you keep clear, you can change course as you please. If you are approaching a port-hand mark, you could bear away under B's stern to try to get an overlap. **(Rule 11)**

You are B:
- You may sail any course but if you luff you must give A room to keep clear. **(Rule 16)**

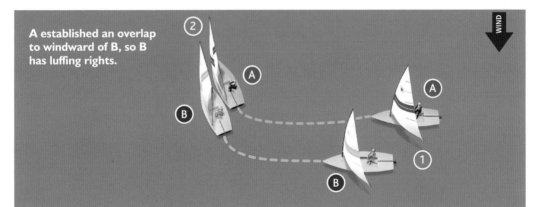

A established an overlap to windward of B, so B has luffing rights.

8

You are A: You must keep clear. **(Rule 11)**

You are B: You may luff or bear away as you please provided you give A room to keep clear. **(Rule 16)**

The 'lock-up' position:
- At position 2, if A luffs, his stern will swing into B. If he bears away their courses will converge and there will be contact almost immediately. The only way in which A can fulfil his obligation to keep clear is to sail straight on. B can luff no more, for to do

so would not be giving A room to keep clear. B may continue sailing straight ahead, or he may bear away. **(Rules 11 & 16)**
- It is for this reason that luffing a boat to windward is rarely worthwhile in fleet racing. B would be wise to luff to clear his wind before A gets an overlap to windward and, unless there is a port rounding mark coming up soon, encourage A to overtake to leeward.
- However, if the lock-up has been caused by A's slowness in luffing to keep clear, then A breaks rule 11.

8

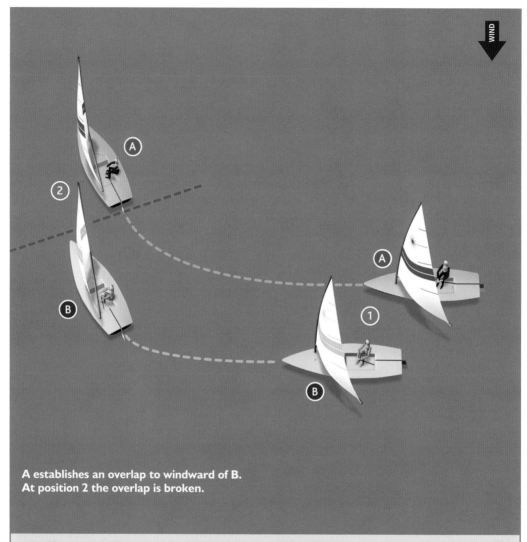

**A establishes an overlap to windward of B.
At position 2 the overlap is broken.**

You are A:
• Position 1: You established the overlap from clear astern to windward of B, so B has luffing rights. You must keep clear. **(Rule 11)**
• Position 2: When the overlap is broken you become the right-of-way boat but obviously if you bear away the overlap will be re-established and you'll be windward boat again, with the obligation to keep clear. **(Rules 12 & 11)**

You are B:
• Position 1: You have luffing rights and may luff as high as you please but you must give A room to keep clear. **(Rules 16 & 17)**
• Position 2: When A draws ahead and the overlap is broken, you become clear astern and must therefore keep clear, but you may sail any course. **(Rule 12)**

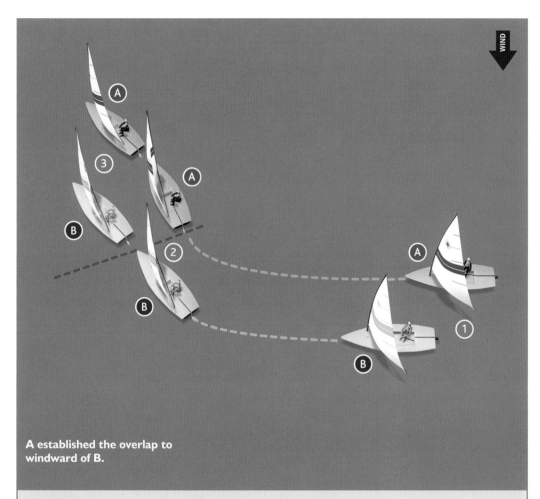

A established the overlap to windward of B.

You are A:
• Position 1: You established the overlap from clear astern to windward of B, so B has luffing rights. You must keep clear. **(Rule 11)**
• Position 2: You can luff to break the overlap so that B becomes clear astern and must keep clear.
• Position 3: When you bear away and an overlap is re-established, B must bear away to his proper course (or lower). However, you are still the keep-clear boat and must keep-clear. Furthermore, because it was your action that put you into a keep-clear position, B does not initially have to give you room to keep clear. **(Rules 11 & 15)**

You are B:
• Position 1: You have luffing rights and may luff as high as you please but you must give A room to keep clear. **(Rule 16)**
• Positions 2 & 3: When A luffs to break the overlap, and then bears away to re-establish an overlap, you lose your luffing rights. You must immediately bear away to your proper course (or lower). If you need to gybe to sail your proper course, then you must gybe. **(Rule 17)**

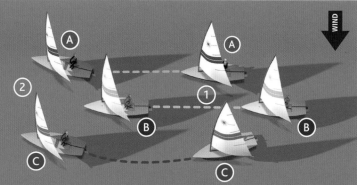

In this scenario, A establishes an overlap to windward of C and draws parallel with her, then B establishes an overlap from clear astern to leeward of A, then while still overlapped with A, B gets an overlap to windward of C.

You are A:
• You are under no obligation to anticipate B getting an overlap, but when he does you must keep clear. Even if B does not luff, you will have to luff to avoid him running into your boom. **(Rules 12 & 11)**

You are B:
• When you first get an overlap to leeward of A, you must give him room to keep clear. Then you may sail up to your proper course, but no higher. **(Rules 15, 16 & 17)**

• Your proper course is a course that will keep you clear of C. **(Definition Proper Course)**
• If C luffs, you must keep clear of C who has luffing rights over both you and A, because you both established overlaps on C's windward side. **(Rule 11)**

You are C:
• You have luffing rights over both A and B so may luff as high as you like, but you must give them room to keep clear. **(Rule 16)**

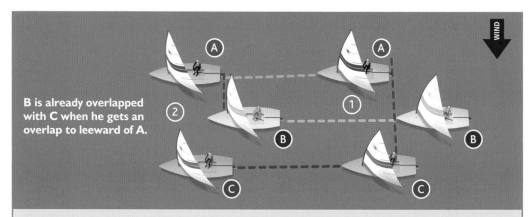

B is already overlapped with C when he gets an overlap to leeward of A.

You are B:
• When you first get the overlap to leeward of A, you become the right-of-way boat in relation to A, but remain the keep-clear boat in relation to C. Although you don't have luffing rights, your proper course is to luff to pass C and A must keep clear. But bear in mind A is not required to change course until you have an overlap, and you must not be so close to A when you get the overlap that A has no room to change course. **(Rules 11, 15 & 19.2(b))**

8

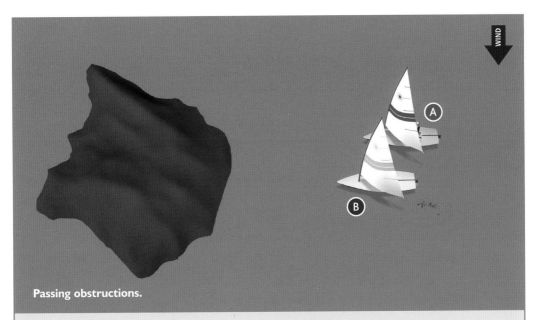

Passing obstructions.

You are A:
• You are the windward boat so you must keep clear of B. **(Rule 11)**
• If B sails to leeward of the obstruction, you may also go to leeward and if you do, B must give you room but you must keep clear. If you break rule 11 when you are taking room between B and the obstruction, you will be exonerated. **(Rules 11, 19.2(b) & 21)**

You are B:
• If you have luffing rights, you may luff A at any time and obviously may go to windward of the obstruction. If you change course you must give A room to keep clear. **(Rules 11 & 16)**
• If you don't have luffing rights you may only pass to windward of the island if that is your proper course. Both sides may sometimes be proper courses. **(Rule 17)**
• Whether or not you have luffing rights, if you choose to go to leeward, and A chooses to do likewise, you must give him room to pass between you and the obstruction. **(Rule 19.2(b))**
• If you both sail to leeward of the obstruction, once the island has been passed, if you have luffing rights you may luff above your proper course, but you must give A room to keep clear. **(Rule 16)**

8

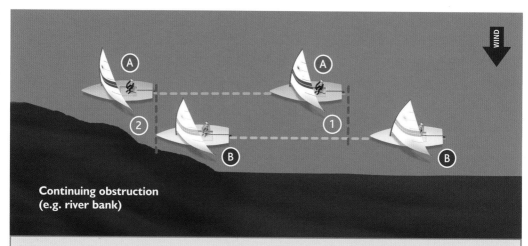

Continuing obstruction (e.g. river bank)

In position 1, B is about to get an overlap between A and the continuing obstruction. At the moment the overlap is established (position 2) there is insufficient room for B to pass between A and the obstruction.

Because B is required to keep clear of A, he has no right to room, and if he gets an overlap rule 11 does not apply and he must keep clear of A. **(Rule 19.2(c))**

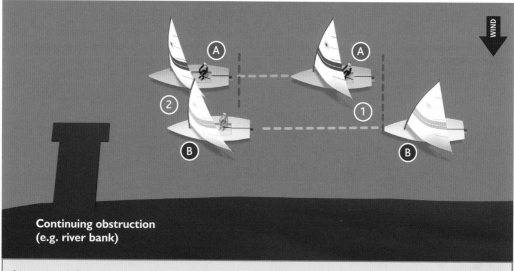

Continuing obstruction (e.g. river bank)

In position 1, B is about to get an overlap between A and the continuing obstruction.

Unlike the situation at the top of the page, at the moment the overlap is established there is sufficient room for B to pass between A and the continuing

obstruction, so B has the right to room. **(Rule 19.2(b))**

At position 2, A will need to luff to give room to B to get round the jetty. **(Rule 19.2(b))**

9. Rounding the Gybe Mark

When the inside boat has to gybe to sail his proper course

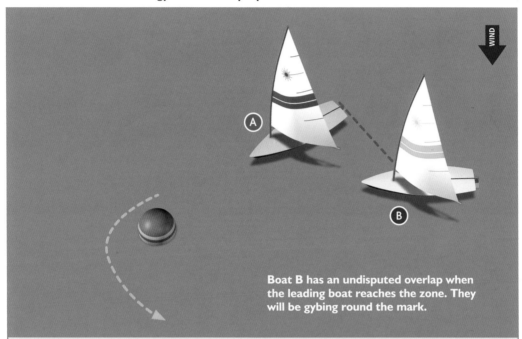

Boat B has an undisputed overlap when the leading boat reaches the zone. They will be gybing round the mark.

You are A:
• B has an overlap when you reach the zone, and you are the keep-clear boat, so you must keep clear and give mark-room. **(Rules 11 & 18.2(b))**
• If you now get clear ahead, you must continue to give mark-room until B has been given mark-room and that is normally when he has left the mark astern. You might do this by staying ahead, but if B is forced to change course to avoid you while rule 18.2(b) still applies, you will have broken a rule. If B does not gybe around the mark but continues beyond the mark, he will break a rule, but you must still keep clear of him. **(Rule 18.2(b), 18.2(c), 18.4)**

You are B:
• Even if you have luffing rights, (for example, if you were more than two of your hull lengths away from

A when you became overlapped, or because A got an overlap on your windward side) then because your proper course is to gybe, as soon as one of you reaches the zone you must sail no farther from the mark than your proper course until you gybe. **(Rule 18.4)**
• As A is overlapped outside you, you must gybe no later than you would have done had A not been there. (If it's very windy and you want to do a loop and tack instead of gybing, you are better off slowing down and letting A go ahead.) **(Rule 18.4)**
• After you have both gybed round the mark, and the mark is 'passed' (left clear astern with no chance of hitting it), then if you are overlapped you will be the windward boat, and you must keep clear of A. A will have luffing rights if there was an overlap when you have both gybed. **(Rule 11)**

How much room must A give?
A is to windward and is, therefore, the keep-clear boat and must keep clear. B must sail a course no higher than his proper course. To comply with that obligation, B will have to gybe. If A believes B has sailed too wide (i.e. above his proper course), he can protest, but he'd be wise to keep clear, because if there is contact, whether or not the protest committee find that B has sailed above his proper course, they will most likely find that A has not kept clear.
(Rules: Definition Proper Course, 18.2(a), 18.4 & 11)

9

When the inside boat does not have to gybe to sail his proper course

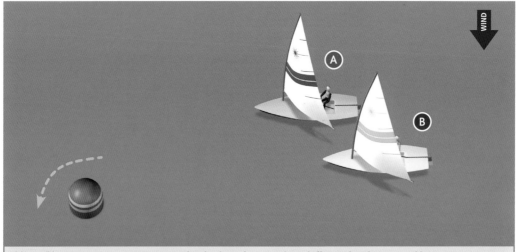

Here, B's proper course is not to gybe (it doesn't matter what A's proper course is). If B has luffing rights (usually because A established the overlap to windward of B) then B may sail straight on past the mark, or luff at any time. If B luffs, he must give room to A to keep clear. A must keep clear. If B does not have luffing rights, he may sail his proper course, but no higher, as he approaches, as he passes, and after he has passed the mark. **(Rules 18.2(a), 11, 16 & 17)**

Here A, the keep-clear boat, will be on the inside. As soon as one of the boats reaches the zone, B must start giving mark-room, whether or not he has luffing rights. Remember 'mark-room' means, 'room for a boat to leave a mark on the required side, room to sail to the mark when his proper course is to sail close to the mark and room to round the mark as necessary to sail the course'. A must keep clear of B, but if he breaks rule 11 while taking mark-room he will be exonerated.

Once B has given A room to round the mark as necessary to sail the course, B may return to his proper course or, if he has luffing rights, may sail as high as he likes, but if he luffs he must give A room to keep clear. **(Rules 18.2(a), 11, 16, 17 & 21)**

9

When there is doubt about the overlap

Often there is doubt whether or not there is an overlap at that critical moment when the leading boat reaches the zone. It is easy to draw a picture in a book, or place models carefully on the protest room table, but in real life the moment passes in an instant. If you are flying a spinnaker and you're preparing for a gybe you'll be reluctant to spare anyone to go to the bow or stern to see if there's an overlap. In addition to knowing whether the boats are overlapped, it is difficult to judge when the leading boat is three hull lengths from the mark. Before you know it, the moment is gone, and the boats are converging towards the mark with the crew of one boat shouting 'No room' and the crew from the other shouting 'Water', plus a fair number of unprintable words and phrases to give emphasis to their respective opinions.

In this diagram, who can say without the use of measuring instruments whether B has an overlap, and whether A is three hull lengths from the mark? If A luffs a little at the critical moment as he is just about to get to the zone, maybe he could break an overlap. If this was happening on the water with boats that are moving rather than being frozen in a picture, and the overlap is in doubt, then the answer to the question 'is B entitled to room?' depends on what was happening before they got to this position: see the next two diagrams.

Here, at position 1 there is no doubt that B has an overlap. So when there is doubt at position 2, it is resolved in B's favour. Even if A surges forward on a wave and gets clear ahead at around three hull lengths, A must keep clear and give mark-room. Both boats should, of course, try to avoid contact.

You are B:
• Unless it is obvious that there is an overlap and A will not draw ahead and break it, try to get A's agreement that you have an overlap well before you reach the critical zone. At least hail 'Overlap' before you get to the 'three-lengths' position. If there is a protest and A claims that he subsequently broke the overlap, any doubt will be resolved in your favour. **(Rules 18.2(e))**
• Your hail does not in itself place any obligation on A, but will usually avoid a disagreement or even a protest.

9

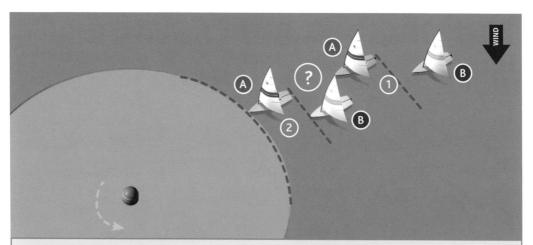

At position I there is no doubt that A is clear ahead. So at position 2, when there is doubt, it is resolved in A's favour. If B surges forward on a wave, A should keep clear and protest. If the water is flat, A could hail something like 'No water' and hold his proper course for the mark. B would be wise to slow down and follow A, because a protest committee is likely to find in favour of A and if A breaks rule 11 while taking mark-room she will be exonerated. There is no obligation on A to give mark-room just because B is claiming he has the right to room. On the other hand, both boats should, of course, try to avoid contact. **(Rules 18.2(e), 14 & 21)**

You are A:
• Unless it is obvious that there is no overlap and B will not get one, hail 'No overlap' long before you get to the zone, and try to get a response from B. If B subsequently claims that he got an inside overlap before the zone, any doubt will be resolved in your favour. **(Rules 18.2(e))**
• Your hail does not in itself place any obligation on B but will usually avoid a disagreement or even a protest.

10. Rounding the Leeward Mark from the Reach

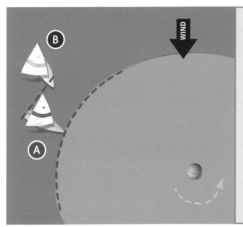

You are A:
• You must give mark-room to B if he can get there in time. If he can't, you could take a risk and round up tight, but if B catches you, even if he hits your transom, you will be in the wrong. Your obligation to give mark-room to B lasts until B has finished rounding the mark, i.e. until he has left the mark astern and it is no longer an issue. **(Rules 18.1, 18.2(b) & (c))**

You are B:
• You have an inside overlap on A as he reaches the critical zone, so you have the right to mark-room – though if you can't get there in time to take advantage of it, it won't be any use to you.

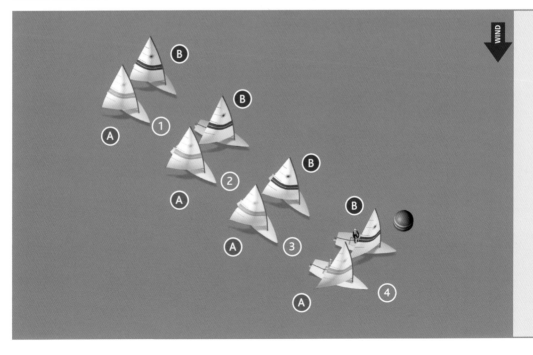

10

You are A:

• At position 1, you haven't reached the zone, so:

- *If you have luffing rights* you may luff and take B to windward of the mark if you want to, but when you change course, you must give him room to keep clear, and if you reach a position where one of you reaches the zone, then you must immediately give mark-room if B is still overlapped, and remember from the previous page, any doubt about an overlap at the zone will go against you. **(Rules 11, 16.1, 18.1 & 18.2(b) & 18.2(e))**

- *If you don't have luffing rights*, you must not sail above your proper course. **(Rule 17)**

• Whether or not you have luffing rights, when you reach the zone (about position 2) you must ignore your proper course and begin to bear away if necessary to give mark-room. **(Rules 18.1 & 18.2(b))**

• Mark-room means room for the other boat to sail to the mark, and then room to round the mark as necessary to sail the course. If there are several boats inside you, or you are sailing fast boats or there is a tide running with you, this often means you will have to begin to bear away before you get to the zone because if you wait until you get to the zone it may no longer be possible for you to give mark-room and you will break rule 18.2(b). At the latest, when one boat has entered the zone you must start giving mark-room, whether or not you have luffing rights. **(Rule 18.2(b) & Definition Mark-Room)**

• If you have managed to get ahead and break the overlap (without 'reasonable doubt' – in other words you must both be sure the overlap is broken) when you get to the zone, then you are no longer required to give mark-room. Remember that if there is reasonable doubt, you must give mark-room. **(Rules 18.2(b) & 18.2(e))**

• From a tactical point of view, it may be better to slow down, let B go ahead, and tighten up round the mark immediately behind B, to prevent yourself getting trapped down to leeward of him as you come away from the mark. Remember that mark-room for B is room to sail to the mark, and then room to round the mark as necessary to sail the course in a seamanlike way. He does **not** have right to room to sail his proper course, which would probably have been to sail wide and come up tight

on the mark.

• If you are still overlapped when the mark is left astern and is no longer an issue, you may return to your proper course or, if you have luffing rights, sail as high as you like, but you must give B room to keep clear when you change course. **(Rule 16.1)**

You are B:

• As you approach the mark, your obligation is to keep clear of A. **(Rule 11)**

• If A has luffing rights, he may luff you to windward of the mark, but when either of you enter the zone, if you are overlapped at that time, A must bear away and give you mark-room. **(Rules 18.1 & 18.2(b))**

• When you enter the zone, you have the right to 'mark-room' to round inside A. Having the right to mark-room means that you can sail a 'seamanlike' course to the mark and then A must give you room to round the mark as necessary to sail the course. If you only take that room and you are forced to break rule 11, you will be exonerated. However, if you sail as wide as you like to be able to round up tight around the mark, and you break rule 11 while doing so, you will **not** be exonerated for that breach as you will have taken more room than 'necessary to sail the course'. If A squeezes you right to the mark while leaving you enough room to round the mark in a seamanlike way, then he is giving you mark-room. If he doesn't give you mark-room, it makes no difference whether you collide with the mark or the boat; whatever you hit (or if you hit both or even neither), if you feel you weren't given mark-room, protest and sail on. If the protest committee agrees he did not give you mark-room you will be exonerated for touching A or the mark or both. **(Rules 18.2(a-b), 21 & 64.1(a))**

• Although A must give mark-room, you remain the keep-clear boat and you must keep clear. When A has given you mark room and the mark is no longer an issue, A may luff to close-hauled (or his proper course if the next leg is a reach) and if he has luffing rights (can you remember how the overlap was established on the last leg?) A may luff up to head to wind and you must keep clear. **(Rule 11)**

When there is doubt about the overlap
See pages 62 & 63. The same principles apply here.

11. On the Run

All of Chapter 8 (On the Reach) applies equally on the run, but there are some additional situations which relate to boats on opposite tacks, and when one or both gybe.

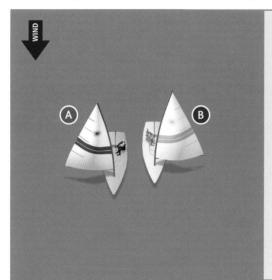

You are A:
• You are on opposite tacks and you are on port tack so your obligation is simple: to keep clear of B. If you are sailing so close to B that B cannot change course without immediately making contact with you, you are not keeping clear. **(Rule 10 & Definition Keep Clear)**

You are B:
• You have the right to sail where you like (your proper course is irrelevant) but if you change course you must give A room to keep clear. **(Rule 16.1)**

11

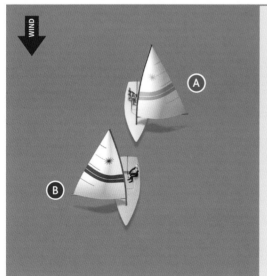

You are A:
• You have the right to sail where you like (your proper course is irrelevant) but if you change course you must give B room to keep clear. **(Rule 16.1)**

You are B:
• Your obligation is simple: to keep clear of A. If A is astern and going faster you'll need to do something. You could gybe on to starboard tack and become the right-of-way boat, or move out of the way. **(Rule 10)**

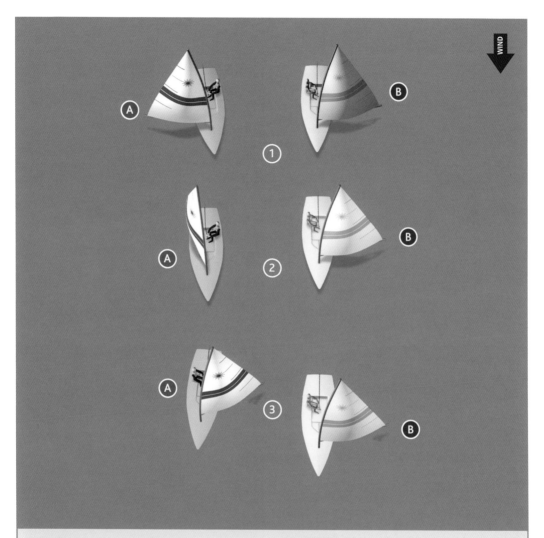

You are A:
- At position 1 you're on port tack and must keep clear. **(Rule 10)**
- At position 2 you are gybing into a 'keep clear' position and your obligation to keep clear continues. **(Rule 11)**
- At position 3 you are windward boat and still required to keep clear. **(Rule 11)**

You are B:
- In position 1 you are the right-of-way boat, and may sail any course, but if you change course you must give A room to keep clear. **(Rules 10 & 16.1)**
- While A is gybing at position 2, you continue to be right-of-way boat, but if you change course you must give A room to keep clear. **(Rules 10, 11 & 16.1)**
- In all three situations you have luffing rights, but if you change course you must give A room to keep clear. **(Rules 11 & 16.1)**

11

You are A:
• At position I you're the right-of-way boat and may luff up to your proper course. If you've got luffing rights, you may luff as high as you like provided you give B room to keep clear. **(Rules 11, 16.1 & 17)**
• As soon as B's mainsail flips to lie on the port side (which means he's on starboard tack) you become the keep-clear boat and if you are on a collision course, as you are in position 2, you must do something to keep clear. **(Rule 10)**

You are B:
• At position I you are windward boat so you must keep clear. **(Rule 11)**
• From the moment you gybe you become the right-of-way boat, but you must gybe in a way that initially gives A room to keep clear, and if you change course you must give A room to keep clear. **(Rules 10, 15 & 16.1)**

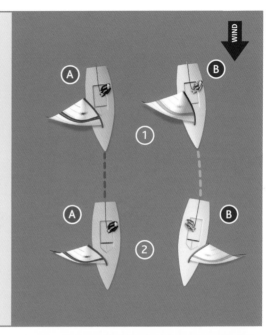

11

You are A:
• In position I you are the right-of-way boat, and may sail up to your proper course if you don't have luffing rights, and as high as you like if you do, but if you change course you must give B room to keep clear. **(Rules 11 & 16.1)**
• At position 2 you have gybed without changing course and you continue to be the right-of-way boat. As you did not change course you were not required to give B room to keep clear, but as I explained in Chapter I, everyone must avoid contact if reasonably possible, so if your boom is going to make contact with B's boom, you should restrain it and protest. However, if there is contact with no damage, you will be exonerated. **(Rule 14)**

You are B:
• At position I you're to windward and must keep clear. **(Rule 11)**
• It is wise to leave sufficient room for A to gybe, because if he does, you'll continue to be the keep-clear boat and he doesn't have to give you room to keep clear. **(Rules 10 & 15)**

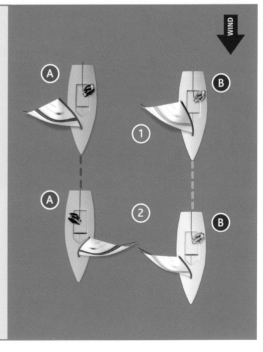

You are A:
• At position 1 you're the right-of-way boat (you are on starboard tack), but if you change course you must give B room to keep clear. **(Rules 10 & 16.1)**
• At position 2 when B gybes you become the keep-clear boat and must keep clear. **(Rule 11)**

You are B:
• In position 1 you are the keep-clear boat, and must keep clear. **(Rule 10)**
• At position 2, when you gybe, you become the right-of-way boat, but A doesn't have to anticipate you being there, and there must be room for him to keep clear when you change tack. **(Rule 15)**
• You may sail any course (you have luffing rights) but if you change course, you must give A room to keep clear. **(Rule 16.1)**

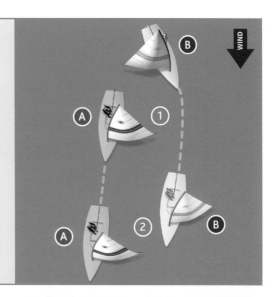

You are A:
You are on port tack, clear astern, gaining on B.
• If there is not room for you to pass between B and the continuing obstruction, and you poke your nose in, you will not be entitled to room and B may luff. Even if you gybe to starboard after you establish the overlap you must keep clear. **(Rule 19.2(c))**
• If there is room for you to pass between B and the continuing obstruction at the moment you get an inside overlap, then you may sail between B and the shore and, although you must keep clear, B must give you room.
• If you cannot keep clear you will be exonerated for breaking rule 11. **(Rules 11, 19.2(b) & 21)**
• If there was room for you to pass between B and the obstruction when you established the overlap and you then gybe to starboard, you become the right-of-way boat with luffing rights and may luff him. If you change course you must give him room to keep clear. **(Rule 11, then 10, 16.1 & 21)**

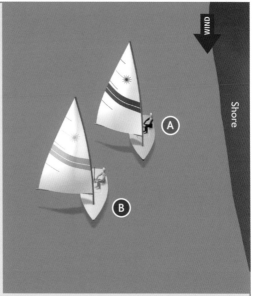

You are B:
• If there is room for A to pass between you and the continuing obstruction, then you must give him room. This is true even if his draft is greater than yours. But you remain the right-of-way boat. **(Rules 10, 19.2(b) & 19.2(c))**

• You should have closed the gap before A got an overlap, so that at that moment there was not enough room for A to pass between you and the obstruction. If his draft is less than yours, there is not a lot you can do.

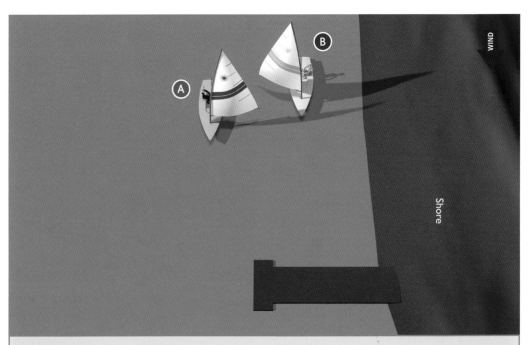

11

You are A:
• Your proper course is irrelevant. You may change course towards B, but only in such a way that B is able to keep clear. **(Rule 10 & 16)**
• Once B cannot, with safety, get any closer to the shore, then you must give him room to sail along between you and the shore. **(Rule 19.2(b))**
• If something sticks out from the shore ahead of B, you'll have to sail out to give B room to pass round it. **(Rule 19.2(b))**
• If B gybes, you become the windward boat and must keep clear. **(Rule 11)**

You are B:
• You must keep clear. When you cannot safely get any closer to the shore, then you may sail along the shoreline (or, more exactly, along the line that is safely close to the shore); A must give you room to do that. If he does not give you room to keep clear along that line, he breaks rule 19.2(b) and although you might break rule 11, if you do you will be exonerated. **(Rules 11, 19.2(b) & 21)**
• There is no requirement to hail if you think he is pushing you too close for safety, but there is no other way he is to know that you think things are getting unsafe, so hail for room when you need it.
• If there is a danger projecting from the shore ahead (or if you think there is) A must give you room to come out round it; again it is advisable, though not essential, to hail for room. **(Rule 19.2(b))**
• If you gybe (looks like a good idea!), you become the right-of-way boat with luffing rights so you may luff above your proper course if you want to, but if you change course you must give A room to keep clear. **(Rules 11 & 16.1)**

You are A:
• You must keep clear. When you cannot safely get any closer to the shore, then you may sail along the shoreline (or, more exactly, along the line that is safely close to the shore); B must give you room to do that. If he does not give you room to keep clear along that line, he breaks rule 19.2(b) and although you might break rule 11, if you do you will be exonerated. **(Rules 11, 19.2(b) & 21)**
• There is no requirement to hail if you think he is pushing you too close for safety, but there is no other way he is to know that you think things are getting unsafe, so hail for room when you need it.
• If there is a danger projecting from the shore ahead (or if you think there is) B must give you room to come out round it; again it is advisable though not essential to hail for room. **(Rule 19.2(b))**

You are B:
• If you have luffing rights and A is some distance from the shore or obstruction, you may luff, but if you change course you must give him room to keep clear. **(Rules 11 & 16.1)**
• When the shore (or other obstruction) impedes A's ability to respond then you must stop luffing and bear away as is necessary to give him room. If he needs more room to come out round a projection, then you must give him room to do so. **(Rule 19.2(b))**
• If you don't have luffing rights, you may luff (in such a way that A can keep clear), up to your proper course. If your proper course is close to the shore, then you may force A towards the shore but must give A room when he gets there, as described in the last paragraph. **(Rule 19.2(b))**

11

12. Rounding the Leeward Mark from the Run

Before the boats are near the mark A, on port tack, must keep clear of B on starboard tack. When one of them enters the zone, B must give room to A to sail to the mark in a seamanlike way, and room to round as necessary to sail the course. However if B is unable to give room by starting to alter course at the edge of the zone (because there isn't time) then she must start giving room earlier. This can happen when the boats are high performance asymmetrics, or there is a tidal stream taking the boats towards the mark.

You are A:
• At position 1 you are outside the zone so you must keep clear. In this situation, you have little choice but to gybe. If you think you or he are entering the zone, it would be a good idea to shout this claim to B to remind him he must start giving mark-room. If he doesn't give mark-room, keep clear and protest. **(Rules 10, 18.1 & 18.2(b))**
• At position 2 when you complete your gybe you are overlapped, so B has luffing rights, and you must keep clear. If neither boat enters the zone, he can sail you as far as he likes the wrong side of the mark. If either boat enters the zone then B must give you room. If you are in the zone and he doesn't give you room, try to keep clear and protest. **(Rules 11, 18.1 & 18.2(b))**
• If you break the overlap (you could luff at position 2) then you become the right-of-way boat (clear ahead). However you can't just gybe in front of B, because as soon as you bear away you'll establish an overlap and be windward (keep-clear) boat. Moreover if you gybe whilst clear ahead, you'll then be on port tack. You want to be clear ahead, without doubt, as you enter the zone. Then you can gybe and must be given mark room. **(Rules 11 & 12)**
• If after luffing to break the overlap at position 2, you bear away so that B is overlapped again,

he doesn't have luffing rights anymore so he must not sail higher than his proper course. His proper course (the course he would sail to finish as soon as possible if you weren't there) is to gybe, so he must gybe. You can then gybe and become leeward (right-of-way) boat. **(Rule 17)**
• When either boat enters the zone then B must give you room to sail to the mark in a seamanlike way, and then room to round the mark as necessary to sail the course. Mark-room will include enough space for you to gybe twice. **(Rule 18.2(b))**

You are B:
• At position 1, you are the right-of-way boat and neither boat is in the zone so you may sail on. However, you are getting into a difficult position. If you are really going to take A the wrong side of the mark (rarely a good tactic when there are other boats that will overtake both of you) then you must stay out of the zone. If you enter the zone, you must immediately give mark-room to A on the inside of you, and if you cannot give room because there is insufficient space or time, you will break the rule requiring you to give room. **(Rules 10 & 18.2(b))**
• When A gybes at position 2, nothing changes; you are still the right-of-way boat and may sail any course you like, but if you change course, you must give room to A to keep clear. **(Rules 11 & 16.1)**
• If the overlap is broken at position 3, you become the keep-clear boat, but provided you keep clear you can sail any course you like. **(Rule 12)**
• If the overlap is re-established you become the right-of-way boat but with the obligation not to sail above your proper course, so you must immediately gybe. **(Rules 11 and 17)**

12

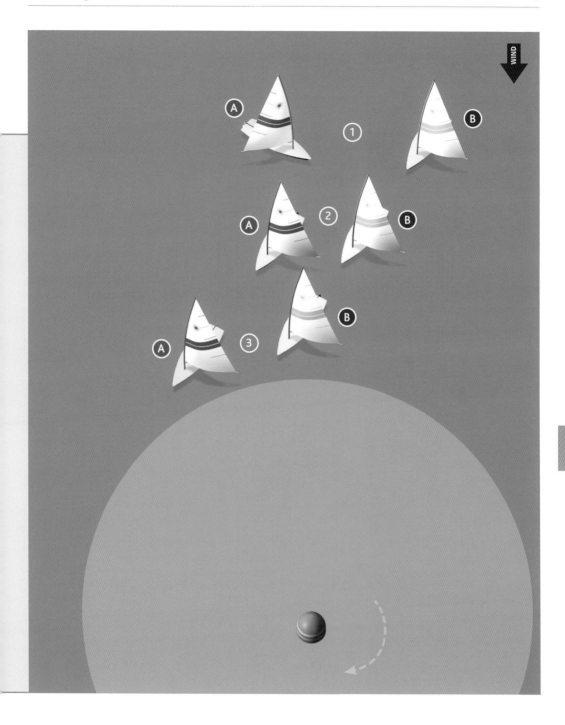

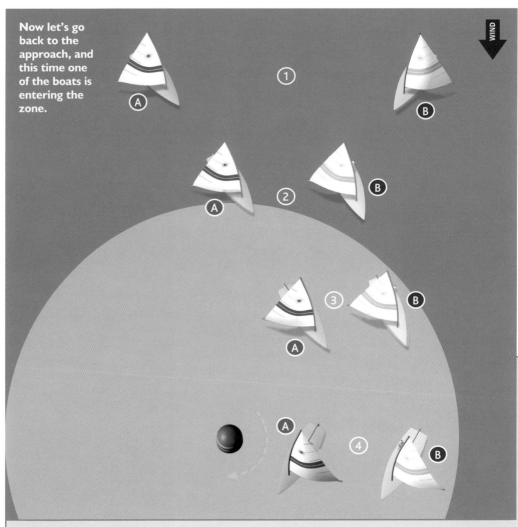

Now let's go back to the approach, and this time one of the boats is entering the zone.

WIND

You are A:
• At position 1 you have an inside overlap but neither boat is in the zone so your obligation is to keep clear. **(Rule 10)**
• As soon as one of you enters the zone, you have the right to mark-room. If your proper course is to sail close to the mark, mark-room includes room for you to do that, then at the mark, room to round the mark as necessary to sail the course. **(Rule 18.2(b) & Definition Mark-Room)**

• If B is not giving you room when one of you first enters the zone, you are required to try to avoid contact but you will be exonerated if you fail to avoid contact and there is no damage or injury, or if it was not reasonably possible to avoid contact. **(Rules 14, 10 & 21)**
• At position 2 you are in the zone and, when B gybes, you become the right-of-way boat, but you must not sail farther from the mark than needed to sail your proper course. **(Rule 18.4)**

12

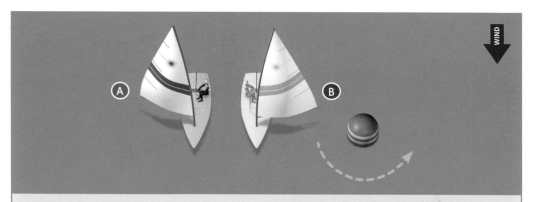

You are A:
* You must keep clear of B. **(Rule 10)**
* Until B gybes, he must not sail above his proper course, so he must gybe in this position. If he doesn't, it's best to continue to keep clear, and protest. **(Rules 10 & 18.4)**

You are B:
* Until you were in the zone you could sail any course, but if you changed course you had to give A room to keep clear. **(Rules 10 & 16.1)**
* Now that you are right-of-way boat in the zone and the boats are overlapped, you must gybe at the mark to sail your proper course – that is, you must not sail farther from the mark than needed to sail your proper course. This will mean gybing of course, but while you have right of way you can swing your stern as you round the mark without worrying about giving room to A. **(Rules 18.2(b) 18.4 & 21)**

* Because you now have right of way, you can sail your proper course to the mark and around the mark. After you gybe to starboard you become keep-clear boat again and must keep clear. You now only have the right to round the mark as necessary to sail the course. **(Rules 18.2(b) & 18.4)**
* After you leave the mark astern, if you are still overlapped remember you are the keep-clear boat. **(Rule 11)**

You are B:
* At position 1, A has an inside overlap, and as soon as one of you enters the zone, you must give him mark-room. That is, the amount of room he needs to sail to the mark and to round the mark as necessary to sail the course. In this case he doesn't need to do any manoeuvring but you will have to anticipate this situation so that from the moment one of you enters the zone you are able to give him mark-room. If he is then forced to gybe to starboard to keep clear of you, you have not given him mark-room. **(Rule 18.2(b))**

* At position 2 after gybing, you become the keep-clear boat. **(Rule 11)**
* A must not sail above his proper course, so at position 4 he must gybe. If he does sail above his proper course, you may protest but you must still keep clear. **(Rules 18.4 & 11)**
* When you both gybe at position 4, you become the right-of-way boat with luffing rights, but you must continue to give mark-room to A so that A can round the mark as necessary to sail the course. A does not have the right to sail his proper course, so even if he thinks his proper course is to 'round wide and come up tight on the mark', you do not have to give him room to do that. If he takes more room than is needed to sail as necessary around the mark, it is best to avoid him and protest. **(Rules 11, 18.2(a) & Definition Mark-Room)**
* If you are still overlapped when you have passed the mark, you may luff right up to head to wind but as this means changing course you must give him room to keep clear. **(Rules 11 & 16.1)**

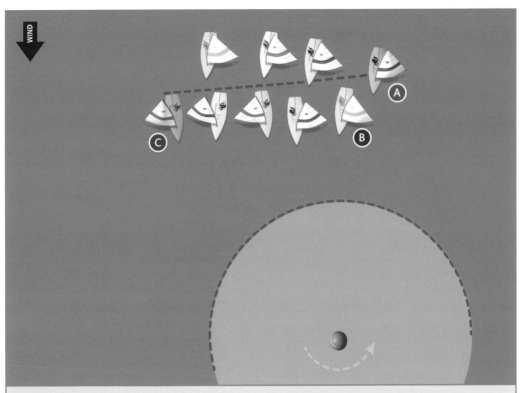

12

You are A:
- Although you may be able to get an overlap inside B before anyone reaches the zone, there is no way B is going to be able to keep clear so that you can sail inside at the mark. Remember B is not required to anticipate your getting the overlap. Therefore you have no right to mark-room from B. **(Rules 11, 15 and 18.2(e))**
- You do have an overlap, without doubt, on the inside of C and, unlike B, C is able to give room. C therefore must keep clear if you maintain the overlap to the zone. **(Rules 18.2(b) & 10)**

You are B:
- As you've had the overlap for some time, those boats outside you must keep clear (either because they are to windward on the same tack, or are on port tack). They must also give you mark-room when you get to the zone. It's usually a good idea to tell A that it's too late for him to get an overlap

now. **(Rules 10, 11, 18.2(b) & 18.2(f))**
- If the outside boats don't keep clear, try to get to the correct side of the mark, even if it means colliding with the mark or the boat outside you (providing there is no chance of damage). If you are forced the wrong side of the mark you might succeed with a protest but you cannot recover the places lost. **(Rules 62.1(b), 64.1(a) & 14)**
- As you need to gybe around this mark, until you gybe you mustn't sail above your proper course. (You can sail the course you would have sailed if the other boat had not been there.) **(Rule 18.4)**

You are C:
- This is not a good place to be! A has an inside overlap, and you are able to keep clear, so keep clear you must, as well as keeping clear of all the boats inside you. Next time, don't get into this position! **(Rules 10 & 18.2(b))**

13. The Leeward Gate

Many courses nowadays include a gate in place of a single leeward mark. The gate reduces congestion at the end of the downwind leg, helps to avoid boats rounding straight into boats still on the run, and sometimes gives you a chance to break free from a rival just ahead.

Instead of rounding a single leeward mark (usually to port in fleet racing or to starboard in match racing), two marks are placed a little more than six hull lengths apart, on an imaginary line at right angles to the wind. However, if, for example, the right side (looking up wind) of the course is favoured, the race committee might place the right gate mark a little further downwind compared to the left gate mark. The idea is to make it difficult for boats to choose which gate mark is favoured (rather like a good starting line where the difficulty in deciding which end to start results in

the fleet being spread out along the line).

When you and your rival just ahead are both sailing for the most favoured mark (usually the one that you judge to be closest to the wind), you might like to round the other mark instead, in order to get out of his dirty wind and perhaps take your chances on the other side of the course. If he would have been in a position to cover you up the beat after rounding the same gate mark, you can break his cover by choosing to round the other mark.

The rule that says 'when boats are overlapped and the rounding includes a gybe for an inside right-of-way boat, that boat must sail no farther from the mark than needed to sail her proper course until she gybes', does not apply at a gate. **(Rule 18.4)**

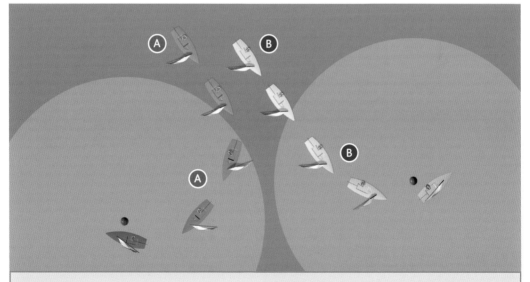

You are A:
• B has chosen to round the right-side mark (looking upwind), which in this case is favoured (a little further upwind). You are free to round the left mark.

You are B:
• You have chosen the favoured mark but A has predictably taken the opportunity to go for the other mark. You'll need to tack soon after rounding to cover.

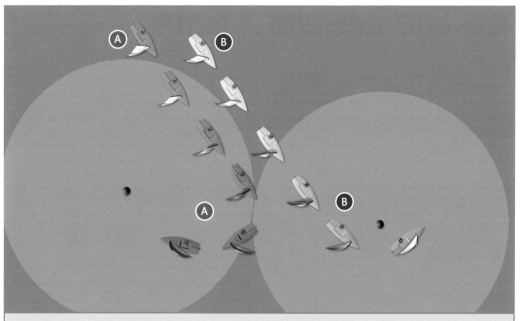

You are A:
- Because this is a gate you are not required to gybe to sail a proper course. You can effectively force B to sail to the less favoured mark, then gybe to round the favoured mark yourself.

You are B:
- Had A gybed early to round the left mark, you could have followed, but now the best you can do is to go for the less-favoured right mark (looking upwind).

13

14. The Finish

You finish when any part of your hull, crew or equipment in normal position first touches the finishing line, from the course side. Typically, the first part of the boat to cross the line is the bow, but your crew's hand held over his head when he's out on the trapeze would count if that was his normal position.

With a downwind finish, the spinnaker is usually the first piece of equipment to cross the line. If the spinnaker head was let out a few centimetres, and the boat often sailed with it like that, that would be OK, but a spinnaker with its head let go several metres would not count, because it would not be in its normal position (whether this had been done intentionally or not). A boat that had let its spinnaker go would be finished on the first piece of the boat to cross the line that was not out of position – probably its stem or pulpit. In match racing the definition is changed so that only the hull is used for deciding when a boat finishes.

You are 'racing' until you have cleared the finishing line and the finishing marks, having completed any penalty turns for hitting a finishing mark or exonerating yourself for breaking a rule in relation to another boat. You have cleared the line when no part of your boat or its equipment is straddling the line. You have cleared the finishing marks when you are first in a position that is not in danger of making contact with the mark. The usual way of doing this is just to keep sailing right over the line near the middle (which would mean you are clear of the marks) or, if you finish near an end, to sail right through the line and get clear of the mark.

You don't have to cross the line completely; having finished with the first part of the boat or its equipment touching the line, you can duck back on to the course side of the line if you want to. **(Rule 28.1)**

When you have finished and cleared the line, you are still subject to the racing rules, but you cannot be penalized (so there is no need to take a penalty) for breaking a 'when boats meet' rule (unless you interfere with a boat that is still racing). **(Rules: Part 2 Preamble & 24.1)**

If you have not sailed the correct course, you can go back and complete the course (provided you haven't finished), and if you crossed the finishing line in the wrong direction you can unwind and finish properly.

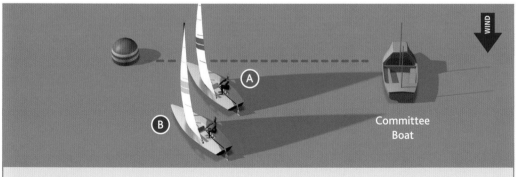

You are A:
* As windward boat you must keep clear. **(Rule 11)**

You are B:
* Even if you don't have luffing rights, you always have the right to sail your proper course which in this situation might be to luff higher than close-hauled to 'shoot the mark', or get to the finishing line as soon as possible. **(Rules 16 & 18.3)**

14

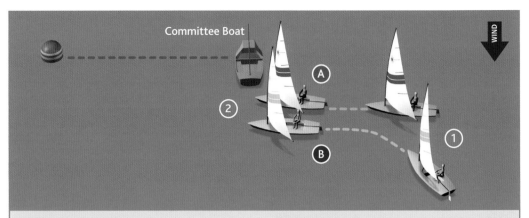

You are A:
• You have the right to mark-room at the mark. A hail is not necessary, but it does no harm to remind B that he must give you room. **(Rule 18.2(b))**

You are B:
• You must give A room to pass the mark, whether or not you have luffing rights and whether or not he hails. **(Rule 18.2(b))**

14

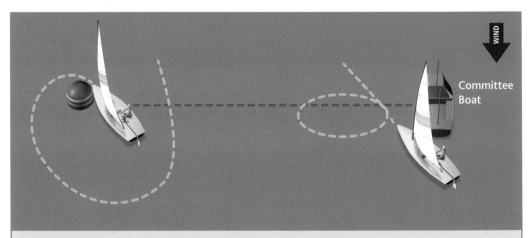

If, before finishing, you touch a finishing mark (a buoy or the committee boat) you must sail clear of other boats and do a turn penalty including a tack and a gybe (it doesn't matter which comes first). You must then sail to where you are wholly on the course side of the line, and finish. **(Rules 31, 44.1, 44.2 & Definition Finish)**

If you hit the mark after finishing but before clearing the line and the mark, you are still racing when you touch the mark so you must sail clear of other boats

as soon as possible and then promptly take a One-Turn Penalty and then finish again. **(Rules 31, 44.1, 44.2 & Definition Finish)**

You don't have to be clear of the line when you do the turn penalty (you can be straddling it or on the post-finish side of it), but if, having completed the penalty, you are not on the course side, you must go back to the course side, and then finish. **(Rules 31, 44.1, 44.2 & Definition Finish)**

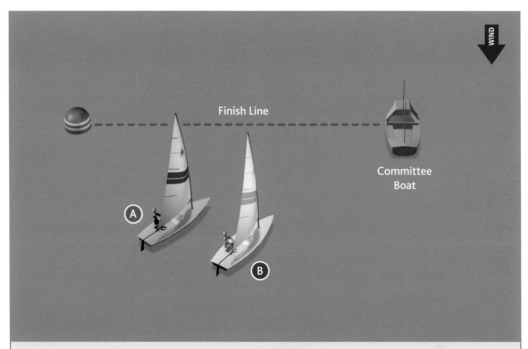

Finish Line

Committee Boat

WIND

You are A:
• As windward boat you must keep clear of B, even if B luffs. Whether or not he has luffing rights, B has the right to luff to head to wind to finish as quickly as he can. **(Rules 11, 17 & Definition Proper Course)**
• Because A is fetching the mark, B does not have the right to hail for room to tack. However, if B hails for room to tack anyway, you must either:
1. Tack, or
2. Hail back 'You tack' and take on the responsibility of giving room to B (typically by ducking B's stern as he tacks).
• You may also protest B for hailing for room to tack when he did not have the right to do so. **(Rules 20.1 & 20.2(c))**

You are B:
• Ahead is a mark that A is fetching. You may not hail A for room to tack, so you may need to slow and tack behind A. You may also try to 'shoot' the line; that is, sail head to wind and hope you will have sufficient way for your bow to touch the line – that's all you need! **(Rules 20.1 & Definition Finish)**
• If you hail without having the right to hail A must still respond, but may protest you. Whether or not A fetches the committee boat without passing head to wind, if you hail for room to tack and he refuses to respond, you may protest him if he doesn't take a penalty. Usually, he cannot respond because of other boats on his windward side. **(Rule 20.2(b))**

14

15. Means of Propulsion

You must not 'increase, maintain or decrease' the speed of your boat by any means other than by using 'wind and water'. At major dinghy championships the sailing instructions usually allow members of the protest committee to go afloat and penalize boats they believe are breaking the rule. **(Rule 42 & Appendix P)**

The differential in speed between a dinghy complying with the propulsion rule and one propelled illegally by a skilled crew paying no attention to it can, in very light winds, be so enormous that in a half-knot zephyr the complying boat wouldn't have reached the windward mark when the boat breaking the rule had completed the course, travelling six times as fast. **(Rule 42)**

The difference lessens as the wind speed increases, but can still be significant in a competitive fleet at a wind speed of 10 knots. Since the difference in boat speed between top competitors in competitive dinghy fleets is often as little as one-tenth of one per cent, breaking rule 42 is an obvious attraction not only to the unscrupulous, but also to the honest sailor when he sees less honest sailors 'getting away with it'.

So what does rule 42 seek to control? If you rock a rig to windward in still air, the sail passing through the still air has the same effect as moving air passing over a still sail (pumping): a driving force is set up. The same sort of effect, though not quite as effective, can be obtained by hauling in the sail: the force drives the boat forward, and the rig or sail can be returned to 'leeward' ready for another go. Waggling the tiller can also drive a hull through calm water (sculling). Moving the trunk of the body forward and backwards, even in strong winds, can flap the leech and increase the sail's drive (ooching).

With practice one can become very efficient at driving a boat through the water on a calm day; it's really quite fun, though very energetic. There is a minority of dinghy sailors who would prefer that there were no restrictions (i.e. most of the prohibitions in rule 42 were removed as they are for boardsailing (see

Appendix B)). Removing the propulsion restrictions would certainly make life easier for race committees and judges, because the rule is not easy to enforce. However, the majority of good sailors do not want 'kinetics' (imparting energy from moving crew weight into forward motion) to be part of sailing. Attitudes might change; up to a few years ago, board sailors did not want to allow kinetics, now they do, resulting in only very fit and strong people being able to win boardsailing championships.

At championships, and at well-organized regional regattas, the judges go afloat to look for offenders. However, this should not change your policy; if you see someone pumping, rocking or sculling, you should protest, and not break the rule yourself.

Several classes now have a rule that allows the race committee to display a flag when the wind speed reaches a certain limit, say, 10 knots or more. The pumping, rocking and ooching prohibitions are then modified or suspended in accordance with the class rule, to the joy of sailors and judges.

15

16. Taking a Penalty

When and where to take a penalty

When you know you've broken a rule (including a sailing instruction), you must take a penalty or retire promptly from the race, unless the rule or sailing instruction broken is one which requires you do or don't do something while racing, and you were not racing at the time of the incident (i.e. it occurred before the preparatory signal or after you finished and cleared the finishing line and marks). In such a case you do not have to take a penalty (but if you've caused damage you may have to pay for the repair).

If you are racing and you break a 'when boats meet' rule, you must take a Two-Turns Penalty promptly. Let's suppose you are sailing up the first beat, and you are close-hauled on port tack, chatting to your crew about tactics. Suddenly you become aware of a starboard-tack boat bearing away under your stern. As he bears away under your stern he shouts something at you so you know he is aggrieved. What should you do? Tell him you're going to take a penalty, and immediately sail clear of other boats and take a Two-Turns Penalty. Actually, if he doesn't hail 'Protest' he cannot protest, but that should not affect whether or not you take the penalty. If you know you have broken a rule, the paragraph named Sportsmanship and the Rules, in the Basic Priciples at the beginning of the rulebook makes it clear that you must take the penalty. Not to do so could result in a protest under rule 2 Fair Sailing or a report resulting in a rule 69 hearing against you for a 'gross breach of good sportsmanship'.

What if you did see him coming and when you were just about to tack, he shouted 'Carry on'? You carry on on port tack and he bears away under your stern. Should you take a penalty? No. By accepting his invitation to carry on, and him ducking your stern, you have in fact kept clear. (By the way, the hail of 'Carry on' did not compel you to sail on; you could have tacked if you had wanted to.)

What if he bears away under your stern, but says nothing? My recommendation is that if he shows no

signs of being aggrieved, then you can assume you kept clear.

If you touch a mark while racing, then you are honour-bound to take a One-Turn Penalty, even if no one saw you. This is the test of a good sportsman. We all need to be good sportsmen if we are going to play this great game of fleet racing without the need for referees or judges. More to the point, it is becoming more common for protest committees to be on the water and when they see a boat clearly and knowingly touching a mark and not taking a penalty, they protest the boat and if upheld the boat might get a DNE for breaking rule 2 Fair Sailing. **(Rules 2, 31, 44.1 & 44.2)**

If you sail the wrong course, or propel the boat by means other than by the use of 'wind and water', or you are on the course side of the starting line at the starting signal, you cannot exonerate yourself by taking a penalty. However, you can often exonerate yourself by doing something else. If you've gone round a mark the wrong way, you can unwind yourself and go round it the right way; if you were a premature starter you can usually go back and start. But having pumped your way down the reaching leg, or paddled, or moored up to the shore for an ice-cream, or – heaven forbid – failed to rescue someone in distress, then there is no exoneration procedure open to you, and you must retire from the race immediately you realize you have broken the rule or sailing instruction.

Remember that if you want to take a Two-Turns Penalty after an incident in the preparatory period, or you hit a starting mark in the preparatory period, then you may (in fact you must) take the penalty as soon as you can; so if the breach is some minutes before the start, you will not be disadvantaged.

If the breach happens on or close to the finishing line, then you must do the Two-Turns Penalty as soon as possible (on either side of the finishing line or its extensions), get your boat wholly on the course side

16

of the line, and then cross the finishing line from the course side. It is possible, therefore, to finish (when the first part of the boat touches the line), then break a rule of Part 2 before clearing the line, do a Two-Turns Penalty, then come back wholly behind the line and 'refinish' when the first part of the boat touches the line again from the course side.

If you break a 'when boats meet' rule (for example, by taking room at a mark to which you are not entitled) and you hit the mark, you can exonerate yourself by doing just a Two-Turns Penalty; you don't have to do the One-Turn Penalty for hitting the mark as well. If you have broken more than one rule in an incident, you need take only one Two-Turns Penalty. **(Rule 44.1)**

How to take the penalty
The standard penalty for breaking a 'when boats meet' rule is the Two-Turns Penalty, which is described in rule 44.2. If there is nothing said about penalties in the sailing instructions, then the Two-Turns Penalty applies.

If you have room, do the penalty immediately (and it costs you nothing to tell the other sailor you're going to do it). If there isn't room, tell the other sailor you're going to do it, immediately sail to where there is room, or slow down to let the surrounding boats pass. Rotate your boat through two tacks and two gybes. When you are training, you should practise doing Two-Turns Penalties so that you can do them as quickly as possible; there's no point in adding to the penalizing effect by getting into irons. When you're on a beat, it's usually best to bear away first rather than tack. **(Rule 44.2)**

Sometimes sailing instructions replace the Two-Turns Penalty with a scoring penalty system (usually for keelboat events in which it is thought unsafe for boats to be doing circles, or because they have different ratings). When the sailing instructions prescribe a scoring penalty then instead of taking a Two-Turns Penalty, you must display a yellow flag and inform the race committee after the finish that you are taking a penalty. **(Rule 44.3)**

Protest, take a penalty, or both?
After the preparatory signal, if you are involved

in an incident with another boat (or several other boats) in which you think a rule has, or may have, been broken, you have to make a decision and you have to make it quickly. If there has been a collision, however small or unavoidable, then almost certainly a rule will have been broken, and of course even without a collision there might have been a breach.

If you know you have broken a rule but think the other boat has broken one too, you can protest and take a penalty. Hail 'Protest', then sail clear and take the Two-Turns Penalty.

If you have a collision or touch a mark, but you were in the right or not given the room to which you were entitled, and there is no damage then you will not be penalized. You can sail on. If there is damage (to either boat) which it would have been reasonably possible to avoid then you can do a Two-Turns Penalty to exonerate yourself. If the damage is serious, then you cannot exonerate yourself with a Two-Turns Penalty, and you must retire. **(Rules 64.1(a) & 44.1(b))**

16

17. Protesting

Some people, even very experienced competitors, say they find protesting unpleasant. Protesting need not be done with any acrimony whatsoever, and unless we want to evolve a breed of referees to blow whistles and penalize on the spot (and there'll need to be lots of them all over the course, because under such a system no one will consider taking a penalty if they don't hear a whistle) then we have to accept that the sport is policed by the following system:

When a competitor knows he has broken a rule he takes a penalty (or retires) whether or not the other sailor hails 'Protest'.

When a competitor involved in or witnessing an incident thinks another competitor has broken a rule, and the other competitor doesn't retire or take a penalty, he protests.

When the race committee (or protest committee if there is one) sees a breach of rule that affects the fairness of the competition and the boat doesn't take a penalty, it protests.

In my opinion (though many judges will not agree with me) there is one other consideration that affects a decision as to whether or not a penalty should be taken or a protest made against another boat when a rule is broken. That is, whether or not the right-of-way boat (or the boat with the right to room) is aggrieved.

Imagine you're on starboard tack a lap ahead of a beginner on port tack and you have to duck under his stern. There is nothing to be gained by protesting; a word over a beer after the race would be much more appropriate – there is no rule requiring you to protest.

But what if you're the one on port tack and a rival ducks under your stern, but says nothing? As I said in the previous chapter, I believe if he is not aggrieved, you can assume there's no breach. That's the criteria I use when I'm racing. If he says even 'tut tut', I'll do

a penalty if I think I've broken a rule. Sometimes I'm not sure if I have broken a rule. If the other sailor thinks I have, that's usually enough for me, and I'll go and do my turns.

When you consider another boat has broken a rule and you feel aggrieved about it, you will want to protest. This chapter is about how to lodge a protest.

There are certain requirements that must be met before a protest can be accepted as valid. The only requirements you actually need to remember are the ones that have to be met out there on the water; the rest you can look up in this book when you are back at the clubhouse.

Things to remember on the water

Any boat may protest, provided that the protesting boat was involved in or witnessed an incident. Even if you have been involved in a previous incident in which you will be disqualified (after a hearing), that doesn't remove your right to protest about a later incident. **(World Sailing Case 1)**

The important thing you need to do at the time of the incident is to hail the word 'Protest'. The rule says this must be done 'at the first reasonable opportunity'. So there is time to ask him whether he's going to take a penalty, and if he says 'no', hail 'Protest'. If you get no reaction to the hail, it's best to repeat it more loudly.

If your hull length is 6 metres or more, you also need to display a protest flag, and this too must be done 'at the first reasonable opportunity'. Don't wait too long. Many protests have been found to be invalid because the flag was not displayed very soon after the incident. The flag must be red. It doesn't matter what the shape is, but it must be red, and it must be a flag, not a red glove or waterproof jacket. The usual flag used to be the flag B which has swallowtails, but a rectangular red flag will do just as well and is now the norm. It must be displayed conspicuously

17

which means it mustn't be too small, and it must be up in the rigging and not lying on the deck. It must be kept displayed until you have finished and cleared the finishing line.

If the flag is already being displayed because of a previous incident, then that's fine; you don't have to pull it down and put it up again, or display another one.

The purpose of the hail and the flag is two-fold. It gives an opportunity for the protestee to take a penalty, and if he decides not to take a penalty, then it marks the moment so that he can recall what happened.

Remember if your hull length is less than 6 metres, you don't need to display a flag (unless the sailing instructions require it, but hopefully the practice of sailing instructions requiring a flag will soon die out).

You cannot lodge a protest if you don't hail, but you don't have to go ahead and lodge the protest if you have hailed.

If the other sailor might not have heard your hail of 'Protest' at the time of the incident, or he is so far away from you there is no chance he will hear a hail, you should inform him again at the next opportunity you get, even if the next opportunity is ashore.

Things to do when you come ashore
You need to fill in a protest form. If you can't find one, unless there is some special sailing instruction (ugh!) then any bit of paper will do provided that you include certain pieces of vital information. Most people make too much of filling in the form. By including too much detail, you're more likely to do yourself harm than good, and you'll certainly wear out the brain unnecessarily. Initially you need only briefly describe the incident including where and when it happened (so that the protestee can identify it), who you are, and the identity of the protestee.

You need to lodge the form with the race committee within the time limit (which is two hours after the last boat finishes unless otherwise specified in the sailing

instructions). If there is a good reason for any delay, the protest committee must extend the time limit. **(Rule 61.3)**

Preparing your witnesses
If there is someone who you think saw the incident, approach him and, having simply identified the incident so that he knows what you're talking about, ask him what he saw. Don't tell him anything and don't ask leading questions. If you think what he saw is what you believe really happened, then ask him if he will be a witness at the hearing.

At the hearing, when you are invited to call witnesses, explain to the chairman that you have not discussed the case with your witness, you merely asked what he saw and considered that as this was more or less what actually happened, you thought he would be a good witness.

When your witness gives his evidence and is questioned, it will invariably become obvious to the protest committee that he has in no way been influenced, and his credibility and the value of his evidence will help you enormously. You'd do better with no witness at all than a 'coached' witness; their complicity is obvious to all but the most inexperienced protest committee.

Conducting yourself at the hearing
If you are an experienced racing skipper sailing in a minor event, there is a good chance that you will know more about the rules and procedures than the protest committee does. Use this knowledge carefully if you wish not to be disadvantaged. At any hearing you should treat the committee members (and indeed the other parties and witnesses) with respect. They are usually fellow sailors doing their best to be fair, but even when this is not the case, losing your cool gains you nothing.

The procedure
Appendix M of the racing rules, which gives a recommended procedure for protest committees, is very well written and easy to follow. Here is a summary.

The protestor and protestee are called to the hearing. You both have the right to be present during all of

17

the taking of evidence (from each of you, and of any witnesses called by you, by your opponent or by the protest committee). If one party chooses not to attend, then the protest committee can proceed without him. **(Rule 63.3)**

Protest committee members must disclose any possible conflict of interest. If both parties agree, or the committee rules it is insignificant (after considering the views of the parties, the level of the conflict, the level of the event, the importance to each party, and the overall perception of fairness) the person can remain. At major events the person with a conflict of interest cannot be a member of a protest committee. Nationality alone would not normally be considered a conflict of interest. **(Rule 63.4)**

The validity of the protest must be considered by the protest committee:

'Was a hail of 'Protest' made, and was it made at the first reasonable opportunity after the incident?' For boats over 6 metres: 'Was the protest flag displayed, and was it displayed at the first reasonable opportunity after the incident?' 'Was it conspicuously displayed?' 'Was it kept displayed till the finish?'. When the evidence from the protestor was that he hailed "protest" and the evidence from the protestee was that there was no hail, it is helpful if the hail was made more than once, and that the protestor got a reaction from the protestee. The protest committee might seek evidence about the hail from sailors who were nearby and heard the hail. It doesn't do the credibility of the protestee any good if he falsely claims 'there was no hail'. After all, the best he can claim is that he didn't hear a hail.

'Was the written protest received by the race committee within the time limit?' 'If not, was there a good reason for it being received late?'

'Did the written protest identify the parties, where and when the incident occured, and the nature of the incident?'

Although the protest committee must extend the time limit for receiving protests if there is a good reason for a delay, it has no power to excuse any of the other requirements, and if they are not met the protest must be found to be invalid, and refused. A protest committee cannot find as a fact that the protestor did not hail 'Protest' and declare 'We'll let you off this time, but don't forget for next time' and proceed to hear the protest.

If a member of the protest committee saw the incident, he must declare that and you can ask him questions in the hearing. **(Rule 63.6)**

If the protest is ruled as valid, the protest committee must proceed to the next stage: the hearing of evidence.

The protestor describes his version of the incident; the protestee then does likewise. Each may question the other and the protest committee members may question both. Each is invited to call witnesses, one at a time, and each witness describes his version of the incident, and is questioned by the parties (the protestor's witnesses should be questioned first by the protestee and vice versa) and the committee. The committee may call witnesses, or the committee members may themselves be witnesses in which case they give their evidence and may be questioned. The protestor summarizes his case; the protestee summarizes his defence.

The protest committee deliberates in private (if there were observers, they too are asked to leave) and produces 'facts found' (what it thinks happened), its decision and the grounds for that decision. The parties are then recalled and the chairman or the 'scribe' (a committee member acting as a secretary) reads out the details.

It is worth noting that the protestor does not have to 'prove' his case. Once the protest is found by the committee to be valid, then it must find the facts and base a decision on them. The committee must apply the standard of proof called 'balance of probability'; that is, what most likely happened, given all the evidence and the protest committee's own experience and knowledge. All evidence must be considered but a claim, for example, that at one moment boat A was clear astern and the next he was clear ahead, is unbelievable and will not be given 'equal weight'.

17

18. Requesting Redress & Appealing

If you think your position in a race, or in a series, has been made significantly worse through no fault of your own, you can sometimes successfully 'request redress' (often erroneously called 'protesting the race committee'). Redress is usually in the form of points that the protest committee considers you would have been awarded had you finished without being prejudiced. **(Rules 62 & 64.2)**

Unlike a protest (for which there are several validity requirements), it is rare for a request for redress to be refused on the grounds it is invalid. The only reasons for refusal to hear a redress request would be either that it does not contain a written reason for making the request, or that it was received after the closing time for receiving protests (usually two hours after the incident), without a good reason.

You can write your request on any bit of paper, but it is usual to use a protest form even though many of the prompts are not relevant. For example, you don't have to display a protest flag, or make a hail.

So it is not difficult to get a hearing; being awarded redress is another matter! Generally the procedure at the hearing is the same as a protest hearing, except that if you are the only one requesting redress, you will take on the 'protestor's' role, and a representative of the race committee will usually act as the 'defendant'.

The protest committee should be independent of the race committee. If you think it isn't, raise the issue early in the proceedings. If the event is anything more than a club race, wise organizers will have appointed a protest committee that is independent of the race committee; at an international event there'll usually be an international jury. At club events the usual practice is for the race committee to arrange a protest committee as independent as is practical, if a request for redress is received by the race committee.

Like a protest hearing, there are the same distinct parts to the hearing: the taking of evidence (from you, your fellow redress requesters if there are any, the race committee, and anyone else you, the race committee, or the protest committee see fit to call); the assessment by the protest committee (sitting in private) as to whether redress is applicable; and lastly, if redress is applicable, what redress will be given.

Redress can be given to you only when:

• Your finishing score or your place in a race or series has been or may be made significantly worse.

• You've done nothing wrong yourself. So if you have been scored OCS ('on course side' for being over the line at the start), and are simply complaining that there were some boats ahead of you that were not scored OCS, you can't get redress. (You could protest the guilty boats, of course.)

• Your finishing score was affected for one of the following reasons:

(a) The race committee (or the protest committee, organizing authority or technical committee) made an improper action or omission. So if some passing whale rammed you, you cannot get redress; a rescue boat would be another matter, as that would be under the control of the race committee. If the race committee fails to make a signal correctly and this affected you, you may be entitled to redress. Redress can be given if there is an act or omission of the race committee even if it adheres to the rules and sailing instructions that govern its conduct.

For example, if the race committee writes itself a sailing instruction saying it can shorten course at any time for any reason, and it shortens course for no apparent reason just as your rival approaches the first mark after 20 minutes of racing – his father is the race officer – you would have a legitimate claim for redress. Conversely, if the sailing instructions said the first leg would be 3 kilometres long and it was only 2.5, it would be impossible to argue that any competitor had been prejudiced and so no redress could be given.

(b) Your boat has been physically damaged, or you or your crew have been injured, by a boat required to keep clear or give room or by a vessel not racing that was required to keep clear of you (for example, under the collision regulations). So if you're on starboard and a boat on port rams you, putting a hole in your side, and you have to retire, you can get redress. You can only get redress if you're damaged; if you simply got tangled up with this port tacker while some close rivals pass you, you cannot get redress. If at a mark you are entitled to room but not given it and forced the wrong side, you must return to round or pass the mark correctly, and although you may successfully protest the boat that didn't give you room, because you were not physically damaged you are not entitled to redress for the 50 places you may have lost.

(c) You went to help someone you had reason to believe was in distress. If you see someone in distress you are required to go to their aid, so if you lose places by your heroic act you are entitled to redress.

(d) You have been significantly affected by someone who is penalized (or given a warning under Rule 69) for cheating, or breaking the 'Fair Sailing' rule.

The protest committee will hear your evidence and that of your witnesses, and if relevant the evidence and advice of the race committee. In private it will then 'find facts' and assess whether these facts meet the criteria for giving redress, and if they do, reconvene to receive submissions on what redress would be appropriate. You can say what you think is fair, but the other skippers can give their opinions too.

If your request meets the above criteria, then you must be given redress. It is not unusual to be awarded points equal to a position the protest committee thinks you would have achieved had you not been prejudiced, or points equal to your 'average to date in the series' (usually also counting any discards when calculating your average score).

In giving redress, the only restriction imposed on the protest committee is that its decision must be as fair as possible to all boats affected. Faced with a complex situation, a protest committee may decide that the fairest arrangement is 'no adjustment to any finishing positions'. To abandon or cancel a race is rarely the fairest solution, although sometimes there is no alternative. **(Rule 64.2)**

Appealing

If you are penalized as a result of a hearing, you usually have the right to appeal against the protest committee's decision or its procedures, but to be eligible you need to be a party directly affected by the decision against which you are appealing. **(Rule 70)**

If you are indirectly affected, for instance, if you find yourself in a lower position as a result of the protest committee giving redress to another boat, then you must first request redress on the grounds that the committee's action materially prejudiced your finishing score, and if you are not satisfied with that decision, you may appeal. You may also appeal against a decision not to hear your protest or your request for redress, or against the fairness of redress awarded as a result of your request.

Sometimes there is no right to appeal. You have no right to appeal:

• When, at an international event, an international jury has been appointed, and it complies with the requirements of Appendix N; or

• When 'it is essential to determine promptly the result of a race that will qualify a boat to compete in a later stage of an event or a subsequent event'. In the UK, the approval from the Royal Yachting Association is also required. In the USA, approval is required from US Sailing. Your country may have such a rule too (a prescription to rule 70.5) and if so it must be included in it's rulebook or be posted on your MNA's website. In all cases, the fact that decisions are not open to appeal must be announced in the notice of the race and in the sailing instructions. **(Rule 70.5(a) & Appendix J 1.2(13))**

Unless the facts found by the protest committee are completely incompatible with all the evidence or with

18

the protest committee's own diagram, you can appeal only on a question of interpretation of the rules or the protest committee's procedures, and not against the facts found by the protest committee.**(Rule 70.1)**

The protest committee may itself refer a case it has decided for confirmation or correction. **(Rule 70.2)**

How to appeal
This varies from country to country, so look at rule 70 and any prescription to the rule that your own national authority may have written.

RACE SIGNALS

The meanings of visual and sound signals are stated below. An arrow pointing up or down (↑↓) means that a visual signal is displayed or removed. A dot (●) means a sound; five short dashes (– – – – –) mean repetitive sounds; a long dash (—) means a long sound. When a visual signal is displayed over a class flag, the signal applies only to that class.

Postponement Signals

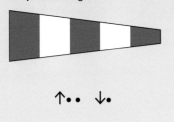

↑●● ↓●

AP Races not started are *postponed*. The warning signal will be made 1 minute after removal unless at that time the race is *postponed* again or *abandoned*.

↑●●

AP over H Races not started are *postponed*. Further signals ashore.

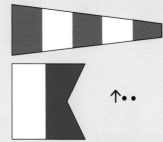

↑●●

AP over A Races not started are *postponed*. No more racing today.

AP over a numeral pennant 1–9

Postponement of 1-9 hours from the scheduled starting time.

Pennant 1	Pennant 2	Pennant 3	Pennant 4
↑●● ↓●	↑●● ↓●	↑●● ↓●	↑●● ↓●

Pennant 5	Pennant 6	Pennant 7	Pennant 8	Pennant 9
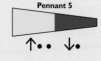				
↑●● ↓●	↑●● ↓●	↑●● ↓●	↑●● ↓●	↑●● ↓●

Abandonment Signals

↑●●● ↓●

N All races that have started are *abandoned*. Return to the starting area. The warning signal will be made 1 minute after removal unless at that time the race is *abandoned* again or *postponed*.

↑●●●

N over H All races are *abandoned*. Further signals ashore.

↑●●●

N over A All races are *abandoned*. No more racing today.

Preparatory Signals

↑• ↓—   ↑• ↓—   ↑• ↓—   ↑• ↓—   ↑• ↓—

P Preparatory signal.   **I** Rule 30.1 is in effect.   **Z** Rule 30.2 is in effect.   **U** Rule 30.3 is in effect.   **Black** flag.
Rule 30.4 is in effect.

Recall Signals   **Shortened Course**

↑•   ↑•• ↓•   ↑••

X Individual recall.   **First Substitute** General recall.   **S** The course has been
The warning signal will be made   shortened. Rule 32.2 is in effect.
1 minute after removal.

Changing the Next Leg

– – – – –

C The position of the next   to starboard;   to port;   to decrease the   to increase the
mark has been changed: length of the leg;   length of the leg.

Other Signals

↑•   – – – – –   ↑•   (no sound)

L Ashore: A notice to   **M** The object displaying this   **Y** Wear a personal flotation   **Blue** flag or shape. This race
competitors has been posted.   signal replaces a missing *mark*.   device (see rule 40).   committee vessel is in position
Afloat: Come within hail or   at the finishing line.
follow this vessel.

The Racing Rules of Sailing for 2017-2020

World Sailing

Published by World Sailing (UK) Limited, Southampton, UK
© World Sailing Limited
June 2016

INTRODUCTION

The *Racing Rules of Sailing* includes two main sections. The first, Parts 1–7, contains rules that affect all competitors. The second, the appendices, provides details of rules, rules that apply to particular kinds of racing, and rules that affect only a small number of competitors or officials.

Terminology

A term used in the sense stated in the Definitions is printed in italics or, in preambles, in bold italics (for example, *racing* and **racing**).

Each of the terms in the table below is used in *The Racing Rules of Sailing* with the meaning given.

Term	Meaning
Boat	A sailboat and the crew on board.
Competitor	A person who races or intends to race in the event.
National authority	A World Sailing member national authority.
Race committee	The race committee appointed under rule 89.2(c) and any other person or committee performing a race committee function.
Racing rule	A rule in *The Racing Rules of Sailing*.
Technical committee	The technical committee appointed under rule 89.2(c) and any other person or committee performing a technical committee function.
Vessel	Any boat or ship.

Other words and terms are used in the sense ordinarily understood in nautical or general use.

Notation   The notation '[DP]' in a *rule* means that the penalty for a breach of the *rule* may, at the discretion of the protest committee, be less than disqualification. Guidelines for discretionary penalties are available on the World Sailing website.

Revision   The racing rules are revised and published every four years by World Sailing, the international authority for the sport. This edition becomes effective on 1 January 2017 except that for an event beginning in 2016 the date may be postponed by the notice of race and sailing instructions. Marginal markings indicate important changes to Parts 1–7 and the Definitions in the 2013–2016 edition. No changes are contemplated before 2021, but any changes determined to be urgent before then will be announced through national authorities and posted on the World Sailing website.

Appendices   When the rules of an appendix apply, they take precedence over any conflicting rules in Parts 1–7 and the Definitions. Each appendix is identified by a letter. A reference to a rule in an appendix will contain the letter and the rule number (for example, 'rule A1'). The letters I, O and Q are not used to designate appendices in this book.

World Sailing Codes   The World Sailing Codes are listed in the table below. The codes are published in the World Sailing Regulations.

Title	Racing Rule	Regulation
Advertising Code	80	20
Anti-Doping Code	5	21
Betting and Anti-Corruption Code	6	37
Disciplinary Code	7	35
Eligibility Code	75.2	19
Sailor Classification Code	79	22

These Codes are referred to in the definition *Rule* but are not included in this book because they can be changed at any time. The most recent versions of the codes are published on the World Sailing website; new versions will be announced through national authorities.

Cases and Calls   World Sailing publishes interpretations of the racing rules in *The Case Book for 2017–2020* and recognizes them as authoritative interpretations and explanations of the rules. It also publishes *The Call Book for Match Racing for 2017–2020* and *The Call Book for Team Racing for 2017–2020*, and it recognizes them as authoritative only for umpired match or team racing. These publications are available on the World Sailing website.

DEFINITIONS

A term used as stated below is shown in italic type or, in preambles, in bold italic type. The meaning of several other terms is given in Terminology in the Introduction.

Abandon   A race that a race committee or protest committee *abandons* is void but may be resailed.

Clear Astern and Clear Ahead; Overlap   One boat is *clear astern* of another when her hull and equipment in normal position are behind a line abeam from the aftermost point of the other boat's hull and equipment in normal position. The other boat is *clear ahead*. They *overlap* when neither is *clear astern*. However, they also *overlap* when a boat between them *overlaps* both. These terms always apply to boats on the same *tack*. They apply to boats on opposite *tacks* only when rule 18 applies between them or when both boats are sailing more than ninety degrees from the true wind.

Conflict of Interest   A person has a *conflict of interest* if he

(a)   may gain or lose as a result of a decision to which he contributes,

(b)   may reasonably appear to have a personal or financial interest which could affect his ability to be impartial, or

(c)   has a close personal interest in a decision.

Fetching   A boat is *fetching* a *mark* when she is in a position to pass to windward of it and leave it on the required side without changing *tack*.

Finish   A boat *finishes* when any part of her hull, or crew or equipment in normal position, crosses the finishing line from the course side. However, she has not *finished* if after crossing the finishing line she

(a)   takes a penalty under rule 44.2,

(b)   corrects an error under rule 28.2 made at the line, or

(c)   continues to sail the course.

Keep Clear   A boat *keeps clear* of a right-of-way boat

(a)   if the right-of-way boat can sail her course with no need to take avoiding action and,

(b)   when the boats are *overlapped*, if the right-of-way boat can also change course in both directions without immediately making contact.

Leeward and Windward   A boat's *leeward* side is the side that is or, when she is head to wind, was away from the wind. However, when sailing by the lee or directly downwind, her *leeward* side is the side on which her mainsail lies. The other side is her *windward* side. When two boats on the same *tack overlap*, the one on the *leeward* side of the other is the *leeward* boat. The other is the *windward* boat.

Mark   An object the sailing instructions require a boat to leave on a specified side, and a race committee vessel surrounded by navigable water from which the starting or finishing line extends. An anchor line or an object attached accidentally to a *mark* is not part of it.

Mark-Room   *Room* for a boat to leave a *mark* on the required side. Also,

(a)   room to sail to the *mark* when her *proper course* is to sail close to it, and

(b)   room to round the *mark* as necessary to sail the course.

However, *mark-room* for a boat does not include *room* to tack unless she is *overlapped* inside and to *windward* of the boat required to give *mark-room* and she would be *fetching* the *mark* after her tack.

Obstruction   An object that a boat could not pass without changing course substantially, if she were sailing directly towards it and one of her hull lengths from it. An object that can be safely passed on only one side and an area so designated by the sailing instructions are also *obstructions*. However, a boat *racing* is not an *obstruction* to other boats unless they are required to *keep clear* of her or, if rule 23 applies, avoid her. A vessel under way, including a boat *racing*, is never a continuing *obstruction*.

Overlap   See **Clear Astern and Clear Ahead; Overlap**.

Party   A *party* to a hearing is

(a)   for a protest hearing: a protestor, a protestee;

(b)   for a request for redress: a boat requesting redress or for which redress is requested, a race committee acting under rule 60.2(b), a technical committee acting under rule 60.4(b);

(c)   for a request for redress under rule 62.1(a): the body alleged to have made an improper action or omission;

(d)   a person against whom an allegation of a breach of rule 69 is made; a person presenting an allegation under rule 69;

(e)   a *support person* subject to a hearing under rule 60.3(d).

However, the protest committee is never a *party*.

Postpone   A *postponed* race is delayed before its scheduled start but may be started or *abandoned* later.

Proper Course   A course a boat would sail to *finish* as soon as possible in the absence of the other boats referred to in the rule using the term. A boat has no *proper course* before her starting signal.

Protest   An allegation made under rule 61.2 by a boat, a race committee, a technical committee or a protest committee that a boat has broken a *rule*.

Racing   A boat is *racing* from her preparatory signal until she *finishes* and clears the finishing line and *marks* or retires, or until the race committee signals a general recall, *postponement* or *abandonment*.

Room   The space a boat needs in the existing conditions, including space to comply with her obligations under the rules of Part 2 and rule 31, while manoeuvring promptly in a seamanlike way.

Rule

(a)   The rules in this book, including the Definitions, Race Signals, Introduction, preambles and the rules of relevant appendices, but not titles;

(b)   World Sailing Advertising Code, Anti-Doping Code, Betting and Anti-Corruption Code, Disciplinary Code, Eligibility Code, Sailor Classification Code, respectively Regulations 20, 21, 37, 35, 19 and 22;

(c)   the prescriptions of the national authority, unless they are changed by the notice of race or sailing instructions in compliance with the national authority's prescription, if any, to rule 88.2;

(d)   the class rules (for a boat racing under a handicap or rating system, the rules of that system are 'class rules');

(e)   the notice of race;

(f)   the sailing instructions; and

(g)   any other documents that govern the event.

Start   A boat *starts* when, having been entirely on the pre-start side of the starting line at or after her starting signal, and having complied with rule 30.1 if it applies, any part of her hull, crew or equipment crosses the starting line in the direction of the first *mark*.

Support Person   Any person who

(a)   provides, or may provide, physical or advisory support to a competitor, including any coach, trainer, manager, team staff, medic, paramedic or any other person working with, treating or assisting a competitor in or preparing for the competition, or

(b)   is the parent or guardian of a competitor.

Tack, Starboard or Port   A boat is on the *tack*, *starboard* or *port*, corresponding to her *windward* side.

Windward   See **Leeward and Windward**.

Zone   The area around a *mark* within a distance of three hull lengths of the boat nearer to it. A boat is in the *zone* when any part of her hull is in the *zone*.

BASIC PRINCIPLES

SPORTSMANSHIP AND THE RULES

Competitors in the sport of sailing are governed by a body of *rules* that they are expected to follow and enforce. A fundamental principle of sportsmanship is that when competitors break a *rule* they will promptly take a penalty, which may be to retire.

ENVIRONMENTAL RESPONSIBILITY

Participants are encouraged to minimize any adverse environmental impact of the sport of sailing.

PART 1

FUNDAMENTAL RULES

1   SAFETY

1.1   Helping Those in Danger

A boat or competitor shall give all possible help to any person or vessel in danger.

1.2   Life-Saving Equipment and Personal Flotation Devices

A boat shall carry adequate life-saving equipment for all persons on board, including one item ready for immediate use, unless her class rules make some other provision. Each competitor is individually responsible for wearing a personal flotation device adequate for the conditions.

2   FAIR SAILING

A boat and her owner shall compete in compliance with recognized principles of sportsmanship and fair play. A boat may be penalized under this rule only if it is clearly established that these principles have been violated. The penalty shall be either disqualification or disqualification that is not excludable.

3   ACCEPTANCE OF THE RULES

3.1   (a)   By participating or intending to participate in a race conducted under these *rules*, each competitor and boat owner agrees to accept these *rules*.

(b)   A *support person* by providing support, or a parent or guardian by permitting their child to enter a race, agrees to accept the *rules*.

3.2   Each competitor and boat owner agrees, on behalf of their *support persons*, that such *support persons* are bound by the *rules*.

3.3   Acceptance of the *rules* includes agreement

(a)   to be governed by the *rules*;

(b)   to accept the penalties imposed and other action taken under the *rules*, subject to the appeal and review procedures provided in them, as the final determination of any matter arising under the *rules*;

(c)   with respect to any such determination, not to resort to any court of law or tribunal not provided for in the *rules*; and

(d)   by each competitor and boat owner to ensure that their *support persons* are aware of the *rules*.

3.4   The person in charge of each boat shall ensure that all competitors in the crew and the boat's owner are aware of their responsibilities under this rule.

3.5   This rule may be changed by a prescription of the national authority of the venue.

4   DECISION TO RACE

The responsibility for a boat's decision to participate in a race or to continue *racing* is hers alone.

5   ANTI-DOPING

A competitor shall comply with the World Anti-Doping Code, the rules of the World Anti-Doping Agency, and World Sailing Regulation 21, Anti-Doping Code. An alleged or actual breach of this rule shall be dealt with under Regulation 21. It shall not be grounds for a *protest* and rule 63.1 does not apply.

6 BETTING AND ANTI-CORRUPTION

Each competitor, boat owner and *support person* shall comply with World Sailing Regulation 37, Betting and Anti-Corruption Code. An alleged or actual breach of this rule shall be dealt with under Regulation 37. It shall not be grounds for a *protest* and rule 63.1 does not apply.

7 DISCIPLINARY CODE

Each competitor, boat owner and *support person* shall comply with World Sailing Regulation 35, Disciplinary, Appeals and Review Code (referred to as 'Disciplinary Code' elsewhere). An alleged or actual breach of this rule shall be dealt with under Regulation 35. It shall not be grounds for a *protest* and rule 63.1 does not apply.

PART 2
WHEN BOATS MEET

The rules of Part 2 apply between boats that are sailing in or near the racing area and intend to **race**, *are* **racing**, *or have been* **racing**. *However, a boat not* **racing** *shall not be penalized for breaking one of these rules, except rule 14 when the incident resulted in injury or serious damage, or rule 24.1.*

When a boat sailing under these rules meets a vessel that is not, she shall comply with the International Regulations for Preventing Collisions at Sea (IRPCAS) *or government right-of-way rules. If the sailing instructions so state, the rules of Part 2 are replaced by the right-of-way rules of the IRPCAS or by government right-of-way rules.*

SECTION A
RIGHT OF WAY

A boat has right of way over another boat when the other boat is required to **keep clear** *of her. However, some rules in Sections B, C and D limit the actions of a right-of-way boat.*

10 ON OPPOSITE TACKS

When boats are on opposite *tacks*, a *port-tack* boat shall *keep clear* of a *starboard-tack* boat.

11 ON THE SAME TACK, OVERLAPPED

When boats are on the same *tack* and *overlapped*, a *windward* boat shall *keep clear* of a *leeward* boat.

12 ON THE SAME TACK, NOT OVERLAPPED

When boats are on the same *tack* and not *overlapped*, a boat

clear astern shall *keep clear* of a boat *clear ahead*.

13 WHILE TACKING

After a boat passes head to wind, she shall *keep clear* of other boats until she is on a close-hauled course. During that time rules 10, 11 and 12 do not apply. If two boats are subject to this rule at the same time, the one on the other's port side or the one astern shall *keep clear*.

SECTION B
GENERAL LIMITATIONS

14 AVOIDING CONTACT

A boat shall avoid contact with another boat if reasonably possible. However, a right-of-way boat or one entitled to *room* or *mark-room*

(a)   need not act to avoid contact until it is clear that the other boat is not *keeping clear* or giving *room* or *mark-room*, and

(b)   shall be exonerated if she breaks this rule and the contact does not cause damage or injury.

15 ACQUIRING RIGHT OF WAY

When a boat acquires right of way, she shall initially give the other boat *room* to *keep clear*, unless she acquires right of way because of the other boat's actions.

16 CHANGING COURSE

16.1   When a right-of-way boat changes course, she shall give the other boat *room* to *keep clear*.

16.2   In addition, when after the starting signal a *port-tack* boat is *keeping clear* by sailing to pass astern of a *starboard-tack* boat, the *starboard-tack* boat shall not change course if as a result the *port-tack* boat would immediately need to change course to continue *keeping clear*.

17 ON THE SAME TACK; PROPER COURSE

If a boat *clear astern* becomes *overlapped* within two of her hull lengths to *leeward* of a boat on the same *tack*, she shall not sail above her *proper course* while they remain on the same *tack* and *overlapped* within that distance, unless in doing so she promptly sails astern of the other boat. This rule does not apply if the *overlap* begins while the *windward* boat is required by rule 13 to *keep clear*.

SECTION C
AT MARKS AND OBSTRUCTIONS

Section C rules do not apply at a starting **mark** *surrounded by navigable water or at its anchor line from the time boats are approaching them to* **start** *until they have passed them.*

18   MARK-ROOM

18.1 When Rule 18 Applies

Rule 18 applies between boats when they are required to leave a *mark* on the same side and at least one of them is in the *zone*. However, it does not apply

(a)   between boats on opposite *tacks* on a beat to windward,

(b)   between boats on opposite *tacks* when the *proper course* at the *mark* for one but not both of them is to tack,

(c)   between a boat approaching a *mark* and one leaving it, or

(d)   if the *mark* is a continuing *obstruction*, in which case rule 19 applies.

18.2 Giving Mark-Room

(a)   When boats are *overlapped* the outside boat shall give the inside boat *mark-room*, unless rule 18.2(b) applies.

(b)   If boats are *overlapped* when the first of them reaches the *zone*, the outside boat at that moment shall thereafter give the inside boat *mark-room*. If a boat is *clear ahead* when she reaches the *zone*, the boat *clear astern* at that moment shall thereafter give her *mark-room*.

(c)   When a boat is required to give *mark-room* by rule 18.2(b),

(1)   she shall continue to do so even if later an *overlap* is broken or a new *overlap* begins;

(2)   if she becomes *overlapped* inside the boat entitled to *mark-room*, she shall also give that boat *room* to sail her *proper course* while they remain *overlapped*.

(d)   Rules 18.2(b) and (c) cease to apply when the boat entitled to *mark-room* has been given that *mark-room*, or if she passes head to wind or leaves the *zone*.

(e)   If there is reasonable doubt that a boat obtained or broke an *overlap* in time, it shall be presumed that she did not.

(f)   If a boat obtained an inside *overlap* from *clear astern* or by tacking to *windward* of the other boat and, from the time the *overlap* began, the outside boat has been unable to give *mark-room*, she is not required to give it.

18.3 Tacking in the Zone

If a boat in the *zone* of a *mark* to be left to port passes head to wind from *port* to *starboard tack* and is then *fetching* the *mark*, she shall not cause a boat that has been on *starboard tack* since entering the *zone* to sail above close-hauled to avoid contact and she shall give *mark-room* if that boat becomes *overlapped* inside her. When this rule applies between boats, rule 18.2 does not apply between them.

18.4 Gybing

When an inside *overlapped* right-of-way boat must gybe at a *mark* to sail her *proper course*, until she gybes she shall sail no farther from the *mark* than needed to sail that course. Rule 18.4 does not apply at a gate *mark*.

19   ROOM TO PASS AN OBSTRUCTION

19.1 When Rule 19 Applies

Rule 19 applies between two boats at an *obstruction* except

(a)   when the *obstruction* is a *mark* the boats are required to leave on the same side, or

(b)   when rule 18 applies between the boats and the *obstruction* is another boat *overlapped* with each of them.

However, at a continuing *obstruction*, rule 19 always applies and rule 18 does not.

19.2 Giving Room at an Obstruction

(a)   A right-of-way boat may choose to pass an *obstruction* on either side.

(b)   When boats are *overlapped*, the outside boat shall give the inside boat *room* between her and the *obstruction*, unless she has been unable to do so from the time the *overlap* began.

(c)   While boats are passing a continuing *obstruction*, if a boat that was *clear astern* and required to *keep clear* becomes *overlapped* between the other boat and the *obstruction* and, at the moment the *overlap* begins, there is not *room* for her to pass between them, she is not entitled to *room* under rule 19.2(b). While the boats remain *overlapped*, she shall *keep clear* and rules 10 and 11 do not apply.

20   ROOM TO TACK AT AN OBSTRUCTION

20.1 Hailing

A boat may hail for *room* to tack and avoid a boat on the same *tack*. However, she shall not hail unless

(a)   she is approaching an *obstruction* and will soon need to make a substantial course change to avoid it safely, and

(b)   she is sailing close-hauled or above.

In addition, she shall not hail if the *obstruction* is a *mark* and a boat that is *fetching* it would be required to change course as a result of the hail.

20.2 Responding

(a)   After a boat hails, she shall give a hailed boat time to respond.

(b)   A hailed boat shall respond even if the hail breaks rule 20.1.

(c)   A hailed boat shall respond either by tacking as soon as possible, or by immediately replying 'You tack' and then giving the hailing boat *room* to tack and avoid her.

(d)   When a hailed boat responds, the hailing boat shall tack as soon as possible.

(e)   From the time a boat hails until she has tacked and avoided a hailed boat, rule 18.2 does not apply between them.

20.3 Passing On a Hail to an Additional Boat

When a boat has been hailed for *room* to tack and she intends to respond by tacking, she may hail another boat on the same *tack* for *room* to tack and avoid her. She may hail even if her hail does not meet the conditions of rule 20.1. Rule 20.2 applies between her and a boat she hails.

SECTION D
OTHER RULES

When rule 22 or 23 applies between two boats, Section A rules do not.

21   EXONERATION

When a boat is sailing within the *room* or *mark-room* to which she is entitled, she shall be exonerated if, in an incident with a boat required to give her that *room* or *mark-room*,

(a)   she breaks a rule of Section A, rule 15 or rule 16, or

(b)   she is compelled to break rule 31.

22   STARTING ERRORS; TAKING PENALTIES; BACKING A SAIL

22.1   A boat sailing towards the pre-start side of the starting line or one of its extensions after her starting signal to *start* or to comply with rule 30.1 shall *keep clear* of a boat not doing so until she is completely on the pre-start side.

22.2   A boat taking a penalty shall *keep clear* of one that is not.

22.3   A boat moving astern, or sideways to windward, through the water by backing a sail shall *keep clear* of one that is not.

23   CAPSIZED, ANCHORED OR AGROUND; RESCUING

If possible, a boat shall avoid a boat that is capsized or has not regained control after capsizing, is anchored or aground, or is trying to help a person or vessel in danger. A boat is capsized when her masthead is in the water.

24   INTERFERING WITH ANOTHER BOAT

24.1   If reasonably possible, a boat not *racing* shall not interfere with a boat that is *racing*.

24.2   If reasonably possible, a boat shall not interfere with a boat that is taking a penalty, sailing on another leg or subject to rule 22.1. However, after the starting signal this rule does not apply when the boat is sailing her *proper course*.

PART 3
CONDUCT OF A RACE

25   NOTICE OF RACE, SAILING INSTRUCTIONS AND SIGNALS

25.1   The notice of race and sailing instructions shall be made available to each boat before a race begins.

25.2   The meanings of the visual and sound signals stated in Race Signals shall not be changed except under rule 86.1(b). The meanings of any other signals that may be used shall be stated in the notice of race or sailing instructions.

25.3   When the race committee is required to display a flag as a visual signal, it may use a flag or other object of a similar appearance.

26   STARTING RACES

Races shall be started by using the following signals. Times shall be taken from the visual signals; the absence of a sound signal shall be disregarded.

Minutes before starting signal	Visual signal	Sound signal	Means
5*	Class flag	One	Warning signal
4	P, I, Z, Z with I, U, or black flag	One	Preparatory signal
1	Preparatory flag removed	One long	One minute
0	Class flag removed	One	Starting signal

*or as stated in the sailing instructions

The warning signal for each succeeding class shall be made with or after the starting signal of the preceding class.

27   OTHER RACE COMMITTEE ACTIONS BEFORE THE STARTING SIGNAL

27.1   No later than the warning signal, the race committee shall signal or otherwise designate the course to be sailed if the sailing instructions have not stated the course, and it may replace one course signal with another and signal that wearing personal flotation devices is required (display flag Y with one sound).

27.2   No later than the preparatory signal, the race committee may move a starting *mark*.

27.3   Before the starting signal, the race committee may for any reason *postpone* (display flag AP, AP over H, or AP over A, with two sounds) or *abandon* the race (display flag N over H, or N over A, with three sounds).

28   SAILING THE COURSE

28.1   A boat shall *start*, sail the course described in the sailing instructions and *finish*. While doing so, she may leave on either side a *mark* that does not begin, bound or end the leg she is sailing. After *finishing* she need not cross the finishing line completely.

28.2   A string representing a boat's track from the time she begins to approach the starting line from its pre-start side to *start* until she *finishes* shall, when drawn taut,

(a)   pass each *mark* on the required side and in the correct order,

(b)   touch each rounding *mark*, and

(c)   pass between the *marks* of a gate from the direction of the previous *mark*.

She may correct any errors to comply with this rule, provided she has not *finished*.

29   RECALLS

29.1   Individual Recall

When at a boat's starting signal any part of her hull, crew or equipment is on the course side of the starting line or she must comply with rule 30.1, the race committee shall promptly display flag X with one sound. The flag shall be displayed until all such boats have sailed completely to the pre-start side of the starting line or one of its extensions and have complied with rule 30.1 if it applies, but no later than four minutes after the starting signal or one minute before any later starting signal, whichever is earlier. If rule 30.3 or 30.4 applies this rule does not.

29.2   General Recall

When at the starting signal the race committee is unable to identify boats that are on the course side of the starting line or to which rule 30 applies, or there has been an error in the starting procedure, the race committee may signal a general recall (display the First Substitute with two sounds). The warning signal for a new start for the recalled class shall be made one minute after the First Substitute is removed (one sound), and the starts for any succeeding classes shall follow the new start.

30   STARTING PENALTIES

30.1   I Flag Rule

If flag I has been displayed, and any part of a boat's hull, crew or equipment is on the course side of the starting line or one of its extensions during the last minute before her starting signal, she shall sail across an extension to the pre-start side before *starting*.

30.2   Z Flag Rule

If flag Z has been displayed, no part of a boat's hull, crew or equipment shall be in the triangle formed by the ends of the starting line and the first *mark* during the last minute before her starting signal. If a boat breaks this rule and is identified, she shall receive, without a hearing, a 20% Scoring Penalty calculated as stated in rule 44.3(c). She shall be penalized even if the race is restarted or resailed, but not if it is *postponed* or *abandoned* before the starting signal. If she is similarly identified during a subsequent attempt to start the same race, she shall receive an additional 20% Scoring Penalty.

30.3   U Flag Rule

If flag U has been displayed, no part of a boat's hull, crew or equipment shall be in the triangle formed by the ends of the starting line and the first *mark* during the last minute before her starting signal. If a boat breaks this rule and is identified, she shall be disqualified without a hearing, but not if the race is restarted or resailed.

30.4   Black Flag Rule

If a black flag has been displayed, no part of a boat's hull, crew or equipment shall be in the triangle formed by the ends of the starting line and the first *mark* during the last minute before her starting signal. If a boat breaks this rule and is identified, she shall be disqualified without a hearing, even if the race is restarted or resailed, but not if it is *postponed* or *abandoned* before the starting signal. If a general recall is signalled or the race is *abandoned* after the starting signal, the race committee shall display her sail number before the next warning signal for that race, and if the race is restarted or resailed she shall not sail in it. If she does so, her disqualification shall not be excluded in calculating her series score.

31   TOUCHING A MARK

While *racing*, a boat shall not touch a starting *mark* before *starting*, a *mark* that begins, bounds or ends the leg of the course on which she is sailing, or a finishing *mark* after *finishing*.

32   SHORTENING OR ABANDONING AFTER THE START

32.1   After the starting signal, the race committee may shorten the course (display flag S with two sounds) or *abandon* the race (display flag N, N over H, or N over A, with three sounds),

(a)   because of foul weather,

(b)   because of insufficient wind making it unlikely that any boat will *finish* within the time limit,

(c)   because a *mark* is missing or out of position, or

(d)   for any other reason directly affecting the safety or fairness of the competition.

In addition, the race committee may shorten the course so that other scheduled races can be sailed, or *abandon* the race because of an error in the starting procedure. However, after one boat has sailed the course and *finished* within the time limit, if any, the race committee shall not *abandon* the race without considering the consequences for all boats in the race or series.

32.2   If the race committee signals a shortened course (displays flag S with two sounds), the finishing line shall be,

(a)   at a rounding *mark*, between the *mark* and a staff displaying flag S;

(b)   a line the course requires boats to cross; or

(c)   at a gate, between the gate *marks*.

The shortened course shall be signalled before the first boat crosses the finishing line.

33   CHANGING THE NEXT LEG OF THE COURSE

The race committee may change a leg of the course that begins at a rounding *mark* or at a gate by changing the position of the next *mark* (or the finishing line) and signalling all boats before they begin the leg. The next *mark* need not be in position at that time.

(a)   If the direction of the leg will be changed, the signal shall be the display of flag C with repetitive sounds and one or both of

    (1)   the new compass bearing,

(2)   a green triangle for a change to starboard or a red rectangle for a change to port.

(b)   If the length of the leg will be changed, the signal shall be the display of flag C with repetitive sounds and a '−' if the length will be decreased or a '+' if it will be increased.

(c)   Subsequent legs may be changed without further signalling to maintain the course shape.

34   MARK MISSING

If a *mark* is missing or out of position, the race committee shall, if possible,

(a)   replace it in its correct position or substitute a new one of similar appearance, or

(b)   substitute an object displaying flag M and make repetitive sound signals.

35   TIME LIMIT AND SCORES

If one boat sails the course as required by rule 28 and *finishes* within the time limit, if any, all boats that *finish* shall be scored according to their finishing places unless the race is *abandoned*. If no boat *finishes* within the time limit, the race committee shall *abandon* the race.

36   RACES RESTARTED OR RESAILED

If a race is restarted or resailed, a breach of a *rule* in the original race, or in any previous restart or resail of that race, shall not

(a)   prohibit a boat from competing unless she has broken rule 30.4; or

(b)   cause a boat to be penalized except under rule 30.2, 30.4 or 69 or under rule 14 when she has caused injury or serious damage.

PART 4
OTHER REQUIREMENTS WHEN RACING

Part 4 rules apply only to boats **racing** *unless the rule states otherwise.*

40   PERSONAL FLOTATION DEVICES

When flag Y is displayed with one sound before or with the warning signal, competitors shall wear personal flotation devices, except briefly while changing or adjusting clothing or personal equipment. When flag Y is displayed ashore, this rule applies at all times while afloat. Wet suits and dry suits are not personal flotation devices.

41   OUTSIDE HELP

A boat shall not receive help from any outside source, except

(a)   help for a crew member who is ill, injured or in danger;

(b)   after a collision, help from the crew of the other vessel

to get clear;

(c)   help in the form of information freely available to all boats;

(d)   unsolicited information from a disinterested source, which may be another boat in the same race.

However, a boat that gains a significant advantage in the race from help received under rule 41(a) may be protested and penalized; any penalty may be less than disqualification.

42   PROPULSION

42.1 Basic Rule

Except when permitted in rule 42.3 or 45, a boat shall compete by using only the wind and water to increase, maintain or decrease her speed. Her crew may adjust the trim of sails and hull, and perform other acts of seamanship, but shall not otherwise move their bodies to propel the boat.

42.2 Prohibited Actions

Without limiting the application of rule 42.1, these actions are prohibited:

(a)   pumping: repeated fanning of any sail either by pulling in and releasing the sail or by vertical or athwartship body movement;

(b)   rocking: repeated rolling of the boat, induced by

    (1)   body movement,

    (2)   repeated adjustment of the sails or centreboard, or

    (3)   steering;

(c)   ooching: sudden forward body movement, stopped abruptly;

(d)   sculling: repeated movement of the helm that is either forceful or that propels the boat forward or prevents her from moving astern;

(e)   repeated tacks or gybes unrelated to changes in the wind or to tactical considerations.

42.3 Exceptions

(a)   A boat may be rolled to facilitate steering.

(b)   A boat's crew may move their bodies to exaggerate the rolling that facilitates steering the boat through a tack or a gybe, provided that, just after the tack or gybe is completed, the boat's speed is not greater than it would have been in the absence of the tack or gybe.

(c)   Except on a beat to windward, when surfing (rapidly accelerating down the front of a wave) or planing is possible, the boat's crew may pull in any sail in order to initiate surfing or planing, but each sail may be pulled in only once for each wave or gust of wind.

(d)   When a boat is above a close-hauled course and either stationary or moving slowly, she may scull to turn to a close-hauled course.

(e)   If a batten is inverted, the boat's crew may pump the sail until the batten is no longer inverted. This action is not permitted if it clearly propels the boat.

(f) A boat may reduce speed by repeatedly moving her helm.

(g) Any means of propulsion may be used to help a person or another vessel in danger.

(h) To get clear after grounding or colliding with a vessel or object, a boat may use force applied by her crew or the crew of the other vessel and any equipment other than a propulsion engine. However, the use of an engine may be permitted by rule 42.3(i).

(i) Sailing instructions may, in stated circumstances, permit propulsion using an engine or any other method, provided the boat does not gain a significant advantage in the race.

Note: Interpretations of rule 42 are available at the World Sailing website or by mail upon request.

43   COMPETITOR CLOTHING AND EQUIPMENT

43.1 (a)   Competitors shall not wear or carry clothing or equipment for the purpose of increasing their weight.

(b) Furthermore, a competitor's clothing and equipment shall not weigh more than 8 kilograms, excluding a hiking or trapeze harness and clothing (including footwear) worn only below the knee. Class rules or sailing instructions may specify a lower weight or a higher weight up to 10 kilograms. Class rules may include footwear and other clothing worn below the knee within that weight. A hiking or trapeze harness shall have positive buoyancy and shall not weigh more than 2 kilograms, except that class rules may specify a higher weight up to 4 kilograms. Weights shall be determined as required by Appendix H.

43.2 Rule 43.1(b) does not apply to boats required to be equipped with lifelines.

44   PENALTIES AT THE TIME OF AN INCIDENT

44.1 Taking a Penalty

A boat may take a Two-Turns Penalty when she may have broken one or more rules of Part 2 in an incident while *racing*. She may take a One-Turn Penalty when she may have broken rule 31. Alternatively, sailing instructions may specify the use of the Scoring Penalty or some other penalty, in which case the specified penalty shall replace the One-Turn and the Two-Turns Penalty. However,

(a) when a boat may have broken a rule of Part 2 and rule 31 in the same incident she need not take the penalty for breaking rule 31;

(b) if the boat caused injury or serious damage or, despite taking a penalty, gained a significant advantage in the race or series by her breach her penalty shall be to retire.

44.2 One-Turn and Two-Turns Penalties

After getting well clear of other boats as soon after the incident as possible, a boat takes a One-Turn or Two-Turns Penalty by

promptly making the required number of turns in the same direction, each turn including one tack and one gybe. When a boat takes the penalty at or near the finishing line, she shall sail completely to the course side of the line before *finishing*.

44.3 Scoring Penalty

(a) A boat takes a Scoring Penalty by displaying a yellow flag at the first reasonable opportunity after the incident.

(b) When a boat has taken a Scoring Penalty, she shall keep the yellow flag displayed until *finishing* and call the race committee's attention to it at the finishing line. At that time she shall also inform the race committee of the identity of the other boat involved in the incident. If this is impracticable, she shall do so at the first reasonable opportunity and within the protest time limit.

(c) The race score for a boat that takes a Scoring Penalty shall be the score she would have received without that penalty, made worse by the number of places stated in the sailing instructions. When the sailing instructions do not state the number of places, the penalty shall be 20% of the score for Did Not *Finish*, rounded to the nearest whole number (0.5 rounded upward). The scores of other boats shall not be changed; therefore, two boats may receive the same score. However, the penalty shall not cause the boat's score to be worse than the score for Did Not *Finish*.

45   HAULING OUT; MAKING FAST; ANCHORING

A boat shall be afloat and off moorings at her preparatory signal. Thereafter, she shall not be hauled out or made fast except to bail out, reef sails or make repairs. She may anchor or the crew may stand on the bottom. She shall recover the anchor before continuing in the race unless she is unable to do so.

46   PERSON IN CHARGE

A boat shall have on board a person in charge designated by the member or organization that entered the boat. See rule 75.

47   LIMITATIONS ON EQUIPMENT AND CREW

47.1 A boat shall use only the equipment on board at her preparatory signal.

47.2 No person on board shall intentionally leave, except when ill or injured, or to help a person or vessel in danger, or to swim. A person leaving the boat by accident or to swim shall be back on board before the boat continues in the race.

48   FOG SIGNALS AND LIGHTS; TRAFFIC SEPARATION SCHEMES

48.1 When safety requires, a boat shall sound fog signals and show lights as required by the *International Regulations for Preventing Collisions at Sea (IRPCAS)* or applicable government rules.

48.2 A boat shall comply with rule 10, Traffic Separation Schemes, of the *IRPCAS*.

49 CREW POSITION; LIFELINES

49.1 Competitors shall use no device designed to position their bodies outboard, other than hiking straps and stiffeners worn under the thighs.

49.2 When lifelines are required by the class rules or any other *rule*, competitors shall not position any part of their torsos outside them, except briefly to perform a necessary task. On boats equipped with upper and lower lifelines, a competitor sitting on the deck facing outboard with his waist inside the lower lifeline may have the upper part of his body outside the upper lifeline. Unless a class rule or any other *rule* specifies a maximum deflection, lifelines shall be taut. If the class rules do not specify the material or minimum diameter of lifelines, they shall comply with the corresponding specifications in the *World Sailing Offshore Special Regulations*.

Note: Those regulations are available at the World Sailing website.

50 SETTING AND SHEETING SAILS

50.1 Changing Sails

When headsails or spinnakers are being changed, a replacing sail may be fully set and trimmed before the replaced sail is lowered. However, only one mainsail and, except when changing, only one spinnaker shall be carried set at a time.

50.2 Spinnaker Poles; Whisker Poles

Only one spinnaker pole or whisker pole shall be used at a time except when gybing. When in use, it shall be attached to the foremost mast.

50.3 Use of Outriggers

(a) No sail shall be sheeted over or through an outrigger, except as permitted in rule 50.3(b) or 50.3(c). An outrigger is any fitting or other device so placed that it could exert outward pressure on a sheet or sail at a point from which, with the boat upright, a vertical line would fall outside the hull or deck. For the purpose of this rule, bulwarks, rails and rubbing strakes are not part of the hull or deck and the following are not outriggers: a bowsprit used to secure the tack of a sail, a bumkin used to sheet the boom of a sail, or a boom of a boomed headsail that requires no adjustment when tacking.

(b) Any sail may be sheeted to or led above a boom that is regularly used for a sail and is permanently attached to the mast from which the head of the sail is set.

(c) A headsail may be sheeted or attached at its clew to a spinnaker pole or whisker pole, provided that a spinnaker is not set.

50.4 Headsails

For the purposes of rules 50 and 54 and Appendix G, the difference between a headsail and a spinnaker is that the width of a headsail, measured between the midpoints of its luff and leech, is less than 75% of the length of its foot. A sail tacked down behind the foremost mast is not a headsail.

51 MOVABLE BALLAST

All movable ballast, including sails that are not set, shall be properly stowed. Water, dead weight or ballast shall not be moved for the purpose of changing trim or stability. Floorboards, bulkheads, doors, stairs and water tanks shall be left in place and all cabin fixtures kept on board. However, bilge water may be bailed out.

52 MANUAL POWER

A boat's standing rigging, running rigging, spars and movable hull appendages shall be adjusted and operated only by the power provided by the crew.

53 SKIN FRICTION

A boat shall not eject or release a substance, such as a polymer, or have specially textured surfaces that could improve the character of the flow of water inside the boundary layer.

54 FORESTAYS AND HEADSAIL TACKS

Forestays and headsail tacks, except those of spinnaker staysails when the boat is not close-hauled, shall be attached approximately on a boat's centreline.

55 TRASH DISPOSAL

A competitor shall not intentionally put trash in the water. This rule applies at all times while afloat. The penalty for a breach of this rule may be less than disqualification.

PART 5

PROTESTS, REDRESS, HEARINGS, MISCONDUCT AND APPEALS

SECTION A
PROTESTS; REDRESS; RULE 69 ACTION

60 RIGHT TO PROTEST; RIGHT TO REQUEST REDRESS OR RULE 69 ACTION

60.1 A boat may

(a) protest another boat, but not for an alleged breach of a rule of Part 2 or rule 31 unless she was involved in or saw the incident; or

(b) request redress.

60.2 A race committee may

(a) protest a boat, but not as a result of information arising from a request for redress or an invalid *protest*, or from a report from a person with a *conflict of interest* other than the representative of the boat herself;

(b) request redress for a boat; or

(c)   report to the protest committee requesting action under rule 69.2(b).

60.3 A protest committee may

(a)   protest a boat, but not as a result of information arising from a request for redress or an invalid *protest*, or from a report from a person with a *conflict of interest* other than the representative of the boat herself. However, it may protest a boat

(1)   if it learns of an incident involving her that may have resulted in injury or serious damage, or

(2)   if during the hearing of a valid *protest* it learns that the boat, although not a *party* to the hearing, was involved in the incident and may have broken a *rule*;

(b)   call a hearing to consider redress;

(c)   act under rule 69.2(b); or

(d)   call a hearing to consider whether a *support person* has broken a *rule*, based on its own observation or information received from any source, including evidence taken during a hearing.

60.4 A technical committee may

(a)   protest a boat, but not as a result of information arising from a request for redress or an invalid *protest*, or from a report from a person with a *conflict of interest* other than the representative of the boat herself. However, it shall protest a boat if it decides that

(1)   a boat has broken a rule of Part 4, but not rules 41, 42, 44 and 46, or

(2)   a boat or personal equipment does not comply with the class rules;

(b)   request redress for a boat; or

(c)   report to the protest committee requesting action under rule 69.2(b).

60.5 However, neither a boat nor a committee may protest for an alleged breach of rule 5, 6, 7 or 69.

61   PROTEST REQUIREMENTS

61.1 Informing the Protestee

(a)   A boat intending to protest shall inform the other boat at the first reasonable opportunity. When her *protest* will concern an incident in the racing area that she was involved in or saw, she shall hail 'Protest' and conspicuously display a red flag at the first reasonable opportunity for each. She shall display the flag until she is no longer *racing*. However,

(1)   if the other boat is beyond hailing distance, the protesting boat need not hail but she shall inform the other boat at the first reasonable opportunity;

(2)   if the hull length of the protesting boat is less than 6 metres, she need not display a red flag;

(3)   if the incident was an error by the other boat in sailing the course, she need not hail or display a

red flag but she shall inform the other boat either before or at the first reasonable opportunity after the other boat *finishes*;

(4)   if as a result of the incident a member of either crew is in danger, or there is injury or serious damage that is obvious to the boat intending to protest, the requirements of this rule do not apply to her, but she shall attempt to inform the other boat within the time limit of rule 61.3.

(b)   If the race committee, technical committee or protest committee intends to protest a boat concerning an incident the committee observed in the racing area, it shall inform her after the race within the time limit of rule 61.3. In other cases the committee shall inform the boat of its intention to protest as soon as reasonably possible.

(c)   If the protest committee decides to protest a boat under rule 60.3(a)(2), it shall inform her as soon as reasonably possible, close the current hearing, proceed as required by rules 61.2 and 63, and hear the original and the new *protests* together.

61.2 Protest Contents

A *protest* shall be in writing and identify

(a)   the protestor and protestee;

(b)   the incident;

(c)   where and when the incident occurred;

(d)   any *rule* the protestor believes was broken; and

(e)   the name of the protestor's representative.

However, if requirement (b) is met, requirement (a) may be met at any time before the hearing, and requirements (d) and (e) may be met before or during the hearing. Requirement (c) may also be met before or during the hearing, provided the protestee is allowed reasonable time to prepare for the hearing.

61.3 Protest Time Limit

A *protest* by a boat, or by the race committee, technical committee or protest committee about an incident the committee observed in the racing area, shall be delivered to the race office within the protest time limit stated in the sailing instructions. If none is stated, the time limit is two hours after the last boat in the race *finishes*. Other race committee, technical committee or protest committee *protests* shall be delivered to the race office no later than two hours after the committee receives the relevant information. The protest committee shall extend the time if there is good reason to do so.

62   REDRESS

62.1 A request for redress or a protest committee's decision to consider redress shall be based on a claim or possibility that a boat's score or place in a race or series has been or may be, through no fault of her own, made significantly worse by

(a)   an improper action or omission of the race committee,

protest committee, organizing authority or technical committee for the event, but not by a protest committee decision when the boat was a *party* to the hearing;

(b) injury or physical damage because of the action of a boat that was breaking a rule of Part 2 or of a vessel not *racing* that was required to keep clear;

(c) giving help (except to herself or her crew) in compliance with rule 1.1; or

(d) an action of a boat, or a member of her crew, that resulted in a penalty under rule 2 or a penalty or warning under rule 69.2(h).

62.2 A request shall be in writing and identify the reason for making it. If the request is based on an incident in the racing area, it shall be delivered to the race office within the protest time limit or two hours after the incident, whichever is later. Other requests shall be delivered as soon as reasonably possible after learning of the reasons for making the request. The protest committee shall extend the time if there is good reason to do so. No red flag is required.

SECTION B
HEARINGS AND DECISIONS

63 HEARINGS

63.1 Requirement for a Hearing

A boat or competitor shall not be penalized without a protest hearing, except as provided in rules 30.2, 30.3, 30.4, 64.3(d), 69, 78.2, A5 and P2. A decision on redress shall not be made without a hearing. The protest committee shall hear all *protests* and requests for redress that have been delivered to the race office unless it allows a *protest* or request to be withdrawn.

63.2 Time and Place of the Hearing; Time for Parties to Prepare

All *parties* to the hearing shall be notified of the time and place of the hearing, the *protest* or redress information shall be made available to them, and they shall be allowed reasonable time to prepare for the hearing.

63.3 Right to Be Present

(a) A representative of each *party* to the hearing has the right to be present throughout the hearing of all the evidence. When a *protest* claims a breach of a rule of Part 2, 3 or 4, the representatives of boats shall have been on board at the time of the incident, unless there is good reason for the protest committee to rule otherwise. Any witness, other than a member of the protest committee, shall be excluded except when giving evidence.

(b) If a *party* to the hearing of a *protest* or request for redress does not come to the hearing, the protest committee may nevertheless decide the *protest* or request. If the *party* was unavoidably absent, the committee may reopen the hearing.

63.4 Conflict of Interest

(a) A protest committee member shall declare any possible *conflict of interest* as soon as he is aware of it. A *party* to the hearing who believes a member of the protest committee has a *conflict of interest* shall object as soon as possible. A *conflict of interest* declared by a protest committee member shall be included in the written information provided under rule 65.2.

(b) A member of a protest committee with a *conflict of interest* shall not be a member of the committee for the hearing, unless

(1) all *parties* consent, or

(2) the protest committee decides that the *conflict of interest* is not significant.

(c) When deciding whether a *conflict of interest* is significant, the protest committee shall consider the views of the *parties*, the level of the conflict, the level of the event, the importance to each *party*, and the overall perception of fairness.

(d) However, for World Sailing major events, or for other events as prescribed by the national authority of the venue, rule 63.4(b) does not apply and a person who has a *conflict of interest* shall not be a member of the protest committee.

63.5 Validity of the Protest or Request for Redress

At the beginning of the hearing the protest committee shall take any evidence it considers necessary to decide whether all requirements for the *protest* or request for redress have been met. If they have been met, the *protest* or request is valid and the hearing shall be continued. If not, the committee shall declare the *protest* or request invalid and close the hearing. If the *protest* has been made under rule 60.3(a)(1), the committee shall also determine whether or not injury or serious damage resulted from the incident in question. If not, the hearing shall be closed.

63.6 Taking Evidence and Finding Facts

The protest committee shall take the evidence of the *parties* present at the hearing and of their witnesses and other evidence it considers necessary. A member of the protest committee who saw the incident shall, while the *parties* are present, state that fact and may give evidence. A *party* present at the hearing may question any person who gives evidence. The committee shall then find the facts and base its decision on them.

63.7 Conflict Between Rules

If there is a conflict between two or more *rules* that must be resolved before the protest committee makes a decision, the committee shall apply the *rule* that it believes will provide the fairest result for all boats affected. Rule 63.7 applies only if the conflict is between rules in the notice of race, the sailing instructions, or any of the other documents that govern the event under item (g) of the definition *Rule*.

63.8 Protests Between Boats in Different Races

A *protest* between boats sailing in different races conducted by different organizing authorities shall be heard by a protest committee acceptable to those authorities.

64 DECISIONS

64.1 Penalties and Exoneration

When the protest committee decides that a boat that is a *party* to a protest hearing has broken a *rule* and is not exonerated, it shall disqualify her unless some other penalty applies. A penalty shall be imposed whether or not the applicable *rule* was mentioned in the *protest*. If a boat has broken a *rule* when not *racing*, her penalty shall apply to the race sailed nearest in time to that of the incident. However,

(a) when as a consequence of breaking a *rule* a boat has compelled another boat to break a *rule*, the other boat shall be exonerated.

(b) if a boat has taken an applicable penalty, she shall not be further penalized under this rule unless the penalty for a *rule* she broke is a disqualification that is not excludable from her series score.

(c) if the race is restarted or resailed, rule 36 applies.

64.2 Decisions on Redress

When the protest committee decides that a boat is entitled to redress under rule 62, it shall make as fair an arrangement as possible for all boats affected, whether or not they asked for redress. This may be to adjust the scoring (see rule A10 for some examples) or finishing times of boats, to *abandon* the race, to let the results stand or to make some other arrangement. When in doubt about the facts or probable results of any arrangement for the race or series, especially before *abandoning* the race, the protest committee shall take evidence from appropriate sources.

64.3 Decisions on Protests Concerning Class Rules

(a) When the protest committee finds that deviations in excess of tolerances specified in the class rules were caused by damage or normal wear and do not improve the performance of the boat, it shall not penalize her. However, the boat shall not *race* again until the deviations have been corrected, except when the protest committee decides there is or has been no reasonable opportunity to do so.

(b) When the protest committee is in doubt about the meaning of a class rule, it shall refer its questions, together with the relevant facts, to an authority responsible for interpreting the rule. In making its decision, the committee shall be bound by the reply of the authority.

(c) When a boat is penalized under a class rule and the protest committee decides that the boat also broke the same rule in earlier races in the same event, the penalty may be imposed for all such races. No further *protest* is necessary.

(d) When a boat penalized under a class rule states in writing that she intends to appeal, she may compete in subsequent races without changes to the boat. However, if she fails to appeal or the appeal is decided against her, she shall be disqualified without a further hearing from all subsequent races in which she competed.

(e) Measurement costs arising from a *protest* involving a class rule shall be paid by the unsuccessful *party* unless the protest committee decides otherwise.

64.4 Decisions Concerning Support Persons

(a) When the protest committee decides that a *support person* who is a *party* to a hearing has broken a *rule*, it may

(1) issue a warning,

(2) exclude the person from the event or venue or remove any privileges or benefits, or

(3) take other action within its jurisdiction as provided by the *rules*.

(b) The protest committee may also penalize a competitor for the breach of a *rule* by a *support person* by changing the boat's score in a single race, up to and including DSQ, when the protest committee decides that

(1) the competitor may have gained a competitive advantage as the result of the breach by the *support person*, or

(2) the *support person* commits a further breach after the competitor has been warned by the protest committee that a penalty may be imposed.

65 INFORMING THE PARTIES AND OTHERS

65.1 After making its decision, the protest committee shall promptly inform the *parties* to the hearing of the facts found, the applicable *rules*, the decision, the reasons for it, and any penalties imposed or redress given.

65.2 A *party* to the hearing is entitled to receive the above information in writing, provided she asks for it in writing from the protest committee no later than seven days after being informed of the decision. The committee shall then promptly provide the information, including, when relevant, a diagram of the incident prepared or endorsed by the committee.

65.3 When the protest committee penalizes a boat under a class rule, it shall send the above information to the relevant class rule authorities.

66 REOPENING A HEARING

The protest committee may reopen a hearing when it decides that it may have made a significant error, or when significant new evidence becomes available within a reasonable time. It shall reopen a hearing when required by the national authority under rule 71.2 or R5. A *party* to the hearing may ask for a reopening no later than 24 hours after being informed of the decision. On the last scheduled day of racing the request shall be delivered

(a) within the protest time limit if the requesting *party* was informed of the decision on the previous day;

(b) no later than 30 minutes after the *party* was informed of the decision on that day.

When a hearing is reopened, a majority of the members of the protest committee shall, if possible, be members of the original protest committee.

67   DAMAGES

The question of damages arising from a breach of any *rule* shall be governed by the prescriptions, if any, of the national authority.

Note: There is no rule 68.

SECTION C
MISCONDUCT

69   MISCONDUCT

69.1   Obligation not to Commit Misconduct; Resolution

(a)   A competitor, boat owner or *support person* shall not commit an act of misconduct.

(b)   Misconduct is:

   (1)   conduct that is a breach of good manners, a breach of good sportsmanship, or unethical behaviour; or

   (2)   conduct that may bring the sport into disrepute.

(c)   An allegation of a breach of rule 69.1(a) shall be resolved in accordance with the provisions of rule 69. It shall not be grounds for a *protest* and rule 63.1 does not apply.

69.2   Action by a Protest Committee

(a)   A protest committee acting under this rule shall have at least three members.

(b)   When a protest committee, from its own observation or from information received from any source, including evidence taken during a hearing, believes a person may have broken rule 69.1(a), it shall decide whether or not to call a hearing.

(c)   When the protest committee needs more information to make the decision to call a hearing, it shall consider appointing a person or persons to conduct an investigation. These investigators shall not be members of the protest committee that will decide the matter.

(d)   When an investigator is appointed, all relevant information he gathers, favourable or unfavourable, shall be disclosed to the protest committee, and if the protest committee decides to call a hearing, to the *parties*.

(e)   If the protest committee decides to call a hearing, it shall promptly inform the person in writing of the alleged breach and of the time and place of the hearing and follow the procedures in rules 63.2, 63.3(a), 63.4 and 63.6 except that:

   (1)   unless a person has been appointed by World Sailing, a person may be appointed by the protest committee to present the allegation.

   (2)   a person against whom an allegation has been made under this rule shall be entitled to have an advisor and a representative with him who may act on his behalf.

(f)   If the person is unable to attend the hearing and

   (1)   provides good reason, the protest committee shall reschedule it; or

   (2)   does not provide good reason and does not come to it, the protest committee may conduct it without the person present.

(g)   The standard of proof to be applied is the test of the comfortable satisfaction of the protest committee, bearing in mind the seriousness of the alleged misconduct. However, if the standard of proof in this rule conflicts with the laws of a country, the national authority may, with the approval of World Sailing, change it with a prescription to this rule.

(h)   When the protest committee decides that a competitor or boat owner has broken rule 69.1(a), it may take one or more of the following actions

   (1)   issue a warning;

   (2)   change their boat's score in one or more races, including disqualification(s) that may or may not be excluded from her series score;

   (3)   exclude the person from the event or venue or remove any privileges or benefits; and

   (4)   take any other action within its jurisdiction as provided by the *rules*.

(i)   When the protest committee decides that a *support person* has broken rule 69.1(a), rule 64.4 applies.

(j)   If the protest committee

   (1)   imposes a penalty greater than one DNE;

   (2)   excludes the person from the event or venue; or

   (3)   in any other case if it considers it appropriate, it shall report its findings, including the facts found, its conclusions and decision to the national authority of the person or, for specific international events listed in the World Sailing Regulations, to World Sailing. If the protest committee has acted under rule 69.2(f)(2), the report shall also include that fact and the reasons for it.

(k)   If the protest committee decides not to conduct the hearing without the person present, or if the protest committee has left the event and a report alleging a breach of rule 69.1(a) is received, the race committee or organizing authority may appoint the same or a new protest committee to proceed under this rule. If it is impractical for the protest committee to conduct a hearing, it shall collect all available information and, if the allegation seems justified, make a report to the national authority of the person or, for specific international events listed in the World Sailing Regulations, to World Sailing.

69.3   Action by a National Authority and World Sailing

The disciplinary powers, procedures and responsibilities of national authorities and World Sailing that apply are specified in World Sailing Regulation 35, Disciplinary Code. National authorities and World Sailing may impose further penalties, including suspension of eligibility, under that regulation.

SECTION D
APPEALS

70 APPEALS AND REQUESTS TO A NATIONAL AUTHORITY

70.1 (a) Provided that the right of appeal has not been denied under rule 70.5, a *party* to a hearing may appeal a protest committee's decision or its procedures, but not the facts found.

(b) A boat may appeal when she is denied a hearing required by rule 63.1.

70.2 A protest committee may request confirmation or correction of its decision.

70.3 An appeal under rule 70.1 or a request by a protest committee under rule 70.2 shall be sent to the national authority with which the organizing authority is associated under rule 89.1. However, if boats will pass through the waters of more than one national authority while *racing*, the sailing instructions shall identify the national authority to which appeals or requests are required to be sent.

70.4 A club or other organization affiliated to a national authority may request an interpretation of the *rules*, provided that no *protest* or request for redress that may be appealed is involved. The interpretation shall not be used for changing a previous protest committee decision.

70.5 There shall be no appeal from the decisions of an international jury constituted in compliance with Appendix N. Furthermore, if the notice of race and the sailing instructions so state, the right of appeal may be denied provided that

(a) it is essential to determine promptly the result of a race that will qualify a boat to compete in a later stage of an event or a subsequent event (a national authority may prescribe that its approval is required for such a procedure);

(b) a national authority so approves for a particular event open only to entrants under its own jurisdiction; or

(c) a national authority after consultation with World Sailing so approves for a particular event, provided the protest committee is constituted as required by Appendix N, except that only two members of the protest committee need be International Judges.

70.6 Appeals and requests shall conform to Appendix R.

71 NATIONAL AUTHORITY DECISIONS

71.1 A person who has a *conflict of interest* or was a member of the protest committee shall not take any part in the discussion or decision on an appeal or a request for confirmation or correction.

71.2 The national authority may uphold, change or reverse a protest committee's decision including a decision on validity or a decision under rule 69. Alternatively, the national authority may order that a hearing be reopened, or that a new hearing be held by the same or a different protest committee. When

the national authority decides that there shall be a new hearing, it may appoint the protest committee.

71.3 When from the facts found by the protest committee the national authority decides that a boat that was a *party* to a protest hearing broke a *rule* and is not exonerated, it shall penalize her, whether or not that boat or that *rule* was mentioned in the protest committee's decision.

71.4 The decision of the national authority shall be final. The national authority shall send its decision in writing to all *parties* to the hearing and the protest committee, who shall be bound by the decision.

PART 6
ENTRY AND QUALIFICATION

75 ENTERING A RACE

75.1 To enter a race, a boat shall comply with the requirements of the organizing authority of the race. She shall be entered by

(a) a member of a club or other organization affiliated to a World Sailing member national authority,

(b) such a club or organization, or

(c) a member of a World Sailing member national authority.

75.2 Competitors shall comply with World Sailing Regulation 19, Eligibility Code.

76 EXCLUSION OF BOATS OR COMPETITORS

76.1 The organizing authority or the race committee may reject or cancel the entry of a boat or exclude a competitor, subject to rule 76.3, provided it does so before the start of the first race and states the reason for doing so. On request the boat shall promptly be given the reason in writing. The boat may request redress if she considers that the rejection or exclusion is improper.

76.2 The organizing authority or the race committee shall not reject or cancel the entry of a boat or exclude a competitor because of advertising, provided the boat or competitor complies with World Sailing Regulation 20, Advertising Code.

76.3 At world and continental championships no entry within stated quotas shall be rejected or cancelled without first obtaining the approval of the relevant World Sailing Class Association (or the Offshore Racing Council) or World Sailing.

77 IDENTIFICATION ON SAILS

A boat shall comply with the requirements of Appendix G governing class insignia, national letters and numbers on sails.

78 COMPLIANCE WITH CLASS RULES; CERTIFICATES

78.1 While a boat is *racing*, her owner and any other person in charge shall ensure that the boat is maintained to comply with her class rules and that her measurement or rating certificate, if any, remains valid. In addition, the boat shall also comply at other times specified in the class rules, the notice of race or the sailing instructions.

78.2 When a *rule* requires a valid certificate to be produced or its existence verified before a boat *races*, and this cannot be done, the boat may *race* provided that the race committee receives a statement signed by the person in charge that a valid certificate exists. The boat shall produce the certificate or arrange for its existence to be verified by the race committee. The penalty for breaking this rule is disqualification without a hearing from all races of the event.

79   CLASSIFICATION

If the notice of race or class rules state that some or all competitors must satisfy classification requirements, the classification shall be carried out as described in World Sailing Regulation 22, Sailor Classification Code.

80   ADVERTISING

A boat and her crew shall comply with World Sailing Regulation 20, Advertising Code.

81   RESCHEDULED EVENT

When an event is rescheduled to dates different from the dates stated in the notice of race, all boats entered shall be notified. The race committee may accept new entries that meet all the entry requirements except the original deadline for entries.

PART 7

RACE ORGANIZATION

84   GOVERNING RULES

The organizing authority, race committee, technical committee, protest committee and other race officials shall be governed by the *rules* in the conduct and judging of races.

85   CHANGES TO RULES

85.1 A change to a *rule* shall refer specifically to the *rule* and state the change. A change to a *rule* includes an addition to it or deletion of all or part of it.

85.2 A change to one of the following types of *rules* may be made only as shown below.

Type of rule	Change only if permitted by
Racing rule	Rule 86
Rule in a World Sailing code	A rule in the code
National authority prescription	Rule 88.2
Class rule	Rule 87

Rule in the notice of race	Rule 89.2(b)
Rule in the sailing instructions	Rule 90.2(c)
Rule in any other document governing the event	A rule in the document itself

86   CHANGES TO THE RACING RULES

86.1 A racing rule shall not be changed unless permitted in the rule itself or as follows:

(a) Prescriptions of a national authority may change a racing rule, but not the Definitions; the Basic Principles; a rule in the Introduction; Part 1, 2 or 7; rule 42, 43, 63.4, 69, 70, 71, 75, 76.3, 79 or 80; a rule of an appendix that changes one of these rules; Appendix H or N; World Sailing Regulation 19, 20, 21, 22, 35 or 37.

(b) The notice of race or sailing instructions may change a racing rule, but not rule 76.1 or 76.2, Appendix R, or a rule listed in rule 86.1(a).

(c) Class rules may change only racing rules 42, 49, 50, 51, 52, 53 and 54.

86.2 In exception to rule 86.1, World Sailing may in limited circumstances (see World Sailing Regulation 28.1.3) authorize changes to the racing rules for a specific international event. The authorization shall be stated in a letter of approval to the event organizing authority and in the notice of race and sailing instructions, and the letter shall be posted on the event's official notice board.

86.3 If a national authority so prescribes, the restrictions in rule 86.1 do not apply if rules are changed to develop or test proposed rules. The national authority may prescribe that its approval is required for such changes.

87   CHANGES TO CLASS RULES

The notice of race or sailing instructions may change a class rule only when the class rules permit the change, or when written permission of the class association for the change is displayed on the official notice board.

88   NATIONAL PRESCRIPTIONS

88.1   Prescriptions that Apply

The prescriptions that apply to an event are the prescriptions of the national authority with which the organizing authority is associated under rule 89.1. However, if boats will pass through the waters of more than one national authority while *racing*, the notice of race or sailing instructions shall identify the prescriptions that will apply and when they will apply.

88.2   Changes to Prescriptions

The notice of race or sailing instructions may change a prescription. However, a national authority may restrict changes to its prescriptions with a prescription to this rule, provided World Sailing approves its application to do so. The restricted prescriptions shall not be changed.

89   ORGANIZING AUTHORITY; NOTICE OF RACE; APPOINTMENT OF RACE OFFICIALS

89.1 Organizing Authority

Races shall be organized by an organizing authority, which shall be

(a)   World Sailing;

(b)   a member national authority of World Sailing;

(c)   an affiliated club;

(d)   an affiliated organization other than a club and, if so prescribed by the national authority, with the approval of the national authority or in conjunction with an affiliated club;

(e)   an unaffiliated class association, either with the approval of the national authority or in conjunction with an affiliated club;

(f)   two or more of the above organizations;

(g)   an unaffiliated body in conjunction with an affiliated club where the body is owned and controlled by the club. The national authority of the club may prescribe that its approval is required for such an event; or

(h)   if approved by World Sailing and the national authority of the club, an unaffiliated body in conjunction with an affiliated club where the body is not owned and controlled by the club.

In rule 89.1, an organization is affiliated if it is affiliated to the national authority of the venue; otherwise the organization is unaffiliated. However, if boats will pass through the waters of more than one national authority while *racing*, an organization is affiliated if it is affiliated to the national authority of one of the ports of call.

89.2 Notice of Race; Appointment of Race Officials

(a)   The organizing authority shall publish a notice of race that conforms to rule J1.

(b)   The notice of race may be changed provided adequate notice is given.

(c)   The organizing authority shall appoint a race committee and, when appropriate, appoint a protest committee, a technical committee and umpires. However, the race committee, an international jury, a technical committee and umpires may be appointed by World Sailing as provided in its regulations.

90   RACE COMMITTEE; SAILING INSTRUCTIONS; SCORING

90.1 Race Committee

The race committee shall conduct races as directed by the organizing authority and as required by the *rules*.

90.2 Sailing Instructions

(a)   The race committee shall publish written sailing instructions that conform to rule J2.

(b)   When appropriate, for an event where entries from other countries are expected, the sailing instructions shall include, in English, the applicable national prescriptions.

(c)   The sailing instructions may be changed provided the change is in writing and posted on the official notice board before the time stated in the sailing instructions or, on the water, communicated to each boat before her warning signal. Oral changes may be given only on the water, and only if the procedure is stated in the sailing instructions.

90.3 Scoring

(a)   The race committee shall score a race or series as provided in Appendix A using the Low Point System, unless the notice of race or sailing instructions specify some other system. A race shall be scored if it is not *abandoned* and if one boat sails the course in compliance with rule 28 and *finishes* within the time limit, if any, even if she retires after *finishing* or is disqualified.

(b)   When a scoring system provides for excluding one or more race scores, any score that is a Disqualification Not Excludable (DNE) shall be included in a boat's series score.

(c)   When the race committee determines from its own records or observations that it has scored a boat incorrectly, it shall correct the error and make the corrected scores available to competitors.

91   PROTEST COMMITTEE

A protest committee shall be

(a)   a committee appointed by the organizing authority or race committee;

(b)   an international jury appointed by the organizing authority or as prescribed in the World Sailing Regulations. It shall be composed as required by rule N1 and have the authority and responsibilities stated in rule N2. A national authority may prescribe that its approval is required for the appointment of international juries for races within its jurisdiction, except World Sailing events or when international juries are appointed by World Sailing under rule 89.2(c); or

(c)   a committee appointed by the national authority under rule 71.2.

92   TECHNICAL COMMITTEE

92.1 A technical committee shall be a committee of at least one member and be appointed by the organizing authority or the race committee or as prescribed in the World Sailing Regulations.

92.2 The technical committee shall conduct equipment inspection and event measurement as directed by the organizing authority and as required by the *rules*.

APPENDIX A
SCORING

See rule 90.3.

A1 NUMBER OF RACES

The number of races scheduled and the number required to be completed to constitute a series shall be stated in the notice of race or sailing instructions.

A2 SERIES SCORES

A2.1 Each boat's series score shall, subject to rule 90.3(b), be the total of her race scores excluding her worst score. (The notice of race or sailing instructions may make a different arrangement by providing, for example, that no score will be excluded, that two or more scores will be excluded, or that a specified number of scores will be excluded if a specified number of races are completed. A race is completed if scored; see rule 90.3(a).) If a boat has two or more equal worst scores, the score(s) for the race(s) sailed earliest in the series shall be excluded. The boat with the lowest series score wins and others shall be ranked accordingly.

A2.2 If a boat has entered any race in a series, she shall be scored for the whole series.

A3 STARTING TIMES AND FINISHING PLACES

The time of a boat's starting signal shall be her starting time, and the order in which boats *finish* a race shall determine their finishing places. However, when a handicap or rating system is used a boat's corrected time shall determine her finishing place.

A4 LOW POINT SYSTEM

The Low Point System will apply unless the notice of race or sailing instructions specify another system; see rule 90.3(a).

A4.1 Each boat *starting* and *finishing* and not thereafter retiring, being penalized or given redress shall be scored points as follows:

Finishing place	Points
First	1
Second	2
Third	3
Fourth	4
Fifth	5
Sixth	6
Seventh	7
Each place thereafter	Add 1 point

A4.2 A boat that did not *start*, did not *finish*, retired or was disqualified shall be scored points for the finishing place one more than the number of boats entered in the series. A boat that is penalized under rule 30.2 or that takes a penalty under rule 44.3(a) shall be scored points as provided in rule 44.3(c).

A5 SCORES DETERMINED BY THE RACE COMMITTEE

A boat that did not *start* or *finish* or comply with rule 30.2, 30.3, 30.4 or 78.2, or that retires or takes a penalty under rule 44.3(a), shall be scored accordingly by the race committee without a hearing. Only the protest committee may take other scoring actions that worsen a boat's score.

A6 CHANGES IN PLACES AND SCORES OF OTHER BOATS

A6.1 If a boat is disqualified from a race or retires after *finishing*, each boat with a worse finishing place shall be moved up one place.

A6.2 If the protest committee decides to give redress by adjusting a boat's score, the scores of other boats shall not be changed unless the protest committee decides otherwise.

A7 RACE TIES

If boats are tied at the finishing line or if a handicap or rating system is used and boats have equal corrected times, the points for the place for which the boats have tied and for the place(s) immediately below shall be added together and divided equally. Boats tied for a race prize shall share it or be given equal prizes.

A8 SERIES TIES

A8.1 If there is a series-score tie between two or more boats, each boat's race scores shall be listed in order of best to worst, and at the first point(s) where there is a difference the tie shall be broken in favour of the boat(s) with the best score(s). No excluded scores shall be used.

A8.2 If a tie remains between two or more boats, they shall be ranked in order of their scores in the last race. Any remaining ties shall be broken by using the tied boats' scores in the next-to-last race and so on until all ties are broken. These scores shall be used even if some of them are excluded scores.

A9 RACE SCORES IN A SERIES LONGER THAN A REGATTA

For a series that is held over a period of time longer than a regatta, a boat that came to the starting area but did not *start*, did not *finish*, retired or was disqualified shall be scored points for the finishing place one more than the number of boats that came to the starting area. A boat that did not come to the starting area shall be scored points for the finishing place one more than the number of boats entered in the series.

A10 GUIDANCE ON REDRESS

If the protest committee decides to give redress by adjusting a boat's score for a race, it is advised to consider scoring her

(a)   points equal to the average, to the nearest tenth of a point (0.05 to be rounded upward), of her points in all the races in the series except the race in question;

(b)   points equal to the average, to the nearest tenth of a point (0.05 to be rounded upward), of her points in all the races before the race in question; or

(c)   points based on the position of the boat in the race at the time of the incident that justified redress.

A11   SCORING ABBREVIATIONS

These scoring abbreviations shall be used for recording the circumstances described:

DNC   Did not *start*; did not come to the starting area

DNS   Did not *start* (other than DNC and OCS)

OCS   Did not *start*; on the course side of the starting line at her starting signal and failed to *start*, or broke rule 30.1

ZFP   20% penalty under rule 30.2

UFD   Disqualification under rule 30.3

BFD   Disqualification under rule 30.4

SCP   Scoring Penalty applied

DNF   Did not *finish*

RET   Retired

DSQ   Disqualification

DNE   Disqualification that is not excludable

RDG   Redress given

DPI   Discretionary penalty imposed

APPENDIX B

WINDSURFING COMPETITION RULES

Windsurfing races shall be sailed under The Racing Rules of Sailing *as changed by this appendix. The term 'boat' elsewhere in the racing rules means 'board' or 'boat' as appropriate. The term 'heat' means one elimination race, a 'round' consists of several heats, and an 'elimination series' consists of one or more rounds. However, in speed competition, a 'round' consists of one or more speed 'runs'.*

A windsurfing event can include one or more of the following disciplines or their formats:

Discipline	Formats
Racing	Course racing; Slalom; Marathon
Expression	Wave performance; Freestyle
Speed	Standard Offshore Speed Course; Speed Crossings; Alpha Speed Course

In racing or expression competition, boards may compete in elimination series, and only a limited number of them may advance from round to round. A marathon race is a race scheduled to last more than one hour.

In expression competition a board's performance is judged on skill and variety rather than speed and is organized using elimination series. Either wave performance or freestyle competition is organized, depending on the wave conditions at the venue.

In speed competition a board's performance is based on her speed over a measured course. Boards take turns sailing runs over the course.

CHANGES TO THE DEFINITIONS

The definitions *Mark-Room*, and *Tack, Starboard or Port* are deleted and replaced by:

Mark-Room   *Mark-Room* for a board is *room* to sail her *proper course* to round or pass the *mark*. However, *mark-room* for a board does not include *room* to tack unless she is *overlapped* inside and to *windward* of the board required to give *mark-room* and she would be *fetching* the *mark* after her tack.

Proper Course   A course a board would sail to *finish* as soon as possible in the absence of other boards referred to in the rule using the term, except that during the last 30 seconds before her starting signal, the *proper course* for a board shall be the shortest course to the first *mark*. A board has no *proper course* until 30 seconds before her starting signal.

Tack, Starboard or Port   A board is on the *tack, starboard* or *port*, corresponding to the competitor's hand that would be nearer the mast if the competitor were in normal sailing position with both hands on the wishbone and arms not crossed. A board is on *starboard tack* when the competitor's right hand would be nearer the mast and is on *port tack* when the competitor's left hand would be nearer the mast.

The definition *Zone* is deleted.

Add the following definitions:

Capsized   A board is *capsized* when she is not under control because her sail or the competitor is in the water.

Rounding or Passing   A board is *rounding or passing* a mark from the time her *proper course* is to begin to manoeuvre to round or pass it, until the *mark* has been rounded or passed.

B1   CHANGES TO THE RULES OF PART 1

[No changes.]

B2   CHANGES TO THE RULES OF PART 2

B2.13   WHILE TACKING

Rule 13 is changed to:

After a board passes head to wind, she shall *keep clear* of other boards until her sail has filled. During that time rules 10, 11 and 12 do not apply. If two boards are subject to this rule at the same time, the one on the other's port side or the one astern shall *keep clear*.

B2.17   ON THE SAME TACK; PROPER COURSE

Rule 17 is changed to:

When, at the warning signal, the course to the first *mark* is approximately ninety degrees from the true wind, a board *overlapped* to *leeward* of another board on the same *tack* during the last 30 seconds before her starting signal shall not sail above her *proper course* while they remain *overlapped* if as a result the other board would need to take action to avoid contact, unless in doing so she promptly sails astern of the other board.

B2.18   MARK-ROOM

Rule 18 is changed as follows:

The first sentence of rule 18.1 is changed to:

Rule B2.18 applies between boards when they are required to leave a *mark* on the same side and at least one of them is *rounding or passing* it.

Rule 18.2(b) is changed to:

(b)   If boards are *overlapped* when the first of them is *rounding or passing* the *mark*, the outside board at that moment shall thereafter give the inside board *mark-room*. If a board is *clear ahead* when she is *rounding or passing* the *mark*, the board *clear astern* at that moment shall thereafter give her *mark-room*.

Rule 18.2(c) is changed to:

(c)   When a board is required to give *mark-room* by rule B2.18.2(b), she shall continue to do so even if later an *overlap* is broken or a new *overlap* begins. However, if the board entitled to *mark-room* passes head to wind, rule B2.18.2(b) ceases to apply.

B2.18.4 Gybing or Bearing Away

Rule 18.4 is changed to:

When an inside *overlapped* right-of-way board must gybe or bear away at a *mark* to sail her *proper course*, until she gybes or bears away she shall sail no farther from the *mark* than needed to sail that course. Rule B2.18.4 does not apply at a gate *mark*.

B2.23   CAPSIZED; AGROUND; RESCUING

Rule 23 is changed to:

B2.23.1 If possible, a board shall avoid a board that is *capsized* or has not regained control after *capsizing*, is aground, or is trying to help a person or vessel in danger.

B2.23.2 If possible, a board that is *capsized* or aground shall not interfere with another board.

B2.24   INTERFERING WITH ANOTHER BOARD; SAIL OUT OF WATER

Add new rule B2.24.3:

B2.24.3 In the last minute before her starting signal, a board shall have her sail out of the water and in a normal position, except when accidentally *capsized*.

PART 2 RULES DELETED

Rule 18.3 is deleted.

B3   CHANGES TO THE RULES OF PART 3

B3.26   STARTING RACES

Rule 26 is changed to:

B3.26.1 System 1

Races shall be started by using the following signals. Times shall be taken from the visual signals; the absence of a sound signal shall be disregarded.

Minutes before starting signal	Visual signal	Sound signal	Means
5*	Class flag	One	Warning signal
4	P, I, Z, Z with I, U, or black flag	One	Preparatory signal
1	Preparatory flag removed	One long	One minute
0	Class flag removed	One	Starting signal

*or as stated in the sailing instructions

The warning signal for each succeeding class shall be made with or after the starting signal of the preceding class.

B3.26.2 System 2

Races shall be started by using the following signals. Times shall be taken from the visual signals; the absence of a sound signal shall be disregarded.

Minutes before starting signal	Visual signal	Sound signal	Means
3	Class flag or heat number		Attention signal
2	Red flag; attention signal removed	One	Warning signal
1	Yellow flag; red flag removed	One	Preparatory signal
1/2	Yellow flag removed		30 seconds
0	Green flag	One	Starting signal

B3.26.3 System 3 (for Beach Starts)

(a)   When the starting line is on the beach, or so close to the beach that the competitor must stand in the water to *start*, the start is a beach start.

(b)   The starting stations shall be numbered so that station 1 is the most windward one. Unless the sailing instructions specify some other system, a board's starting station shall be determined

(1)   for the first race or round of the event, by draw, or

(2)   for any race or round after the first one, by her

place in the previous race or heat (The first place on station 1, the second place on station 2, and so on.).

(c) After boards have been called to take their positions, the race committee shall make the preparatory signal by displaying a red flag with one sound. The starting signal shall be made, at any time after the preparatory signal, by removing the red flag with one sound.

(d) After the starting signal each board shall take the shortest route from her starting station to the water and then to her sailing position without interfering with other boards. Part 2 rules will apply when both of the competitor's feet are on the board.

B3.31　TOUCHING A MARK

Rule 31 is changed to:

A board may touch a *mark* but shall not hold on to it.

B4　CHANGES TO THE RULES OF PART 4

B4.42　PROPULSION

Rule 42 is changed to:

A board shall be propelled only by the action of the wind on the sail, by the action of the water on the hull and by the unassisted actions of the competitor. However, significant progress shall not be made by paddling, swimming or walking.

B4.43　COMPETITOR CLOTHING AND EQUIPMENT

Rule 43.1(a) is changed to:

(a) Competitors shall not wear or carry clothing or equipment for the purpose of increasing their weight. However, a competitor may wear a drinking container that shall have a capacity of at least one litre and weigh no more than 1.5 kilograms when full.

B4.44　PENALTIES AT THE TIME OF AN INCIDENT

Rule 44 is changed to:

B4.44.1 Taking a Penalty

A board may take a 360°-Turn Penalty when she may have broken one of more rules of Part 2 in an incident while *racing*. The sailing instructions may specify the use of some other penalty. However, if the board caused injury or serious damage or, despite taking a penalty, gained a significant advantage in the race or series by her breach, her penalty shall be to retire.

B4.44.2 360°-Turn Penalty

After getting well clear of other boards as soon after the incident as possible, a board takes a 360°-Turn Penalty by promptly making a 360° turn with no requirement for a tack or a gybe. When a board takes the penalty at or near the finishing line, she shall sail completely to the course side of the line before *finishing*.

PART 4 RULES DELETED

Rules 43.2, 44.3, 45, 47.2, 48.1, 49, 50, 51, 52 and 54 are deleted.

B5　CHANGES TO THE RULES OF PART 5

B5.60　RIGHT TO PROTEST; RIGHT TO REQUEST REDRESS OR RULE 69 ACTION

Rule 60.1(a) is changed by deleting 'or saw'.

B5.61　PROTEST REQUIREMENTS

The first three sentences of rule 61.1(a) are changed to:

A board intending to protest shall inform the other board at the first reasonable opportunity. When her *protest* will concern an incident in the racing area that she was involved in or saw, she shall hail 'Protest'. She shall also inform the race committee of her intention to protest as soon as practicable after she *finishes* or retires.

B5.62　REDRESS

Rule 62.1(b) is changed to:

(b) injury, physical damage or *capsize* because of the action of

(1) a board that broke a rule of Part 2 and took the appropriate penalty or was penalized, or

(2) a vessel not *racing* that was required to keep clear.

B5.64　DECISIONS

Rule 64.3(b) is changed to:

(b) When the protest committee is in doubt about a matter concerning the measurement of a board, the meaning of a class rule, or damage to a board, it shall refer its questions, together with the relevant facts, to an authority responsible for interpreting the rule. In making its decision, the committee shall be bound by the reply of the authority.

B6　CHANGES TO THE RULES OF PART 6

B6.78　COMPLIANCE WITH CLASS RULES; CERTIFICATES

Add to rule 78.1: 'When so prescribed by World Sailing, a numbered and dated device on a board and her centreboard, fin and rig shall serve as her measurement certificate.'

B7　CHANGES TO THE RULES OF PART 7

B7.90　RACE COMMITTEE; SAILING INSTRUCTIONS; SCORING

The last sentence of rule 90.2(c) is changed to: 'Oral instructions may be given only if the procedure is stated in the sailing instructions.'

B8　CHANGES TO APPENDIX A

B8.A1　NUMBER OF RACES; OVERALL SCORES

Rule A1 is changed to:

The number of races scheduled and the number required to be completed to constitute a series shall be stated in the notice of race or sailing instructions. If an event includes more than one discipline or format, the notice of race or sailing instructions shall state how the overall scores are to be calculated.

B8.A2.1 SERIES SCORES

Rule A2.1 is changed to:

Each board's series score shall, subject to rule 90.3(b), be the total of her race scores excluding her

(a) worst score when from 5 to 11 races have been completed, or

(b) two worst scores when 12 or more races have been completed.

(The notice of race or sailing instructions may make a different arrangement. A race is completed if scored; see rule 90.3(a).) If a board has two or more equal worst scores, the score(s) for the race(s) sailed earliest in the series shall be excluded. The board with the lowest series score wins and others shall be ranked accordingly.

B8.A8 SERIES TIES

Rule A8 is changed to:

B8.A8.1 If there is a series-score tie between two or more boards, they shall be ranked in order of their best excluded race score.

B8.A8.2 If a tie remains between two or more boards, each board's race scores, including excluded scores, shall be listed in order of best to worst, and at the first point(s) where there is a difference the tie shall be broken in favour of the board(s) with the best score(s). These scores shall be used even if some of them are excluded scores.

B8.A8.3 If a tie still remains between two or more boards, they shall be ranked in order of their scores in the last race. Any remaining ties shall be broken by using the tied boards' scores in the next-to-last race and so on until all ties are broken. These scores shall be used even if some of them are excluded scores.

B9   CHANGES TO APPENDIX G

B9.G1 WORLD SAILING CLASS BOARDS

B9.G1.3 Positioning

Rule G1.3(a) is changed to:

(a) The class insignia shall be displayed once on each side of the sail in the area above a line projected at right angles from a point on the luff of the sail one-third of the distance from the head to the wishbone. The national letters and sail numbers shall be in the central third of that part of the sail above the wishbone, clearly separated from any advertising. They shall be black and applied back to back on an opaque white background. The background shall extend a minimum of 30 mm beyond the characters. There shall be a '–' between the national letters and the sail number, and the spacing between characters shall be adequate for legibility.

APPENDIX G RULES DELETED

The first sentence of rule G1.3(b) is deleted. Rules G1.3(c), G1.3(d) and G1.3(e) are deleted.

B10   CHANGES TO RULES FOR EVENTS THAT INCLUDE ELIMINATION SERIES

B10.29 RECALLS

For a race of an elimination series that will qualify a board to compete in a later stage of an event, rule 29 is changed to:

(a) When at a board's starting signal any part of her hull, crew or equipment is on the course side of the starting line, the race committee shall signal a general recall.

(b) If the race committee acts under rule B10.29(a) and the board is identified, she shall be disqualified without a hearing, even if the race is *abandoned*. The race committee shall hail or display her sail number, and she shall leave the course area immediately. If the race is restarted or resailed, she shall not sail in it.

(c) If the race was completed but was later *abandoned* by the protest committee, and if the race is resailed, a board disqualified under rule B10.29(b) may sail in it.

B10.37 ELIMINATION SERIES INCLUDING HEATS

Add new rule B10.37:

Rule B10.37 applies in elimination series in which boards compete in heats.

B10.37.1 Elimination Series Procedure

(a) Competition shall take the form of one or more elimination series. Each of them shall consist of either rounds in a single elimination series where only a number of the best scorers advance, or rounds in a double elimination series where boards have more than one opportunity to advance.

(b) Boards shall sail one against another in pairs, or in groups determined by the elimination ladder. The selected form of competition shall not be changed while a round remains uncompleted.

B10.37.2 Seeding and Ranking Lists

(a) When a seeding or ranking list is used to establish the heats of the first round, places 1–8 (four heats) or 1–16 (eight heats) shall be distributed evenly among the heats.

(b) For a subsequent elimination series, if any, boards shall be reassigned to new heats according to the ranking in the previous elimination series.

(c) The organizing authority's seeding decisions are final and are not grounds for a request for redress.

B10.37.3 Heat Schedule

The schedule of heats shall be posted on the official notice board no later than 30 minutes before the starting signal for the first heat.

B10.37.4 Advancement and Byes

(a) In racing and expression competition, the boards

in each heat to advance to the next round shall be announced by the race committee no later than 10 minutes before the starting signal for the first heat. The number advancing may be changed by the protest committee as a result of a redress decision.

(b) In expression competition, any first-round byes shall be assigned to the highest-seeded boards.

(c) In wave performance competition, only the winner of each heat shall advance to the next round.

(d) In freestyle competition, boards shall advance to the next round as follows: from an eight-board heat, the best four advance, and the winner will sail against the fourth and the second against the third; from a four-board heat, the best two advance and will sail against each other.

B10.37.5   Finals

(a) The final shall consist of a maximum of three races. The race committee shall announce the number of races to be sailed in the final no later than 5 minutes before the warning signal for the first final race.

(b) A runners-up final may be sailed after the final. All boards in the semi-final heats that failed to qualify for the final may compete in it.

B10.63 HEARINGS

For a race of an elimination series that will qualify a board to compete in a later stage of an event, rules 61.2 and 65.2 are deleted and rule 63.6 is changed to:

B10.63.6   Taking Evidence and Finding Facts

Protests and requests for redress need not be in writing; they shall be made orally to a member of the protest committee as soon as reasonably possible following the race. The protest committee may take evidence in any way it considers appropriate and may communicate its decision orally.

B10.70 APPEALS AND REQUESTS TO A NATIONAL AUTHORITY

Add new rule B10.70.7:

B10.70.7   Appeals are not permitted in disciplines and formats with elimination series.

B10.A2.1   SERIES SCORES

Rule A2.1 is changed to:

Each board's elimination series score shall, subject to rule 90.3(b), be the total of her race scores excluding her

(a) worst score when 3 or 4 races are completed,

(b) two worst scores when from 5 to 7 races are completed,

(c) three worst scores when 8 or more races are completed.

Each board's final series score shall be the total of her race scores excluding her worst score when 3 races are completed. (The notice of race or sailing instructions may make a different arrangement. A race is completed if

scored; see rule 90.3(a).) If a board has two or more equal worst scores, the score(s) for the race(s) sailed earliest in the series shall be excluded. The board with the lowest series score wins and others shall be ranked accordingly.

B10.A4 LOW POINT SYSTEM

Add at the end of the first sentence of rule A4.2: 'or, in a race of an elimination series, the number of boards in that heat'.

Add new rule B10.A4.3:

B10.A4.3   When a heat cannot be completed, the points for the unscored places shall be added together and divided by the number of places in that heat. The resulting number of points, to the nearest tenth of a point (0.05 to be rounded upward), shall be given to each board entered in the heat.

B11   CHANGES TO RULES FOR EXPRESSION COMPETITION

Add the following definitions:

Coming In* and *Going Out   A board sailing in the same direction as the incoming surf is *coming in*. A board sailing in the direction opposite to the incoming surf is *going out*.

Jumping   A board is *jumping* when she takes off at the top of a wave while *going out*.

Overtaking   A board is *overtaking* from the moment she gains an *overlap* from *clear astern* until the moment she is *clear ahead* of the *overtaken* board.

Possession   The first board sailing shoreward immediately in front of a wave has *possession* of that wave. However, when it is impossible to determine which board is first the *windward* board has *possession*.

Recovering   A board is *recovering* from the time her sail or, when water-starting, the competitor is out of the water until she has steerage way.

Surfing   A board is *surfing* when she is on or immediately in front of a wave while *coming in*.

Transition   A board changing *tacks*, or taking off while *coming in*, or one that is not *surfing*, *jumping*, *capsized* or *recovering* is in *transition*.

B11.PART 2 – WHEN BOARDS MEET

The rules of Part 2 are deleted and replaced by:

(a) COMING IN AND GOING OUT

A board *coming in* shall *keep clear* of a board *going out*. When two boards are *going out* or *coming in* while on the same wave, or when neither is *going out* or *coming in*, a board on *port tack* shall *keep clear* of the one on *starboard tack*.

(b) BOARDS ON THE SAME WAVE, COMING IN

When two or more boards are on a wave *coming in*, a board that does not have *possession* shall *keep clear*.

(c) CLEAR ASTERN, CLEAR AHEAD AND OVERTAKING

A board *clear astern* and not on a wave shall *keep clear*

of a board *clear ahead*. An *overtaking* board that is not on a wave shall *keep clear*.

(d) TRANSITION

A board in *transition* shall *keep clear* of one that is not. When two boards are in *transition* at the same time, the one on the other's port side or the one astern shall *keep clear*.

(e) JUMPING

A board that is *jumping* shall *keep clear* of one that is not.

B11.26 STARTING AND ENDING HEATS

Rule 26 is changed to:

Heats shall be started and ended by using the following signals:

(a) STARTING A HEAT

Each flag shall be removed when the next flag is displayed.

Minutes before starting signal	Visual signal	Sound signal	Means
Beginning of transition period	Heat number with red flag	One	Warning
1	Yellow flag	One	Preparatory
0	Green flag	One	Starting signal

(b) ENDING A HEAT

Minutes before ending signal	Visual signal	Sound signal	Means
1	Green flag removed	One	End warning
0	Red flag	One	Ending signal

B11.38 REGISTRATION; COURSE AREA; HEAT DURATION; ADVANCEMENT AND BYES

Add new rule B11.38:

(a) Boards shall register with the race committee the colours and other particulars of their sails, or their identification according to another method stated in the sailing instructions, no later than the starting signal for the heat two heats before their own.

(b) The course area shall be defined in the sailing instructions and posted on the official notice board no later than 10 minutes before the starting signal for the first heat. A board shall be scored only while sailing in the course area.

(c) Any change in heat duration shall be announced by the race committee no later than 15 minutes before the starting signal for the first heat in the next round.

(d) Rule B10.37.4 applies.

B11.41 OUTSIDE HELP

Change the number of rule 41 to B11.41.1 and add new rule B11.41.2:

B11.41.2 An assistant may provide replacement equipment to a board. The assistant shall not interfere with other competing boards. A board whose assistant interferes with another board may be penalized at the discretion of the protest committee.

APPENDIX A – SCORING

The rules of Appendix A are deleted and replaced by:

B11.A1 EXPRESSION COMPETITON SCORING

(a) Expression competition shall be scored by a panel of three judges. However, the panel may have a greater odd number of members, and there may be two such panels. Each judge shall give points for each manoeuvre based on the scale stated in the notice of race or sailing instructions.

(b) The criteria of scoring shall be decided by the race committee and announced on the official notice board no later than 30 minutes before the starting signal for the first heat.

(c) A board's heat standing shall be determined by adding together the points given by each judge. The board with the highest score wins and others shall be ranked accordingly.

(d) Both semi-final heats shall have been sailed for an elimination series to be valid.

(e) Except for members of the race committee responsible for scoring the event, only competitors in the heat shall be allowed to see judges' score sheets for the heat. Each score sheet shall bear the full name of the judge.

(f) Scoring decisions of the judges shall not be grounds for a request for redress by a board.

B11.A2 SERIES TIES

(a) In a heat, if there is a tie in the total points given by one or more judges, it shall be broken in favour of the board with the higher single score in the priority category. If the categories are weighted equally, in wave performance competition the tie shall be broken in favour of the board with the higher single score in wave riding, and in freestyle competition in favour of the board with the higher score for overall impression. If a tie remains, in wave performance competition it shall be broken in favour of the board with the higher single score in the category without priority, and in freestyle competition it shall stand as the final result.

(b) If there is a tie in the series score, it shall be broken in favour of the board that scored better more times than the other board. All scores shall be used even if some of them are excluded scores.

(c) If a tie still remains, the heat shall be resailed. If this is not possible, the tie shall stand as the final result.

B12   CHANGES TO RULES FOR SPEED COMPETITION

The rules of Part 2 are deleted and replaced by:

B12.PART 2 – GENERAL RULES

(a)   WATER STARTING

A board shall not water start on the course or in the starting area, except to sail off the course to avoid boards that are making, or about to make, a run.

(b)   LEAVING THE COURSE AREA

A board leaving the course area shall *keep clear* of boards making a run.

(c)   COURSE CONTROL

When the race committee points an orange flag at a board, she is penalized and the run shall not be counted.

(d)   RETURNING TO THE STARTING AREA

A board returning to the starting area shall keep clear of the course.

(e)   MAXIMUM NUMBER OF RUNS FOR EACH BOARD

The maximum number of runs that may be made by each board in a round shall be announced by the race committee no later than 15 minutes before the starting signal for the first round.

(f)   DURATION OF A ROUND

The duration of a round shall be announced by the race committee no later than 15 minutes before the starting signal for the next round.

(g)   CONDITIONS FOR ESTABLISHING A RECORD

The minimum distance for a world record is 500 metres. Other records may be established over shorter distances. The course shall be defined by posts and transits ashore or by buoys afloat. Transits shall not converge.

(h)   VERIFICATION RULES

(1)   An observer appointed by the World Sailing Speed Record Council shall be present and verify run times and speeds at world record attempts. The race committee shall verify run times and speeds at other record attempts.

(2)   A competitor shall not enter the timing control area or discuss any timing matter directly with the timing organization. Any timing question shall be directed to the race committee.

B12.26   STARTING AND ENDING A ROUND

Rule 26 is changed to:

Rounds shall be started and ended by using the following signals. Each flag shall be removed when the next flag is displayed.

(a)   STARTING A ROUND

Signal	Flag	Means
Stand-by	AP flag	Course closed. Races are *postponed*
Course closed	Red flag	Course closed; will open shortly
Preparatory	Red and yellow flag	Course will open in 5 minutes
Starting	Green flag	Course is open

(b)   ENDING A ROUND

Signal	Flag	Means
End warning	Green and yellow flag	Course will be closed in 5 minutes
Extension	Yellow flag	Current round extended by 15 minutes
Round ended	Red flag	A new round will be started shortly

B12.64   DECISIONS

Rule 64.1 is deleted and replaced by:

B12.64.1   Penalties

(a)   If a board fails to comply with a rule, she may be warned. If a board is warned a second time during the same round, she shall be excluded by the race committee from the remainder of the round. A list of the sail numbers of boards that have received warnings or have been excluded shall be posted on a notice board near the finishing line.

(b)   A board observed in the course area after having been excluded from a round shall be excluded from the competition without a hearing, and none of her previous times or results shall be valid.

(c)   Any breach of the verification rules may result in exclusion from one or more rounds or from the competition.

APPENDIX A – SCORING

The rules of Appendix A are deleted and replaced by:

B12.A1   SPEED COMPETITON SCORING

(a)   On Standard Offshore Speed Courses, the speeds of a board's fastest two runs in a round shall be averaged to determine her standing in that round. The board with the highest average wins and others shall be ranked accordingly. If boards are tied, the tie shall be broken in favour of the board with the fastest run in the round.

(b)   On Speed Crossings and Alpha Speed Courses, boards shall be ranked based on their fastest run in the round.

(c) If there is a series-score tie between two or more boards, it shall be broken in favour of the board(s) with the fastest run during the competition. If a tie remains, it shall be broken by applying rules B8.A8.2 and B8.A8.3.

APPENDIX C
MATCH RACING RULES

Match races shall be sailed under The Racing Rules of Sailing *as changed by this appendix. Matches shall be umpired unless the notice of race and sailing instructions state otherwise.*

Note: A Standard Notice of Race, Standard Sailing Instructions, and Match Racing Rules for Blind Competitors are available at the World Sailing website.

C1   TERMINOLOGY

'Competitor' means the skipper, team or boat as appropriate for the event. 'Flight' means two or more matches started in the same starting sequence.

C2   CHANGES TO THE DEFINITIONS AND THE RULES OF PARTS 1, 2, 3 AND 4

C2.1 The definition *Finish* is changed to:

Finish   A boat *finishes* when any part of her hull crosses the finishing line in the direction of the course from the last *mark* after completing any penalties. However, when penalties are cancelled under rule C7.2(d) after one or both boats have *finished* each shall be recorded as *finished* when she crossed the line.

C2.2 The definition *Mark-Room* is changed to:

Mark-Room   Room for a boat to sail her *proper course* to round or pass the *mark* on the required side.

C2.3 Add to the definition *Proper Course*: 'A boat taking a penalty or manoeuvring to take a penalty is not sailing a *proper course*.'

C2.4 In the definition *Zone* the distance is changed to two hull lengths.

C2.5 Add new rule 8 to Part 1:

8   LAST POINT OF CERTAINTY

The umpires will assume that the state of a boat, or her relationship to another boat, has not changed, until they are certain that it has changed.

C2.6 Rule 13 is changed to:

13   WHILE TACKING OR GYBING

13.1 After a boat passes head to wind, she shall *keep clear* of other boats until she is on a close-hauled course.

13.2 After the foot of the mainsail of a boat sailing downwind crosses the centreline she shall *keep clear* of other boats until her mainsail has filled or she is no longer sailing downwind.

13.3 While rule 13.1 or 13.2 applies, rules 10, 11 and 12 do not. However, if two boats are subject to rule 13.1 or 13.2 at the same time, the one on the other's port side or the one astern shall *keep clear*.

C2.7 Rule 16.2 is deleted.

C2.8 Rule 17 is deleted.

C2.9 Rule 18 is changed to:

18   MARK-ROOM

18.1   When Rule 18 Applies

Rule 18 applies between boats when they are required to leave a *mark* on the same side and at least one of them is in the *zone*. However, it does not apply between a boat approaching a *mark* and one leaving it.

18.2   Giving Mark-Room

(a)   When the first boat reaches the *zone*,

(1)   if boats are *overlapped*, the outside boat at that moment shall thereafter give the inside boat *mark-room*.

(2)   if boats are not *overlapped*, the boat that has not reached the *zone* shall thereafter give *mark-room*.

(b)   If the boat entitled to *mark-room* leaves the *zone*, the entitlement to *mark-room* ceases and rule 18.2(a) is applied again if required based on the relationship of the boats at the time rule 18.2(a) is re-applied.

(c)   If a boat obtained an inside *overlap* and, from the time the *overlap* began, the outside boat is unable to give *mark-room*, she is not required to give it.

18.3   Tacking or Gybing

(a)   If *mark-room* for a boat includes a change of *tack*, such tack or gybe shall be done no faster than a tack or gybe to sail her *proper course*.

(b)   When an inside *overlapped* right-of-way boat must change *tack* at a *mark* to sail her *proper course*, until she changes *tack* she shall sail no farther from the *mark* than needed to sail that course. Rule 18.3(b) does not apply at a gate *mark* or a finishing *mark* and a boat shall not be penalized for breaking this rule unless the course of another boat was affected by the breach of this rule.

C2.10 When rule 20 applies, the following arm signals by the helmsman are required in addition to the hails:

(a)   for 'Room to tack', repeatedly and clearly pointing to windward; and

(b)   for 'You tack', repeatedly and clearly pointing at the other boat and waving the arm to windward.

C2.11 Rule 22.3 is deleted.

C2.12 Rule 24.1 is changed to: 'If reasonably possible, a boat not *racing* shall not interfere with a boat that is *racing* or an umpire boat.'

C2.13 Add new rule 24.3: 'When boats in different matches meet, any change of course by either boat shall be consistent with complying with a *rule* or trying to win her own match.'

C2.14 Rule 31 is changed to:

31   TOUCHING A MARK

While *racing*, neither the crew nor any part of a boat's hull shall touch a starting *mark* before *starting*, a *mark* that begins, bounds or ends the leg of the course on which she is sailing, or a finishing *mark* after *finishing*. In addition, while *racing*, a boat shall not touch a race committee vessel that is also a *mark*.

C2.15   Rule 42 shall also apply between the warning and preparatory signals.

C2.16   Rule 42.2(d) is changed to: 'sculling: repeated movement of the helm to propel the boat forward;'.

C3   RACE SIGNALS AND CHANGES TO RELATED RULES

C3.1 Starting Signals

The signals for starting a match shall be as follows. Times shall be taken from the visual signals; the failure of a sound signal shall be disregarded. If more than one match will be sailed, the starting signal for one match shall be the warning signal for the next match.

Time in minutes	Visual signal	Sound signal	Means
10	Flag F displayed	One	Attention signal
6	Flag F removed	None	
5	Numeral pennant displayed*	One	Warning signal
4	Flag P displayed	One	Preparatory signal
2	Blue or yellow flag or both displayed**	One**	End of pre-start entry time
1	Flag P removed	One long	
0	Warning signal removed	One	Starting signa

*Within a flight, numeral pennant 1 means Match 1, pennant 2 means Match 2, etc., unless the sailing instructions state otherwise.

**These signals shall be made only if one or both boats fail to comply with rule C4.2. The flag(s) shall be displayed until the umpires have signalled a penalty or for one minute, whichever is earlier.

C3.2 Changes to Related Rules

(a)   Rule 29.1 is changed to:

(1)   When at a boat's starting signal any part of her hull, crew or equipment is on the course side of the starting line or one of its extensions, the race committee shall promptly display a blue or yellow flag identifying the boat with one sound. The flag shall be displayed until the boat is completely on the pre-start side of the starting line or one of its extensions or until two minutes after her starting signal, whichever is earlier.

(2)   When after her starting signal a boat sails from the pre-start side to the course side of the starting line across an extension without having *started* correctly, the race committee shall promptly display a blue or yellow flag identifying the boat. The flag shall be displayed until the boat is completely on the pre-start side of the starting line or one of its extensions or until two minutes after her starting signal, whichever is earlier.

(b)   In the race signal AP the last sentence is changed to: 'The attention signal will be made 1 minute after removal unless at that time the race is *postponed* again or *abandoned*.'

(c)   In the race signal N the last sentence is changed to: 'The attention signal will be made 1 minute after removal unless at that time the race is *abandoned* again or *postponed*.'

C3.3 Finishing Line Signals

The race signal Blue flag or shape shall not be used.

C4   REQUIREMENTS BEFORE THE START

C4.1   At her preparatory signal, each boat shall be outside the line that is at a 90° angle to the starting line through the starting *mark* at her assigned end. In the pairing list, the boat listed on the left-hand side is assigned the port end and shall display a blue flag at her stern while *racing*. The other boat is assigned the starboard end and shall display a yellow flag at her stern while *racing*.

C4.2 Within the two-minute period following her preparatory signal, a boat shall cross and clear the starting line, the first time from the course side to the pre-start side.

C5   SIGNALS BY UMPIRES

C5.1   A green and white flag with one long sound means 'No penalty'.

C5.2   A blue or yellow flag identifying a boat with one long sound means 'The identified boat shall take a penalty by complying with rule C7.'

C5.3   A red flag with or soon after a blue or yellow flag with one long sound means 'The identified boat shall take a penalty by complying with rule C7.3(d).'

C5.4   A black flag with a blue or yellow flag and one long sound means 'The identified boat is disqualified, and the match is terminated and awarded to the other boat.'

C5.5   One short sound means 'A penalty is now completed.'

C5.6   Repetitive short sounds mean 'A boat is no longer taking a penalty and the penalty remains.'

C5.7   A blue or yellow flag or shape displayed from an umpire boat means 'The identified boat has an outstanding penalty.'

C6   PROTESTS AND REQUESTS FOR REDRESS BY BOATS

C6.1 A boat may protest another boat

(a)   under a rule of Part 2, except rule 14, by clearly displaying flag Y immediately after an incident in which she was involved;

(b)   under any rule not listed in rule C6.1(a) or C6.2 by clearly displaying a red flag as soon as possible after the incident.

C6.2 A boat may not protest another boat under

(a)   rule 14, unless damage or injury results;

(b)   a rule of Part 2, unless she was involved in the incident;

(c)   rule 31 or 42; or

(d)   rule C4 or C7.

C6.3 A boat intending to request redress because of circumstances that arise before she *finishes* or retires shall clearly display a red flag as soon as possible after she becomes aware of those circumstances, but no later than two minutes after *finishing* or retiring.

C6.4 (a)   A boat protesting under rule C6.1(a) shall remove flag Y before or as soon as possible after the umpires' signal.

(b)   A boat protesting under rule C6.1(b) or requesting redress under rule C6.3 shall, for her *protest* or request to be valid, keep her red flag displayed until she has so informed the umpires after *finishing* or retiring. No written *protest* or request for redress is required.

C6.5 Umpire Decisions

(a)   After flag Y is displayed, the umpires shall decide whether to penalize any boat. They shall signal their decision in compliance with rule C5.1, C5.2 or C5.3. However, when the umpires penalize a boat under rule C8.2 and in the same incident there is a flag Y from a boat, the umpires may disregard the flag Y.

(b)   The red-flag penalty in rule C5.3 shall be used when a boat has gained a controlling position as a result of breaking a *rule*, but the umpires are not certain that the conditions for an additional umpire-initiated penalty have been fulfilled.

C6.6 Protest Committee Decisions

(a)   The protest committee may take evidence in any way it considers appropriate and may communicate its decision orally.

(b)   If the protest committee decides that a breach of a *rule* has had no significant effect on the outcome of the match, it may

(1)   impose a penalty of one point or part of one point;

(2)   order a resail; or

(3)   make another arrangement it decides is equitable, which may be to impose no penalty.

(c)   The penalty for breaking rule 14 when damage or injury results will be at the discretion of the protest committee, and may include exclusion from further races in the event.

C6.7 Add new rule N1.10 to Appendix N:

N1.10   In rule N.1, one International Umpire may be appointed to the jury, or a panel of it, in place of one International Judge.

C7   PENALTY SYSTEM

C7.1 Deleted Rule

Rule 44 is deleted.

C7.2 All Penalties

(a)   A penalized boat may delay taking a penalty within the limitations of rule C7.3 and shall take it as follows:

(1)   When on a leg of the course to a windward *mark*, she shall gybe and, as soon as reasonably possible, luff to a close-hauled course.

(2)   When on a leg of the course to a leeward *mark* or the finishing line, she shall tack and, as soon as reasonably possible, bear away to a course that is more than ninety degrees from the true wind.

(b)   Add to rule 2: 'When *racing*, a boat need not take a penalty unless signalled to do so by an umpire.'

(c)   A boat completes a leg of the course when her bow crosses the extension of the line from the previous *mark* through the *mark* she is rounding, or on the last leg when she *finishes*.

(d)   A penalized boat shall not be recorded as having *finished* until she takes her penalty and sails completely to the course side of the line and then *finishes*, unless the penalty is cancelled before or after she crosses the finishing line.

(e)   If a boat has one or two outstanding penalties and the other boat in her match is penalized, one penalty for each boat shall be cancelled except that a red-flag penalty shall not cancel or be cancelled by another penalty.

(f)   If a boat has more than two outstanding penalties, the umpires shall signal her disqualification under rule C5.4.

C7.3 Penalty Limitations

(a)   A boat taking a penalty that includes a tack shall have the spinnaker head below the main-boom gooseneck from the time she passes head to wind until she is on a close-hauled course.

(b)   No part of a penalty may be taken inside the *zone* of a rounding *mark* that begins, bounds or ends the leg the boat is on.

(c)   If a boat has one outstanding penalty, she may take the penalty any time after *starting* and before *finishing*. If a boat has two outstanding penalties, she shall take one of them as soon as reasonably possible, but not before *starting*.

(d)   When the umpires display a red flag with or soon after a penalty flag, the penalized boat shall take a penalty as soon as reasonably possible, but not before *starting*.

C7.4 Taking and Completing Penalties

(a) When a boat with an outstanding penalty is on a leg to a windward *mark* and gybes, or is on a leg to a leeward *mark* or the finishing line and passes head to wind, she is taking a penalty.

(b) When a boat taking a penalty either does not take the penalty correctly or does not complete the penalty as soon as reasonably possible, she is no longer taking a penalty. The umpires shall signal this as required by rule C5.6.

(c) The umpire boat for each match shall display blue or yellow flags or shapes, each flag or shape indicating one outstanding penalty. When a boat has taken a penalty, or a penalty has been cancelled, one flag or shape shall be removed, with the appropriate sound signal. Failure of the umpires to signal correctly shall not change the number of penalties outstanding.

C8   PENALTIES INITIATED BY UMPIRES

C8.1 Rule Changes

(a) Rules 60.2(a) and 60.3(a) do not apply to *rules* for which penalties may be imposed by umpires.

(b) Rule 64.1(a) is changed so that the provision for exonerating a boat may be applied by the umpires without a hearing, and it takes precedence over any conflicting rule of this appendix.

C8.2 When the umpires decide that a boat has broken rule 31, 42, C4, C7.3(c) or C7.3(d) she shall be penalized by signalling her under rule C5.2 or C5.3. However, if a boat is penalized for breaking a rule of Part 2 and if she in the same incident breaks rule 31, she shall not be penalized for breaking rule 31. Furthermore, a boat that displays an incorrect flag or does not display the correct flag shall be warned orally and given an opportunity to correct the error before being penalized.

C8.3 When the umpires decide that a boat has

(a) gained an advantage by breaking a *rule* after allowing for a penalty,

(b) deliberately broken a *rule*, or

(c) committed a breach of sportsmanship,

she shall be penalized under rule C5.2, C5.3 or C5.4.

C8.4 If the umpires or protest committee members decide that a boat may have broken a *rule* other than those listed in rules C6.1(a) and C6.2, they shall so inform the protest committee for its action under rule 60.3 and rule C6.6 when appropriate.

C8.5 When, after one boat has *started*, the umpires are satisfied that the other boat will not *start*, they may signal under rule C5.4 that the boat that did not *start* is disqualified and the match is terminated.

C8.6 When the match umpires, together with at least one other umpire, decide that a boat has broken rule 14 and damage resulted, they may impose a points-penalty without a hearing. The competitor shall be informed of the penalty as soon as practicable and, at the time of being so informed, may request

a hearing. The protest committee shall then proceed under rule C6.6. Any penalty decided by the protest committee may be more than the penalty imposed by the umpires. When the umpires decide that a penalty greater than one point is appropriate, they shall act under rule C8.4.

C9   REQUESTS FOR REDRESS OR REOPENING; APPEALS; OTHER PROCEEDINGS

C9.1 There shall be no request for redress or an appeal from a decision made under rule C5, C6, C7 or C8. In rule 66 the third sentence is changed to: 'A *party* to the hearing may not ask for a reopening.'

C9.2 A competitor may not base a request for redress on a claim that an action by an official boat was improper. The protest committee may decide to consider giving redress in such circumstances but only if it believes that an official boat, including an umpire boat, may have seriously interfered with a competing boat.

C9.3 No proceedings of any kind may be taken in relation to any action or non-action by the umpires, except as permitted in rule C9.2.

C10 SCORING

C10.1 The winning competitor of each match scores one point (half a point each for a dead heat); the loser scores no points.

C10.2 When a competitor withdraws from part of an event the scores of all completed races shall stand.

C10.3 When a single round robin is terminated before completion, or a multiple round robin is terminated during the first round robin, a competitor's score shall be the average points scored per match sailed by the competitor. However, if any of the competitors have completed less than one third of the scheduled matches, the entire round robin shall be disregarded and, if necessary, the event declared void. For the purposes of tie-breaking in rule C11.1(a), a competitor's score shall be the average points scored per match between the tied competitors.

C10.4 When a multiple round robin is terminated with an incomplete round robin, only one point shall be available for all the matches sailed between any two competitors, as follows:

Number of matches completed between any two competitors	Points for each win
1	One point
2	Half a point
3	A third of a point
(etc.)	

C10.5 In a round-robin series,

(a) competitors shall be placed in order of their total scores, highest score first;

(b) a competitor who has won a match but is disqualified

for breaking a *rule* against a competitor in another match shall lose the point for that match (but the losing competitor shall not be awarded the point); and

(c) the overall position between competitors who have sailed in different groups shall be decided by the highest score.

C10.6 In a knockout series the sailing instructions shall state the minimum number of points required to win a series between two competitors. When a knockout series is terminated it shall be decided in favour of the competitor with the higher score.

C11 TIES

C11.1 Round-Robin Series

In a round-robin series competitors are assigned to one or more groups and scheduled to sail against all other competitors in their group one or more times. Each separate stage identified in the event format shall be a separate round-robin series irrespective of the number of times each competitor sails against each other competitor in that stage.

Ties between two or more competitors in a round-robin series shall be broken by the following methods, in order, until all ties are broken. When one or more ties are only partially broken, rules C11.1(a) to C11.1(e) shall be reapplied to them. Ties shall be decided in favour of the competitor(s) who

(a) placed in order, has the highest score in the matches between the tied competitors;

(b) when the tie is between two competitors in a multiple round robin, has won the last match between the two competitors;

(c) has the most points against the competitor placed highest in the round-robin series or, if necessary, second highest, and so on until the tie is broken. When two separate ties have to be resolved but the resolution of each depends upon resolving the other, the following principles shall be used in the rule C11.1(c) procedure:

   (1) the higher-place tie shall be resolved before the lower-place tie, and

   (2) all the competitors in the lower-place tie shall be treated as a single competitor for the purposes of rule C11.1(c);

(d) after applying rule C10.5(c), has the highest place in the different groups, irrespective of the number of competitors in each group;

(e) has the highest place in the most recent stage of the event (fleet race, round robin, etc.).

C11.2 Knockout Series

Ties (including 0–0) between competitors in a knockout series shall be broken by the following methods, in order, until the tie is broken. The tie shall be decided in favour of the competitor who

(a) has the highest place in the most recent round-robin series, applying rule C11.1 if necessary;

(b) has won the most recent match in the event between the tied competitors.

C11.3 Remaining Ties

When rule C11.1 or C11.2 does not resolve a tie,

(a) if the tie needs to be resolved for a later stage of the event (or another event for which the event is a direct qualifier), the tie shall be broken by a sail-off when practicable. When the race committee decides that a sail-off is not practicable, the tie shall be decided in favour of the competitor who has the highest score in the round-robin series after eliminating the score for the first race for each tied competitor or, should this fail to break the tie, the second race for each tied competitor and so on until the tie is broken. When a tie is partially resolved, the remaining tie shall be broken by reapplying rule C11.1 or C11.2.

(b) to decide the winner of an event that is not a direct qualifier for another event, or the overall position between competitors eliminated in one round of a knockout series, a sail-off may be used (but not a draw).

(c) when a tie is not broken any monetary prizes or ranking points for tied places shall be added together and divided equally among the tied competitors.

APPENDIX D

TEAM RACING RULES

Team races shall be sailed under The Racing Rules of Sailing *as changed by this appendix.*

D1 CHANGES TO THE RACING RULES

D1.1 Definitions and the Rules of Parts 2 and 4

(a) In the definition *Zone* the distance is changed to two hull lengths.

(b) Rule 18.2(b) is changed to:

If boats are *overlapped* when the first of them reaches the zone, the outside boat at that moment shall thereafter give the inside boat *mark-room*. If a boat is *clear ahead* when she reaches the *zone*, or she later becomes *clear ahead* when another boat passes head to wind, the boat *clear astern* at that moment shall thereafter give her *mark-room*.

(c) Rule 18.4 is deleted.

(d) When rule 20 applies the following arm signals by the helmsman are required in addition to the hails:

   (1) for 'Room to tack', repeatedly and clearly pointing to windward; and

   (2) for 'You tack', repeatedly and clearly pointing at the other boat and waving the arm to windward.

   Sailing instructions may delete this requirement.

(e) Rule 24.1 is changed to: 'If reasonably possible, a boat not *racing* shall not interfere with a boat that is *racing*, and a boat that has *finished* shall not act to interfere with a boat that has not *finished*.'

(f) Add new rule 24.3: 'When boats in different races meet, any change of course by either boat shall be consistent with complying with a *rule* or trying to win her own race.'

(g) Add to rule 41:

(e) help from another boat on her team provided electronic communication is not used.

(h) Rule 45 is deleted.

D1.2 Protests and Requests for Redress

(a) Rule 60.1 is changed to:

A boat may

(a) protest another boat, but not for an alleged breach of a rule of Part 2 unless she was involved in the incident or the incident involved contact between members of the other team; or

(b) request redress.

(b) Rule 61.1(a) is changed so that a boat may remove her red flag after it has been conspicuously displayed.

(c) A boat intending to request redress for an incident in the racing area shall display a red flag at the first reasonable opportunity after the incident. She shall display the red flag until it is acknowledged by the race committee or by an umpire.

(d) The race committee or protest committee shall not protest a boat for breaking a rule of Part 2 or rule 31 or 42 except

(1) based on evidence in a report from an umpire after a black and white flag has been displayed; or

(2) under rule 14 upon receipt of a report from any source alleging damage or injury.

(e) *Protests* and requests for redress need not be in writing. The protest committee may take evidence in any way it considers appropriate and may communicate its decision orally.

(f) A boat is not entitled to redress based on damage or injury caused by another boat on her team.

(g) When a supplied boat suffers a breakdown, rule D5 applies.

D1.3 Penalties

(a) Rule 44.1 is changed to:

A boat may take a One-Turn Penalty when she may have broken one or more rules of Part 2, or rule 31 or 42, in an incident while *racing*. However, when she may have broken a rule of Part 2 and rule 31 in the same incident she need not take the penalty for breaking rule 31.

(b) A boat may take a penalty by retiring, in which case she shall notify the race committee as soon as possible and 6 points shall be added to her score.

(c) There shall be no penalty for breaking a rule of Part 2 when the incident is between boats on the same team

and there is no contact.

D2   UMPIRED RACES

D2.1 When Rule D2 Applies

Rule D2 applies to umpired races. Races to be umpired shall be identified either in the sailing instructions or by the display of flag J no later than the warning signal.

D2.2 Protests by Boats

When a boat protests under a rule of Part 2 or under rule 31 or 42 for an incident in the racing area, she is not entitled to a hearing and the following applies:

(a) She shall hail 'Protest' and conspicuously display a red flag at the first reasonable opportunity for each.

(b) The boats shall be given time to respond. A boat involved in the incident may respond by promptly taking an appropriate penalty or clearly indicating that she will do so as soon as possible.

(c) If no boat takes a penalty, an umpire shall decide whether to penalize any boat.

(d) If more than one boat broke a rule and was not exonerated, an umpire may penalize any boat that broke a rule and did not take an appropriate penalty.

(e) An umpire shall signal a decision in compliance with rule D2.4.

(f) A boat penalized by an umpire shall take a Two-Turns Penalty.

D2.3 Penalties Initiated by an Umpire

An umpire may penalize a boat without a *protest* by another boat, or report the incident to the protest committee, or both, when the boat

(a) breaks rule 31 or 42 and does not take a penalty;

(b) breaks a rule of Part 2 and makes contact with another boat on her team or with a boat in another race, and no boat takes a penalty;

(c) breaks a *rule* and her team gains an advantage despite her, or another boat on her team, taking a penalty;

(d) breaks rule 14 and there is damage or injury;

(e) clearly indicates that she will take a One-Turn Penalty, and then fails to do so;

(f) fails to take a penalty signalled by an umpire;

(g) commits a breach of sportsmanship.

The umpire shall signal a decision in compliance with rule D2.4. A boat penalized by an umpire shall take a Two-Turns Penalty except that, when an umpire hails a number of turns, the boat shall take that number of One-Turn Penalties.

D2.4 Signals by an Umpire

An umpire shall signal a decision with one long sound and the display of a flag as follows:

(a) For no penalty, a green and white flag.

(b) To penalize one or more boats, a red flag. The umpire

shall hail or signal to identify each boat penalized.

(c)   To report the incident to the protest committee, a black and white flag.

D2.5 Two-Flag Protest Procedure

This rule applies only if the sailing instructions so state and it then replaces rule D2.2.

When a boat protests under a rule of Part 2 or under rule 31 or 42 for an incident in the racing area, she is not entitled to a hearing and the following applies:

(a)   She shall hail 'Protest' and conspicuously display a red flag at the first reasonable opportunity for each.

(b)   The boats shall be given time to respond. A boat involved in the incident may respond by promptly taking an appropriate penalty or clearly indicating that she will do so as soon as possible.

(c)   If the protested boat fails to respond, the protesting boat may request a decision by conspicuously displaying a yellow flag and hailing 'Umpire'.

(d)   An umpire shall then decide whether to penalize any boat.

(e)   An umpire shall signal a decision in compliance with rule D2.4.

(f)   If a boat hails for an umpire decision without complying with the protest procedure, an umpire shall signal No Penalty.

(g)   A boat penalized by an umpire shall take a Two-Turns Penalty.

D2.6 Limited Umpiring

This rule applies only if the sailing instructions so state and it then changes rules D2.2 and D2.5.

When a boat protests and either there is no decision signalled, or an umpire displays a yellow flag with one long sound signalling he has insufficient facts to make a decision, the protesting boat is entitled to a hearing.

D2.7 Limitations on Other Proceedings

A decision, action or non-action of an umpire shall not be

(a)   grounds for redress,

(b)   subject to an appeal under rule 70, or

(c)   grounds for *abandoning* a race after it has started.

The protest committee may decide to consider giving redress when it believes that an official boat, including an umpire boat, may have seriously interfered with a competing boat.

D3   SCORING A RACE

D3.1 (a)

Each boat *finishing* a race shall be scored points equal to her finishing place. All other boats shall be scored points equal to the number of boats entitled to *race*.

(b)   When a boat is scored OCS, 10 points shall be added to her score unless she retired as soon as possible after the starting signal.

(c)   When a boat fails to take a penalty imposed by an umpire

at or near the finishing line, she shall be scored points for last place and other scores shall be adjusted accordingly.

(d)   When a protest committee decides that a boat that is a *party* to a protest hearing has broken a *rule* and is not exonerated,

(1)   if the boat has not taken a penalty, 6 points shall be added to her score;

(2)   if the boat's team has gained an advantage despite any penalty taken or imposed, the boat's score may be increased;

(3)   when the boat has broken rule 1 or 2, rule 14 when she has caused damage or injury, or a *rule* when not *racing*, half or more race wins may be deducted from her team, or no penalty may be imposed. Race wins deducted shall not be awarded to any other team.

D3.2 When all boats on one team have *finished*, retired or failed to *start*, the other team's boats *racing* at that time shall be scored the points they would have received had they *finished*.

D3.3 The team with the lower total points wins the race. If the totals are equal, the team that does not have first place wins.

D4   SCORING A STAGE

D4.1 Terminology

(a)   The racing format at an event will consist of one or more stages.

(b)   In a round-robin stage teams are assigned to one or more groups and scheduled to sail one or more round-robins. A round robin is a schedule of races in which each team sails once against each other team in the same group.

(c)   In a knock-out stage teams are scheduled to sail in matches. A match is one or more races between two teams.

(d)   The notice of race or sailing instructions may specify other formats and scoring methods.

D4.2 Terminating a Stage

(a)   The race committee may terminate a stage at any reasonable time taking into account the entries, weather, time constraints and other relevant factors.

(b)   When a round-robin stage is terminated, any round-robin in the stage in which 80% or more of the full schedule of races has been completed shall be scored as complete; if fewer races have been completed, the round-robin shall not be scored, but may be used to break ties.

D4.3 Scoring a Round-Robin Stage

(a)   In a round-robin stage the teams shall be ranked in order of number of race wins, highest number first. If the teams have not completed an equal number of races, they shall be ranked in order of the percentage of races won, highest number first.

(b)   If a round-robin in the stage is not completed, teams shall be ranked according to the results from all completed round-robins in the stage.

D4.4 Ties in a Completed Round-Robin Stage

Ties in a completed round-robin stage shall be broken by using, in the following order, only results in the stage,

(a) the highest number of race wins in all races between the tied teams;

(b) the lowest total points scored in all races between the tied teams;

(c) if two teams remain tied, the winner of the last race between them;

(d) the lowest average points scored in all races against common opponents;

(e) a sail-off if possible, otherwise a game of chance.

If a tie is partially broken by one of these, the remaining tie shall be broken by starting again at rule D4.4(a).

D4.5 Ties in an Incomplete Round-Robin Stage

Ties in an incomplete round-robin stage shall be broken whenever possible using the results from races between the tied teams in any incomplete round-robin. Other ties shall be broken in accordance with rule D4.4.

D4.6 Scoring a Knock-Out Stage

The winner of a match is the first team to score the number of race wins stated in the sailing instructions.

D4.7 Incomplete Knock-Out Stage

If a match in a knock-out stage is not completed (including 0-0), the result of the match shall be determined using, in order,

(a) the higher number of race wins in the incomplete match;

(b) the higher number of race wins in all races in the event between the tied teams;

(c) the higher place in the most recent stage, applying rule D4.4(a) if necessary;

(d) the winner of the most recent race between the teams.

If this rule fails to determine a result, the stage shall be tied unless the sailing instructions provide for some other result.

D5 BREAKDOWNS WHEN BOATS ARE SUPPLIED BY THE ORGANIZING AUTHORITY

D5.1 Rule D5 applies when boats are supplied by the organizing authority.

D5.2 When a boat suffers a breakdown in the racing area, she may request a score change by displaying a red flag at the first reasonable opportunity after the breakdown until it is acknowledged by the race committee or by an umpire. If possible, she shall continue *racing*.

D5.3 The race committee shall decide requests for a score change in accordance with rules D5.4 and D5.5. It may take evidence in any way it considers appropriate and may communicate its decision orally.

D5.4 When the race committee decides that the team's finishing position was made significantly worse, that the breakdown

was through no fault of the crew, and that in the same circumstances a reasonably competent crew would not have been able to avoid the breakdown, it shall make as equitable a decision as possible. This may be to *abandon* and resail the race or, when the boat's finishing position was predictable, award her points for that position. Any doubt about a boat's position when she broke down shall be resolved against her.

D5.5 A breakdown caused by defective supplied equipment or a breach of a *rule* by an opponent shall not normally be determined to be the fault of the crew, but one caused by careless handling, capsizing or a breach by a boat on the same team shall be. If there is doubt, it shall be presumed that the crew are not at fault.

APPENDIX E
RADIO SAILING RACING RULES

Radio sailing races shall be sailed under The Racing Rules of Sailing *as changed by this appendix.*

E1 CHANGES TO THE DEFINITIONS, TERMINOLOGY AND THE RULES OF PARTS 1, 2 AND 7

E1.1 Definitions

Add to the definition *Conflict of Interest*:

However, an observer does not have a *conflict of interest* solely by being a competitor.

In the definition *Zone* the distance is changed to four hull lengths.

Add new definition:

Disabled A boat is *disabled* while she is unable to continue in the heat.

E1.2 Terminology

The Terminology paragraph of the Introduction is changed so that:

(a) 'Boat' means a sailboat controlled by radio signals and having no crew. However, in the rules of Part 1 and Part 5, rule E6 and the definitions *Party* and *Protest*, 'boat' includes the competitor controlling her.

(b) 'Competitor' means the person designated to control a boat using radio signals.

(c) In the racing rules, but not in its appendices, replace the noun 'race' with 'heat'. In Appendix E a race consists of one or more heats and is completed when the last heat in the race is completed.

E1.3 Rules of Parts 1, 2 and 7

(a) Rule 1.2 is deleted.

(b) In rule 20, hails and replies shall be made by the competitor controlling the boat.

(c) Rule 23 is changed to: 'If possible, a boat shall avoid a boat that is *disabled*.'

(d) Rule 90.2(c) is changed to:

Changes to the sailing instructions may be communicated orally to all affected competitors before the warning signal of the relevant race or heat. When appropriate, changes shall be confirmed in writing.

E2   ADDITIONAL RULES WHEN RACING

*Rule E2 applies only while boats are **racing**.*

E2.1 Hailing Requirements

(a) A hail shall be made so that the competitors to whom the hail is directed might reasonably be expected to hear it.

(b) The individual digits of a boat's sail number shall be hailed; for example 'one five', not 'fifteen'.

E2.2 Giving Advice

A competitor shall not give tactical or strategic advice to a competitor controlling a boat that is *racing*.

E2.3 Boat Out of Radio Control

A competitor who loses radio control of his boat shall promptly hail and repeat '(The boat's sail number) out of control' and the boat shall retire.

E2.4 Transmitter Aerials

If a transmitter aerial is longer than 200mm when extended, the extremity shall be adequately protected.

E2.5 Radio Interference

Transmission of radio signals that cause interference with the control of other boats is prohibited. A competitor that has broken this rule shall not *race* again until permitted to do so by the race committee.

E3   CONDUCT OF A RACE

E3.1 Control Area

The sailing instructions may specify a control area; if not specified, it shall be unrestricted. Competitors shall be in this area when controlling boats that are *racing*, except briefly to handle and then release or relaunch the boat.

E3.2 Launching Area

The sailing instructions may specify a launching area and its use; if not specified it shall be unrestricted.

E3.3 Course Board

The sailing instructions may require the course to be displayed on a board and, if so, the board shall be located in or adjacent to the control area.

E3.4 Starting and Finishing

(a) Rule 26 is changed to:

Heats shall be started using warning, preparatory and starting signals at one-minute intervals. During the minute before the starting signal, additional sound or oral signals shall be made at ten-second intervals, and during the final ten seconds at one-second intervals. Each signal shall be timed from the beginning of its sound.

(b) The starting and finishing lines shall be between the course sides of the starting and finishing *marks*.

E3.5 Individual Recall

Rule 29.1 is changed to:

When at a boat's starting signal any part of the boat is on the course side of the starting line or when she must comply with rule 30.1, the race committee shall promptly hail 'Recall (sail numbers)' and repeat the hail as appropriate. If rule 30.3 or 30.4 applies this rule does not.

E3.6 General Recall

Rule 29.2 is changed to:

When at the starting signal the race committee is unable to identify boats that are on the course side of the starting line or to which rule 30 applies, or there has been an error in the starting procedure, the race committee may hail and repeat as appropriate 'General recall' and make two loud sounds. The warning signal for a new start will normally be made shortly thereafter.

E3.7 U Flag and Black Flag Rules

When the race committee informs a boat that she has broken rule 30.3 or 30.4, the boat shall immediately leave the course area.

E3.8 Other Changes to the Rules of Part 3

(a) Rules 30.2 and 33 are deleted.

(b) All race committee signals shall be made orally or by other sounds. No visual signals are required unless specified in the sailing instructions.

(c) Courses shall not be shortened.

(d) Rule 32.1(b) is changed to: 'because of foul weather or thunderstorms,'.

E3.9 Disabled Competitors

To enable a disabled competitor to compete on equal terms, the race committee shall make as fair an arrangement as possible.

E4   RULES OF PART 4

E4.1 Deleted Rules in Part 4

Rules 40, 43, 44.3, 45, 47, 48, 49, 50, 52 and 54 are deleted.

E4.2 Outside Help

Rule 41 is changed to:

A boat or the competitor controlling her shall not receive help from any outside source, except

(a) help needed as a direct result of a competitor becoming ill, injured or in danger;

(b) when the boat is entangled with another boat, help from the other competitor;

(c) when the boat is entangled, or she is aground or in danger, help from a race committee vessel;

(d) help in the form of information freely available to all competitors;

(e) unsolicited information from a disinterested source. A competitor is not a disinterested source unless acting as an observer.

However, a boat that gains a significant advantage in the heat or race from help received under rule 41 may be protested and penalized; any penalty may be less than disqualification.

E4.3 Taking a Penalty

Rule 44.1 is changed to:

A boat may take a One-Turn Penalty when she may have broken one or more rules of Part 2, or rule 31, in an incident while *racing*. However,

(a) when she may have broken a rule of Part 2 and rule 31 in the same incident she need not take the penalty for breaking rule 31;

(b) if the boat gained a significant advantage in the heat or race by her breach despite taking a penalty, her penalty shall be an additional One-Turn Penalty;

(c) if the boat caused serious damage, or as a result of breaking a rule of Part 2 she caused another boat to become *disabled* and retire, her penalty shall be to retire.

E4.4 Person in Charge

Rule 46 is changed to: 'The member or organization that entered the boat shall designate the competitor. See rule 75.'

E5 RACING WITH OBSERVERS AND UMPIRES

E5.1 Observers

(a) The race committee may appoint observers, who may be competitors.

(b) Observers shall hail the sail numbers of boats that make contact with a *mark* or another boat and shall repeat the hail as appropriate.

(c) At the end of a heat, observers shall report to the race committee all unresolved incidents, and any failure to sail the course as required by rule 28.

E5.2 Umpired Races

The International Radio Sailing Association Addendum Q shall apply to umpired races. Races to be umpired may be identified in the sailing instructions or orally before the warning signal.

Note: The addendum is available at the website: **radiosailing. org**.

E5.3 Rules for Observers and Umpires

Observers and umpires shall be located in the control area. They shall not use any aid or device that gives them a visual advantage over competitors.

E6 PROTESTS AND REQUESTS FOR REDRESS

E6.1 Right to Protest

Rule 60.1 is changed to:

A boat may

(a) protest another boat, but not for an alleged breach of a

rule of Part 2, 3 or 4 unless she was scheduled to sail in that heat; or

(b) request redress.

However, a boat or competitor may not protest for an alleged breach of rules E2 or E3.7.

E6.2 Protest for a Rule Broken by a Competitor

When a race committee or protest committee learns that a competitor may have broken a *rule*, it may protest the boat controlled by that competitor.

E6.3 Informing the Protestee

Rule 61.1(a) is changed to:

A boat intending to protest shall inform the other boat at the first reasonable opportunity. When her *protest* concerns an incident in the racing area that she was involved in or saw, she shall hail twice '(Her own sail number) protest (the sail number of the other boat)'.

E6.4 Informing the Race Committee

A boat intending to protest or request redress about an incident in the racing area or control area shall inform the race officer as soon as reasonably possible after *finishing* or retiring.

E6.5 Time Limits

A *protest*, request for redress or request for reopening shall be delivered to the race officer no later than ten minutes after the last boat in the heat *finishes* or after the relevant incident, whichever is later.

E6.6 Redress

Add to rule 62.1:

(e) external radio interference acknowledged by the race committee, or

(f) becoming *disabled* because of the action of a boat that was breaking a rule of Part 2 or of a vessel not *racing* that was required to keep clear.

E6.7 Right to Be Present

In rule 63.3(a) 'the representatives of boats shall have been on board' is changed to 'the representative of each boat shall be the competitor designated to control her'.

E6.8 Taking Evidence and Finding Facts

Add to rule 63.6:

When the *protest* concerns an alleged breach of a rule of Part 2, 3 or 4, any witness shall have been in the control area at the time of the incident. If the witness is a competitor who was not acting as an observer, he shall also have been scheduled to race in the relevant heat.

E6.9 Decisions on Redress

Add to rule 64.2:

If a boat is given redress because she was damaged, her redress shall include reasonable time, but not more than 30 minutes, to make repairs before her next heat.

E7 PENALTIES

When a protest committee decides that a boat that is a *party* to a protest hearing has broken a *rule* other than a *rule* of Part 2, 3 or 4, it shall either

(a) disqualify her or add any number of points (including zero and fractions of points) to her score. The penalty shall be applied, if possible, to the heat or race in which the *rule* was broken; otherwise it shall be applied to the next heat or race for that boat. When points are added, the scores of other boats shall not be changed; or

(b) require her to take one or more One-Turn Penalties that shall be taken as soon as possible after the starting signal of her next heat that is started and not subsequently recalled or *abandoned*.

However, if the boat has broken a rule in Appendix G or rule E8, the protest committee shall act in accordance with rule G4.

E8 CHANGES TO APPENDIX G, IDENTIFICATION ON SAILS

Rule G1, except the table of National Sail Letters, is changed to:

G1 WORLD SAILING AND IRSA CLASS BOATS

This rule applies to every boat of a class administered or recognised by World Sailing or by the International Radio Sailing Association (IRSA).

G1.1 Identification

(a) A boat of a World Sailing or IRSA Class shall display her class insignia, national letters and sail number as specified in rule G1, unless her class rules state otherwise.

(b) At world and continental championships, sails shall comply with these rules. At other events they shall comply with these rules or the rules applicable at the time of their initial certification.

G1.2 National Letters

At all international events, a boat shall display national letters in accordance with the table of National Sail Letters denoting:

(a) when entered under rule 75.1(a), the national authority of the nationality, place of residence, or affiliation of the owner or the member.

(b) when entered under rule 75.1(b), the national authority of the organisation which entered her.

For the purposes of this rule, international events are world and continental championships and events described as international events in their notices of race and sailing instructions.

Note: An up-to-date version of the National Sail Letters table is available on the World Sailing website.

G1.3 Sail numbers

(a) The sail number shall be the last two digits of the boat's registration number or the competitor's or owner's personal number, allotted by the relevant issuing authority.

(b) When there is conflict between sail numbers, or when a sail number may be misread, the race committee shall require that the sail numbers of one or more boats be changed to numeric alternatives.

G1.4 Specifications

(a) National letters and sail numbers shall be in capital letters and Arabic numerals, clearly legible and of the same colour. Commercially available typefaces giving the same or better legibility than Helvetica are acceptable.

(b) The height and spacing of letters and numbers shall be as follows:

Dimension	Minimum	Maximum
Height of sail numbers	100 mm	110 mm
Spacing of adjacent sail numbers	20 mm	30 mm
Height of national letters	60 mm	70 mm
Spacing of adjacent national letters	13 mm	23 mm

G1.5 Positioning

(a) Class insignia, sail numbers and national letters shall be positioned

(1) on both sides of the sail;

(2) with those on the starboard side uppermost;

(3) approximately horizontally;

(4) with no less than 40 mm vertical spacing between numbers and letters on opposite sides of the sail;

(5) with no less than 20 mm vertical spacing between class insignia on opposite sides of the sail.

However, symmetrical or reversed class insignia may be positioned back to back.

(b) On a mainsail, sail numbers shall be positioned

(1) below class insignia;

(2) above the line perpendicular to the luff through the quarter leech point;

(3) above national letters;

(4) with sufficient space in front of the sail number for a prefix '1'.

G1.6 Exceptions

(a) Where the size of the sail prevents compliance with rule G1.2, National Letters, then exceptions to rules G1.2, G1.4, and G1.5 shall be made in the following order of precedence. National letters shall

(1) be spaced vertically below sail numbers by less an 30 mm, but no less than 20 mm;

(2) be spaced on opposite sides of the sail by less than 30 mm, but no less than 20 mm;

    (3)   be reduced in height to less than 45 mm, but no less than 40 mm;

    (4)   be omitted.

  (b) Where the size of the sail prevents compliance with rule G1.3, Sail Numbers, then exceptions to rules G1.4 and G1.5 shall be made in the following order of precedence. Sail numbers shall

    (1)   extend below the specified line;

    (2)   be spaced on opposite sides of the sail by less than 30 mm, but no less than 20 mm apart;

    (3)   be reduced in height to less than 90 mm, but no less than 80 mm;

    (4)   be omitted on all except the largest sail;

    (5)   be reduced in height until they do fit on the largest sail.

APPENDIX F

KITEBOARD RACING RULES

Kiteboard course races shall be sailed under The Racing Rules of Sailing as changed by this appendix. The term 'boat' elsewhere in the racing rules means 'kiteboard' or 'boat' as appropriate.

Note: Rules for other kiteboard racing formats (such as Short Track, Kitecross, Slalom, Boarder X) or other kiteboard competitions (such as Freestyle, Wave, Big Air, Speed) are not included in this appendix. Links to current versions of these rules can be found on the World Sailing website.

CHANGES TO THE DEFINITIONS

The definitions *Clear Astern* and *Clear Ahead; Overlap, Finish, Keep Clear, Leeward* and *Windward, Mark-Room, Obstruction, Start, Tack, Starboard* or *Port* and *Zone* are changed to:

Clear Astern and Clear Ahead; Overlap One kiteboard is *clear astern* of another when her hull is behind a line abeam from the aftermost point of the other kiteboard's hull. The other kiteboard is *clear ahead*. They *overlap* when neither is *clear astern*. However, they also *overlap* when a kiteboard between them *overlaps* both. These terms always apply to kiteboards on the same *tack*. They do not apply to kiteboards on opposite *tacks* unless both kiteboards are sailing more than ninety degrees from the true wind.

Finish A kiteboard *finishes* when, while the competitor is in contact with the hull, any part of her hull, or the competitor in normal position, crosses the finishing line from the course side. However, she has not *finished* if after crossing the finishing line she

  (a) takes a penalty under rule 44.2,

  (b) corrects an error under rule 28.2 made at the line, or

  (c) continues to sail the course.

Keep Clear A kiteboard *keeps clear* of a right-of-way kiteboard

  (a) if the right-of-way kiteboard can sail her course with no need to take avoiding action and,

  (b) when the kiteboards are *overlapped*, if the right-of-way kiteboard can also, without immediately making contact, change course in both directions or move her kite in any direction.

Leeward and Windward A kiteboard's *leeward* side is the side that is or, when she is head to wind, was away from the wind. However, when sailing by the lee or directly downwind, her *leeward* side is the side on which her kite lies. The other side is her *windward* side. When two kiteboards on the same *tack overlap*, the one whose hull is on the *leeward* side of the other's hull is the *leeward* kiteboard. The other is the *windward* kiteboard.

Mark-Room Room for a kiteboard to sail her *proper course* to round or pass the *mark* on the required side.

Obstruction An object that a kiteboard could not pass without changing course substantially, if she were sailing directly towards it and 10 metres from it. An object that can be safely passed on only one side and an area so designated by the sailing instructions are also *obstructions*. However, a kiteboard *racing* is not an *obstruction* to other kiteboards unless they are required to *keep clear* of her or, if rule 23 applies, avoid her. A vessel under way, including a kiteboard *racing*, is never a continuing *obstruction*.

Start A kiteboard *starts* when, her hull and the competitor having been entirely on the pre-start side of the starting line at or after her starting signal, and having complied with rule 30.1 if it applies, any part of her hull, or the competitor crosses the starting line in the direction of the first *mark*.

Tack, Starboard or Port A kiteboard is on the *tack*, *starboard* or *port*, corresponding to the competitor's hand that would be forward if the competitor were in normal riding position (riding heel side with both hands on the control bar and arms not crossed). A kiteboard is on *starboard tack* when the competitor's right hand would be forward and is on the *port tack* when the competitor's left hand would be forward.

Zone The area around a *mark* within a distance of 30 metres. A kiteboard is in the *zone* when any part of her hull is in the *zone*.

Add the following definitions:

Capsized A kiteboard is *capsized* if

  (a) her kite is in the water,

  (b) her lines are tangled with another kiteboard's lines, or

  (c) the competitor has, clearly by accident and for a significant period of time,

    (1)   fallen into the water or

    (2)   become disconnected from the hull.

Jumping A kiteboard is *jumping* when her hull, its appendages and the competitor are clear of the water.

Recovering A kiteboard is *recovering* from the time her kite is out of the water until she has steerage way.

F1   CHANGES TO THE RULES OF PART 1

   [No changes.]

F2   CHANGES TO THE RULES OF PART 2

PART 2 - PREAMBLE

In the second sentence of the preamble, 'injury or serious damage' is changed to 'injury, serious damage or a tangle'.

13   WHILE TACKING

Rule 13 is deleted.

14   AVOIDING CONTACT

Rule 14(b) is changed to:

(b)   shall be exonerated if she breaks this rule and the contact does not cause damage, injury or a tangle.

16   CHANGING COURSE OR KITE POSITION

Rule 16 is changed to:

16.1 When a right-of-way kiteboard changes course or the position of her kite, she shall give the other kiteboard *room* to *keep clear*.

16.2 In addition, when after the starting signal a *port-tack* kiteboard is *keeping clear* by sailing to pass astern of a *starboard-tack* kiteboard, the *starboard-tack* kiteboard shall not change course or the position of her kite if as a result the *port-tack* kiteboard would immediately need to change course or the position of her kite to continue *keeping clear*.

17   ON THE SAME TACK; PROPER COURSE

Rule 17 is deleted.

18   MARK-ROOM

Rule 18 is changed to:

18.1   When Rule 18 Applies

Rule 18 applies between kiteboards when they are required to leave a *mark* on the same side and at least one of them is in the *zone*. However, it does not apply

(a)   between a kiteboard approaching a *mark* and one leaving it, or

(b)   between kiteboards on opposite *tacks*.

18.2   Giving Mark-Room

(a)   When the first kiteboard reaches the *zone*,

   (1)   if kiteboards are *overlapped*, the outside kiteboard at that moment shall thereafter give the inside kiteboard *mark-room*.

   (2)   if kiteboards are not *overlapped*, the kiteboard that has not reached the *zone* shall thereafter give *mark-room*.

(b)   If the kiteboard entitled to *mark-room* leaves the *zone*, the entitlement to *mark-room* ceases and rule 18.2(a) is applied again if required based on the relationship of the kiteboards at the time rule 18.2(a) is re-applied.

(c)   If a kiteboard obtained an inside *overlap* and, from the time the *overlap* began, the outside kiteboard is unable to give *mark-room*, she is not required to give it.

18.3   Tacking and Gybing

When an inside *overlapped* right-of-way kiteboard must change *tack* at a *mark* to sail her *proper course*, until she changes *tack* she shall sail no farther from the *mark* than needed to sail that course. Rule 18.3 does not apply at a gate *mark* or a finishing *mark* and a kiteboard shall not be penalized for breaking this rule unless the course of another kiteboard was affected by the breach of this rule.

20   ROOM TO TACK AT AN OBSTRUCTION

Add new rule 20.4:

20.4   Arm Signals

The following arm signals are required in addition to the hails

(a)   for 'Room to tack', repeatedly and clearly circling one hand over the head; and

(b)   for 'You tack', repeatedly and clearly pointing at the other kiteboard and waving the arm to windward.

22   STARTING ERRORS; TAKING PENALTIES; JUMPING

Rule 22.3 is changed and new rule 22.4 is added:

22.3 During the last minute before her starting signal, a kiteboard that stops, slows down significantly, or one that is not making significant forward progress shall *keep clear* of all others unless she is accidentally *capsized*.

22.4 A kiteboard that is *jumping* shall *keep clear* of one that is not.

23   CAPSIZED; RECOVERING; AGROUND; RESCUING

Rule 23 is changed to:

23.1 If possible, a kiteboard shall avoid a kiteboard that is *capsized* or has not regained control after *capsizing*, is aground, or is trying to help a person or vessel in danger.

23.2 A kiteboard that is *recovering* shall *keep clear* of a kiteboard that is not.

F3   CHANGES TO THE RULES OF PART 3

29   RECALLS

In rule 29.1 'crew or equipment' is changed to 'competitor'.

30   STARTING PENALTIES

In rules 30.1, 30.2, 30.3 and 30.4, 'crew or equipment' is changed to 'or competitor'.

In rule 30.4, 'sail number' is changed to 'competitor number'.

31   TOUCHING A MARK

Rule 31 is changed to:

While *racing*, a kiteboard shall not touch a windward *mark*.

36   RACES RESTARTED OR RESAILED

Rule 36(b) is changed to:

(b)   cause a kiteboard to be penalized except under rule 30.2, 30.4 or 69 or under rule 14 when she has caused injury, serious damage or a tangle.

F4   CHANGES TO THE RULES OF PART 4

41   OUTSIDE HELP

Add new rules 41(e) and 41(f):

(e)   help from another competitor in the same race to assist a relaunch;

(f) help to change equipment, but only in the launching area.

42 PROPULSION

Rule 42 is changed to:

A kiteboard shall be propelled only by the action of the wind on the kite, by the action of the water on the hull and by the unassisted actions of the competitor. However, the competitor shall not make significant progress by paddling, swimming or walking.

43 COMPETITOR CLOTHING AND EQUIPMENT

Rule 43.1(a) is changed to:

(a) Competitors shall not wear or carry clothing or equipment for the purpose of increasing their weight. However, a competitor may wear a drinking container that shall have a capacity of at least one litre and weigh no more than 1.5 kilograms when full.

44 PENALTIES AT THE TIME OF AN INCIDENT

Rules 44.1 and 44.2 are changed to:

44.1 Taking a Penalty

A kiteboard may take a One-Turn Penalty when she may have broken one or more rules of Part 2 or rule 31 in an incident while *racing*. Alternatively, the notice of race or sailing instructions may specify the use of the Scoring Penalty or some other penalty, in which case the specified penalty shall replace the One-Turn Penalty. However,

(a) when a kiteboard may have broken a rule of Part 2 and rule 31 in the same incident she need not take the penalty for breaking rule 31; and

(b) if the kiteboard caused injury, damage or a tangle or, despite taking a penalty, gained a significant advantage in the race or series by her breach, her penalty shall be to retire.

44.2 One-Turn Penalty

After getting well clear of other kiteboards as soon after the incident as possible, a kiteboard takes a One-Turn Penalty by promptly making one turn with her hull in the water. The turn shall include one completed tack and one completed gybe. Forward motion shall be established between the tack and the gybe (or vice versa) with the competitor on the correct side of the hull in normal sailing position. When a kiteboard takes the penalty at or near the finishing line, she shall sail completely to the course side of the line before *finishing*.

PART 4 RULES DELETED

Rules 43.2, 45, 47, 48.1, 49, 50, 51, 52 and 54 are deleted.

F5 CHANGES TO THE RULES OF PART 5

61 PROTEST REQUIREMENTS

Rule 61.1(a) is changed to:

(a) A kiteboard intending to protest shall inform the other kiteboard at the first reasonable opportunity. When her *protest* will concern an incident in the racing area that she was involved in or saw, she shall hail 'Protest' at the first reasonable opportunity. However,

(1) if the other kiteboard is beyond hailing distance, the protesting kiteboard need not hail but she shall inform the other kiteboard at the first reasonable opportunity;

(2) no red flag need be displayed;

(3) if the incident was an error by the other kiteboard in sailing the course, she need not hail but she shall inform the other kiteboard before that kiteboard *finishes* or at the first reasonable opportunity after she *finishes*;

(4) if as a result of the incident either competitor is in danger, or there is injury, serious damage or a tangle that is obvious to the kiteboard intending to protest, the requirements of this rule do not apply to her, but she shall attempt to inform the other kiteboard within the time limit of rule 61.3.

62 REDRESS

Rule 62.1(b) is changed to:

(b) injury, physical damage or a tangle because of the action of a kiteboard that was breaking a rule of Part 2 or of a vessel not *racing* that was required to keep clear;

63 HEARINGS

For a race of an elimination series that will qualify a kiteboard to compete in a later stage of an event, rules 61.2 and 65.2 are deleted and rule 63.6 is changed to:

63.6 *Protests* and requests for redress need not be in writing; they shall be made orally to a member of the protest committee as soon as reasonably possible following the race. The protest committee may take evidence in any way it considers appropriate and may communicate its decision orally.

64 DECISIONS

Add new rule 64.1(d):

(d) when a kiteboard has broken a rule of Part 2 and, as a result, caused a tangle for which redress was given, she shall be scored RCT if she retired or DCT if she was disqualified. When she does this a second or subsequent time in the series, her penalty shall be DNE.

Rules 64.3(a) and 64.3(b) are changed to:

(a) When the protest committee finds that deviations in excess of acceptable manufacturing tolerances were caused by damage or normal wear and do not improve the performance of the kiteboard, it shall not penalize her. However, the kiteboard shall not *race* again until the deviations have been corrected, except when the protest committee decides there is or has been no reasonable opportunity to do so.

(b) When the protest committee is in doubt about any matter concerning the measurement of a kiteboard, the interpretation of a class rule, or a matter involving damage to a kiteboard, it shall refer its questions, together with the relevant facts, to an authority responsible for interpreting the rule. In making its decision, the committee shall be bound by the reply of the authority.

70 APPEALS AND REQUESTS TO A NATIONAL AUTHORITY

Add new rule 70.7:

70.7 Appeals are not permitted in disciplines and formats with elimination series.

F6 CHANGES TO THE RULES OF PART 6

[No changes.]

F7 CHANGES TO THE RULES OF PART 7

90 RACE COMMITTEE; SAILING INSTRUCTIONS; SCORING

The last sentence of rule 90.2(c) is changed to: 'Oral instructions may be given only if the procedure is stated in the sailing instructions.'

F8 CHANGES TO APPENDIX A

A1 NUMBER OF RACES; OVERALL SCORES

Rule A1 is changed to:

The number of races scheduled and the number required to be completed to constitute a series shall be stated in the notice of race or sailing instructions. If an event includes more than one discipline or format, the notice of race or sailing instructions shall state how the overall scores are to be calculated.

A4 LOW POINT SYSTEM

Rule A4.2 is changed to:

A4.2 A kiteboard that did not *start*, did not *finish*, retired or was disqualified shall be scored points for the finishing place one more than the number of kiteboards entered in the series or, in a race of an elimination series, the number of kiteboards in that heat. A kiteboard that is penalized under rule 30.2 shall be scored points as provided in rule 44.3(c).

A11 SCORING ABBREVIATIONS

Add to Rule A11:

DCT Disqualified after causing a tangle in an incident

RCT Retired after causing a tangle

F9 CHANGES TO APPENDIX G

Appendix G is changed to:

Appendix G – Identification on Competitors

G1 Every kiteboard shall be identified as follows:

(a) Each competitor shall be provided with and wear a shirt with a personal competition number of no more than three digits.

(b) The numbers shall be displayed on the front and back of the shirts and be at least 15 cm high.

(c) The numbers shall be Arabic numerals, all of the same solid colour, clearly legible and in a commercially available typeface giving the same or better legibility as Helvetica. The colour of the numbers shall contrast with the colour of the shirt.

APPENDIX G

IDENTIFICATION ON SAILS

See rule 77.

G1 WORLD SAILING CLASS BOATS

G1.1 Identification

Every boat of a World Sailing Class shall carry on her mainsail and, as provided in rules G1.3(d) and G1.3(e) for letters and numbers only, on her spinnaker and headsail

(a) the insignia denoting her class;

(b) at all international events, except when the boats are provided to all competitors, national letters denoting her national authority from the table below. For the purposes of this rule, international events are World Sailing events, world and continental championships, and events described as international events in their notices of race and sailing instructions; and

(c) a sail number of no more than four digits allotted by her national authority or, when so required by the class rules, by the class association. The four-digit limitation does not apply to classes whose World Sailing membership or recognition took effect before 1 April 1997. Alternatively, if permitted in the class rules, an owner may be allotted a personal sail number by the relevant issuing authority, which may be used on all his boats in that class.

Sails measured before 31 March 1999 shall comply with rule G1.1 or with the rules applicable at the time of measurement.

Note: An up-to-date version of the table below is available on the World Sailing website.

NATIONAL SAIL LETTERS

National authority	Letters
Algeria	ALG
American Samoa	ASA
Andorra	AND
Angola	ANG
Antigua	ANT
Argentina	ARG
Armenia	ARM
Aruba	ARU
Australia	AUS
Austria	AUT
Azerbaijan	AZE

National authority	Letters	National authority	Letters
Bahamas	BAH	Indonesia	INA
Bahrain	BRN	Iraq	IRQ
Barbados	BAR	Ireland	IRL
Belarus	BLR	Israel	ISR
Belgium	BEL	Italy	ITA
Belize	BIZ	Jamaica	JAM
Bermuda	BER	Japan	JPN
Brazil	BRA	Kazakhstan	KAZ
British Virgin Islands	IVB	Kenya	KEN
Bulgaria	BUL	Korea, DPR	PRK
Canada	CAN	Korea, Republic of	KOR
Cayman Islands	CAY	Kosovo	KOS
Chile	CHI	Kuwait	KUW
China, PR	CHN	Kyrgyzstan	KGZ
Chinese Taipei	TPE	Latvia	LAT
Colombia	COL	Lebanon	LIB
Cook Islands	COK	Libya	LBA
Croatia	CRO	Liechtenstein	LIE
Cuba	CUB	Lithuania	LTU
Cyprus	CYP	Luxembourg	LUX
Czech Republic	CZE	Macedonia (FYRO)	MKD
Denmark	DEN	Madagascar	MAD
Djibouti	DJI	Malaysia	MAS
Dominican Republic	DOM	Malta	MLT
Ecuador	ECU	Mauritius	MRI
Egypt	EGY	Mexico	MEX
El Salvador	ESA	Moldova	MDA
Estonia	EST	Monaco	MON
Fiji	FIJ	Montenegro	MNE
Finland	FIN	Morocco	MAR
France	FRA	Mozambique	MOZ
Georgia	GEO	Myanmar	MYA
Germany	GER	Namibia	NAM
Great Britain	GBR	Netherlands	NED
Greece	GRE	Netherlands Antilles	AHO
Grenada	GRN	New Zealand	NZL
Guam	GUM	Nicaragua	NCA
Guatemala	GUA	Nigeria	NGR
Hong Kong	HKG	Norway	NOR
Hungary	HUN	Oman	OMA
Iceland	ISL	Pakistan	PAK
India	IND	Palestine	PLE

National authority	Letters
Panama	PAN
Papua New Guinea	PNG
Paraguay	PAR
Peru	PER
Philippines	PHI
Poland	POL
Portugal	POR
Puerto Rico	PUR
Qatar	QAT
Romania	ROU
Russia	RUS
Samoa	SAM
San Marino	SMR
Saudi Arabia	KSA
Senegal	SEN
Serbia	SRB
Seychelles	SEY
Singapore	SIN
Slovak Republic	SVK
Slovenia	SLO
South Africa	RSA
Spain	ESP
Sri Lanka	SRI
St Lucia	LCA
St Vincent & Grenadines	VIN
Sudan	SUD
Sweden	SWE
Switzerland	SUI
Tahiti	TAH
Tanzania	TAN
Thailand	THA
Trinidad & Tobago	TTO
Tunisia	TUN
Turkey	TUR
Uganda	UGA
Ukraine	UKR
United Arab Emirates	UAE
United States of America	USA
Uruguay	URU
US Virgin Islands	ISV
Vanuatu	VAN
Venezuela	VEN

National authority	Letters
Vietnam	VIE
Zimbabwe	ZIM

G1.2 Specifications

(a) National letters and sail numbers shall be in capital letters and Arabic numerals, clearly legible and of the same colour. Commercially available typefaces giving the same or better legibility than Helvetica are acceptable.

(b) The height of characters and space between adjoining characters on the same and opposite sides of the sail shall be related to the boat's overall length as follows:

Overall length	Minimum height	Minimum space between characters and from edge of sail
Under 3.5 m	230 mm	45 mm
3.5 m – 8.5 m	300 mm	60 mm
8.5 m – 11 m	375 mm	75 mm
Over 11 m	450 mm	90 mm

G1.3 Positioning

Class insignia, national letters and sail numbers shall be positioned as follows:

(a) Except as provided in rules G1.3(d) and G1.3(e), class insignia, national letters and sail numbers shall, if possible, be wholly above an arc whose centre is the head point and whose radius is 60% of the leech length. They shall be placed at different heights on the two sides of the sail, those on the starboard side being uppermost.

(b) The class insignia shall be placed above the national letters. If the class insignia is of such a design that two of them coincide when placed back to back on both sides of the sail, they may be so placed.

(c) National letters shall be placed above the sail number.

(d) The national letters and sail number shall be displayed on the front side of a spinnaker but may be placed on both sides. They shall be displayed wholly below an arc whose centre is the head point and whose radius is 40% of the foot median and, if possible, wholly above an arc whose radius is 60% of the foot median.

(e) The national letters and sail number shall be displayed on both sides of a headsail whose clew can extend behind the mast 30% or more of the mainsail foot length. They shall be displayed wholly below an arc whose centre is the head point and whose radius is half the luff length and, if possible, wholly above an arc whose radius is 75% of the luff length.

G2　OTHER BOATS

Other boats shall comply with the rules of their national authority or class association in regard to the allotment, carrying and size of insignia, letters and numbers. Such rules shall, when practicable, conform to the above requirements.

G3 CHARTERED OR LOANED BOATS

When so stated in the notice of race or sailing instructions, a boat chartered or loaned for an event may carry national letters or a sail number in contravention of her class rules.

G4 WARNINGS AND PENALTIES

When a protest committee finds that a boat has broken a rule of this appendix, it shall either warn her and give her time to comply or penalize her.

G5 CHANGES BY CLASS RULES

World Sailing Classes may change the rules of this appendix provided the changes have first been approved by World Sailing.

APPENDIX H
WEIGHING CLOTHING AND EQUIPMENT

See rule 43. This appendix shall not be changed by sailing instructions or prescriptions of national authorities.

H1 Items of clothing and equipment to be weighed shall be arranged on a rack. After being saturated in water the items shall be allowed to drain freely for one minute before being weighed. The rack must allow the items to hang as they would hang from clothes hangers, so as to allow the water to drain freely. Pockets that have drain-holes that cannot be closed shall be empty, but pockets or items that can hold water shall be full.

H2 When the weight recorded exceeds the amount permitted, the competitor may rearrange the items on the rack and the member of the technical committee in charge shall again soak and weigh them. This procedure may be repeated a second time if the weight still exceeds the amount permitted.

H3 A competitor wearing a dry suit may choose an alternative means of weighing the items.

(a) The dry suit and items of clothing and equipment that are worn outside the dry suit shall be weighed as described above.

(b) Clothing worn underneath the dry suit shall be weighed as worn while *racing*, without draining.

(c) The two weights shall be added together.

APPENDIX J
NOTICE OF RACE AND SAILING INSTRUCTIONS

See rules 89.2 and 90.2. In this appendix, the term 'race' includes a regatta or other series of races.

Care should be taken to ensure that there is no conflict between a rule in the notice of race and a rule in the sailing instructions.

J1 NOTICE OF RACE CONTENTS

J1.1 The notice of race shall include the following information:

(1) the title, place and dates of the race and name of the organizing authority;

(2) that the race will be governed by the *rules* as defined in *The Racing Rules of Sailing*;

(3) a list of any other documents that will govern the event (for example, *The Equipment Rules of Sailing*, to the extent that they apply), stating where or how each document or a copy of it may be seen;

(4) the classes to race, any handicap or rating system that will be used and the classes to which it will apply, conditions of entry and any restrictions on entries;

(5) the times of registration and warning signals for the practice race, if one is scheduled, and the first race, and succeeding races if known.

J1.2 The notice of race shall include any of the following that will apply and that would help competitors decide whether to attend the event or that conveys other information they will need before the sailing instructions become available:

(1) changes to the racing rules permitted by rule 86, referring specifically to each rule and stating the change (also, if rule 86.2 applies, include the statement from World Sailing authorizing the change);

(2) that boats will be required to display advertising chosen and supplied by the organizing authority (see rule 80 and World Sailing Regulation 20, Advertising Code) and other information related to Regulation 20;

(3) any classification requirements that some or all competitors must satisfy (see rule 79 and World Sailing Regulation 22, Sailor Classification Code);

(4) for an event where entries from other countries are expected, any national prescriptions that may require advance preparation (see rule 88);

(5) the procedures for registration or entry, including fees and any closing dates;

(6) an entry form, to be signed by the boat's owner or owner's representative, containing words such as 'I agree to be bound by *The Racing Rules of Sailing* and by all other *rules* that govern this event.';

(7) times or procedures for equipment inspection or event measurement, or requirements for measurement or

rating certificates;

(8) the time and place at which the sailing instructions will be available;

(9) changes to class rules, as permitted under rule 87, referring specifically to each rule and stating the change;

(10) the courses to be sailed;

(11) the time after which no warning signal will be made on the last scheduled day of racing;

(12) the penalty for breaking a rule of Part 2, other than the Two-Turns Penalty;

(13) denial of the right of appeal, subject to rule 70.5;

(14) the scoring system, if different from the Low Point System in Appendix A, included by reference to class rules or other *rules* governing the event. State the number of races scheduled and the minimum number that must be completed to constitute a series;

(15) for chartered or loaned boats, whether rule G3 applies;

(16) prizes.

J2   SAILING INSTRUCTION CONTENTS

J2.1 The sailing instructions shall include the following information:

(1) that the race will be governed by the *rules* as defined in *The Racing Rules of Sailing*;

(2) a list of any other documents that will govern the event (for example, *The Equipment Rules of Sailing*, to the extent that they apply);

(3) the schedule of races, the classes to race and times of warning signals for each class;

(4) the course(s) to be sailed, or a list of *marks* from which the course will be selected and, if relevant, how courses will be signalled;

(5) descriptions of *marks*, including starting and finishing *marks*, stating the order in which *marks* are to be passed and the side on which each is to be left and identifying all rounding *marks* (see rule 28.2);

(6) descriptions of the starting and finishing lines, class flags and any special signals to be used;

(7) the time limit, if any, for *finishing*;

(8) the handicap or rating system to be used, if any, and the classes to which it will apply;

(9) unless stated in the notice of race, the scoring system, if different from the Low Point System in Appendix A, included by reference to class rules or other *rules* governing the event, or stated in full. State the number of races scheduled and the minimum number that must be completed to constitute a series;

(10) unless stated in the notice of race, location(s) of official notice board(s) or address of online notice board.

J2.2 The sailing instructions shall include those of the following that will apply:

(1) that boats will be required to display advertising chosen and supplied by the organizing authority (see rule 80 and World Sailing Regulation 20, Advertising Code) and other information related to Regulation 20;

(2) replacement of the rules of Part 2 with the right-of-way rules of the *International Regulations for Preventing Collisions at Sea* or other government right-of-way rules, the time(s) or place(s) they will apply, and any night signals to be used by the race committee;

(3) changes to the racing rules permitted by rule 86, referring specifically to each rule and stating the change (also, if rule 86.2 applies, include the statement from World Sailing authorizing the change);

(4) changes to the national prescriptions (see rule 88.2);

(5) prescriptions that will apply if boats will pass through the waters of more than one national authority while *racing*, and when they will apply (see rule 88.1);

(6) when appropriate, at an event where entries from other countries are expected, a copy in English of the national prescriptions that will apply;

(7) changes to class rules, as permitted under rule 87, referring specifically to each rule and stating the change;

(8) restrictions controlling changes to boats when supplied by the organizing authority;

(9) unless included in the notice of race, times or procedures for equipment inspection or event measurement;

(10) procedure for changing the sailing instructions;

(11) procedure for giving oral changes to the sailing instructions on the water (see rule 90.2(c));

(12) safety requirements, such as requirements and signals for personal flotation devices, check-in at the starting area, and check-out and check-in ashore;

(13) declaration requirements;

(14) signals to be made ashore and location of signal station(s);

(15) the racing area (a chart is recommended);

(16) approximate course length and approximate length of windward legs;

(17) description of any area designated by the race committee to be an *obstruction* (see the definition *Obstruction*);

(18) the time after which no warning signal will be made on the last scheduled day of racing;

(19) the time limit, if any, for the first boat to *finish* and the time limit, if any, for boats other than the first boat to *finish*;

(20) time allowances;

(21) location of the starting area and any restrictions on entering it;

(22) any special procedures or signals for individual or general recall;

(23) boats identifying *mark* locations;

(24) any special procedures or signals for changing a leg of the course (see rule 33);

(25) any special procedures for shortening the course or for *finishing* a shortened course;

(26) restrictions on use of support boats, plastic pools, radios, etc.; on trash disposal; on hauling out; and on outside assistance provided to a boat that is not *racing*;

(27) the penalty for breaking a rule of Part 2, other than the Two-Turns Penalty;

(28) whether Appendix P will apply;

(29) when and under what circumstances propulsion is permitted under rule 42.3(i);

(30) time limits, place of hearings, and special procedures for *protests*, requests for redress or requests for reopening;

(31) if rule N1.4(b) will apply, the time limit for requesting a hearing under that rule;

(32) denial of the right of appeal, subject to rule 70.5;

(33) when required by rule 70.3, the national authority to which appeals and requests may be sent;

(34) the national authority's approval of the appointment of an international jury, when required under rule 91(b);

(35) substitution of competitors;

(36) the minimum number of boats appearing in the starting area required for a race to be started;

(37) when and where races *postponed* or *abandoned* for the day will be sailed;

(38) tides and currents;

(39) prizes;

(40) other commitments of the race committee and obligations of boats.

APPENDIX K
NOTICE OF RACE GUIDE

This guide provides a notice of race designed primarily for major championship regattas for one or more classes. It therefore will be particularly useful for world, continental and national championships and other events of similar importance. It can be downloaded from the World Sailing website as a basic text for producing a notice of race for any particular event.

The guide can also be useful for other events. However, for such events some of the paragraphs will be unnecessary or undesirable. Organizing authorities should therefore be careful in making their choices.

This guide relates closely to Appendix L, Sailing Instructions Guide, and its expanded version Appendix LE on the World Sailing website, the introduction to which contains principles that also apply to a notice of race.

Rule references within the notice of race use RRS, NoR and SI to denote the source of the rule. 'RRS x' is a rule in The Racing Rules of Sailing. 'NoR x' is a rule in the notice of race, and 'SI x' is a rule in the sailing instructions.

To use this guide, first review rule J1 and decide which paragraphs will be needed. Paragraphs that are required by rule J1.1 are marked with an asterisk (*). Delete all inapplicable or unnecessary paragraphs. Select the version preferred where there is a choice. Follow the directions in the left margin to fill in the spaces where a solid line (_____) appears and select the preferred wording if a choice or option is shown in brackets ([. . .]).

After deleting unused paragraphs, renumber all paragraphs in sequential order. Be sure that paragraph numbers are correct where one paragraph refers to another.

Care should be taken to ensure that there is no conflict between a rule in the notice of race and a rule in the sailing instructions.

If the notice of race is made available electronically, printed copies should be provided on request.

The items listed below, when applicable, should be distributed with the notice of race, but should not be included as numbered paragraphs in the notice.

1   An entry form, to be signed by the boat's owner or owner's representative, containing words such as 'I agree to be bound by The Racing Rules of Sailing and by all other rules that govern this event.'

2   For an event where entries from other countries are expected, the applicable national prescriptions in English.

3   List of sponsors, if appropriate.

4   Lodging and camping information.

5   Description of meal facilities.

6   Race committee and protest committee members.

7   Special mooring or storage requirements.

8   Sail and boat repair facilities and ship's chandlers.

9   Availability of chartered or loaned boats and whether rule G3 will apply.

On separate lines, insert the full name of the regatta, the inclusive dates from equipment inspection, event measurement or the practice race until the final race or closing ceremony, the name of the organizing authority, and the city and country.

_____
_____
_____
_____

NOTICE OF RACE

The notation '[DP]' in a rule in the NoR means that the penalty for a breach of that rule may, at the discretion of the protest committee, be less than disqualification.

1   RULES

1.1*   The regatta will be governed by the rules as defined in *The Racing Rules of Sailing*.

Use the first sentence if appropriate. Insert the name. List by number and title the prescriptions that will not apply (see RRS 88). Use the second sentence if it applies and if entries from other countries are expected, and state the relevant prescriptions in full.

1.2   [The following prescriptions of the _____ national authority will not apply: _____.] [The prescriptions that may require advance preparation are stated in full below.]

(OR)

Use if appropriate, but only if the national authority for the venue of the event has not adopted a prescription to RRS 88.

1.2   No national prescriptions will apply.

List by name any other documents that govern the event; for example, The Equipment Rules of Sailing, to the extent that they apply.

1.3*   _____ will apply.

See RRS 86. Insert the rule number(s) and summarize the changes.

1.4   Racing rule(s) _____ will be changed as follows: _____. The changes will appear in full in the sailing instructions. The sailing instructions may also change other racing rules.

(OR)

See RRS 86. Either insert here the rule number(s) and state the changes, or, if not using this NoR, do the same in each NoR that changes a racing rule.

1.4   Racing rule(s) _____ will be changed as follows: _____.

Insert the rule number(s) and class name. Make a separate statement for the rules of each class.

1.5   Under RRS 87, rule(s) _____ of the _____ class rules [will not apply] [is (are) changed as follows: _____].

1.6   If there is a conflict between languages the English text will take precedence.

Use only if RRS Appendix S, Standard Sailing Instructions, will be used. Insert the location.

1.7   The sailing instructions will consist of the instructions in RRS Appendix S, Standard Sailing Instructions, and supplementary sailing instructions that will be on the official notice board located at _____.

	2	**ADVERTISING**
See World Sailing Regulation 20, Advertising Code. Include other applicable information related to Regulation 20.	**2.1**	Competitor advertising will be restricted as follows: _____.
See World Sailing Regulation 20.4.	**2.2**	Boats [shall] [may be required to] display advertising chosen and supplied by the organizing authority. If this rule is broken, World Sailing Regulation 20.9.2 applies. [DP]

	3*	**ELIGIBILITY AND ENTRY**
Insert the class(es).	**3.1**	The regatta is open to all boats of the _____ class(es).
	(OR)	
Insert the class(es) and eligibility requirements.	**3.1**	The regatta is open to boats of the _____ class(es) that _____.
Insert the postal, fax and email addresses and entry closing date.	**3.2**	Eligible boats may enter by completing the attached form and sending it, together with the required fee, to _____ by _____.
Insert any conditions.	**3.3**	Late entries will be accepted under the following conditions: _____.
Insert any restrictions.	**3.4**	The following restrictions on the number of boats apply: _____.

	4	**CLASSIFICATION**
Insert any requirements.		The following classification requirements will apply (see RRS 79): _____.

	5	**FEES**
Insert all required fees for racing.	**5.1**	Required fees are as follows:
		Class *Fee*
		_____ _____
		_____ _____
		_____ _____
Insert optional fees (for example, for social events).	**5.2**	Other fees:
		_____
		_____

	6	**QUALIFYING SERIES AND FINAL SERIES**
Use only when a class is divided into fleets racing a qualifying series and a final series.		The regatta will consist of a qualifying series and a final series.

	7	**SCHEDULE**
Insert the day, date and times.	**7.1***	Registration:
		Day and date _____
		From _____ To _____
Insert the day, date and times.	**7.2**	Equipment inspection and event measurement:
		Day and date _____
		From _____ To _____

Revise as desired and insert the dates and classes. Include a practice race if any. When the series consists of qualifying races and final races, specify them. The schedule can also be given in an attachment.	**7.3***		

7.3* Dates of racing:

Date	Class _____	Class_____
_____	racing	racing
_____	racing	reserve day
_____	reserve day	racing
_____	racing	racing
_____	racing	racing

Insert the classes and numbers.

7.4 Number of races:

Class	Number	Races per day
_____	_____	_____
_____	_____	_____

Insert the time.

7.5* The scheduled time of the warning signal for the [practice race] [first race] [each day] is _____.

Use when it would be helpful to competitors to know this time before the event. Insert the time.

7.6 On the last scheduled day of racing no warning signal will be made after _____.

8 MEASUREMENT

8.1 Each boat shall produce a valid [measurement] [rating] certificate.

(OR)

List the equipment with appropriate references to the class rules.

8.1 Each boat shall produce a valid [measurement] [rating] certificate. In addition the following equipment [may] [will] be inspected or measured: _____.

Insert the time(s).

8.2 A boat shall comply with RRS 78.1 at _____.

9 SAILING INSTRUCTIONS

Insert the time, date and location.

The sailing instructions will be available after _____ on _____ at _____.

10 VENUE

Insert a number or letter. Provide a marked map with driving instructions.

10.1 Attachment _____ shows the location of the regatta harbour.

Insert a number or letter. Provide a marked map or chart.

10.2 Attachment _____ shows the location of the racing areas.

11 THE COURSES

Include the description.

The courses to be sailed will be as follows: _____.

(OR)

Insert a number or letter. A method of illustrating various courses is shown in Addendum A of Appendix L or LE. Insert the course length if applicable.

The diagrams in Attachment _____ show the courses, including the approximate angles between legs, the order in which marks are to be passed, and the side on which each mark is to be left. [The approximate course length will be _____.]

	12	**PENALTY SYSTEM**
Include paragraph 12.1 only when the Two-Turns Penalty will not be used. Insert the number of places or describe the penalties.	**12.1** **(OR)**	The Scoring Penalty, RRS 44.3, will apply. The penalty will be _____ places.
	12.1	The penalties are as follows: _____.
Insert the class(es).	**12.2**	For the _____ class(es) RRS 44.1 is changed so that the Two-Turns Penalty is replaced by the One-Turn Penalty.
Include only if the protest committee is an international jury or another provision of RRS 70.5 applies.	**12.3**	Decisions of the [protest committee] [international jury] will be final as provided in RRS 70.5.

	13	**SCORING**
Include only if the Low Point System of Appendix A will not be used. Describe the system.	**13.1**	The scoring system is as follows: _____.
Insert the number.	**13.2**	_____ races are required to be completed to constitute a series.
Insert the numbers throughout.	**13.3**	(a) When fewer than _____ races have been completed, a boat's series score will be the total of her race scores.
		(b) When from _____ to _____ races have been completed, a boat's series score will be the total of her race scores excluding her worst score.
		(c) When _____ or more races have been completed, a boat's series score will be the total of her race scores excluding her two worst scores.

	14	**SUPPORT BOATS**
Insert the identification markings. National letters are suggested for international events.		Support boats shall be marked with _____. [DP]

	15	**BERTHING**
		Boats shall be kept in their assigned places while they are in the [boat park] [harbour]. [DP]

	16	**HAUL-OUT RESTRICTIONS**
		Keelboats shall not be hauled out during the regatta except with and according to the terms of prior written permission of the race committee. [DP]

	17	**DIVING EQUIPMENT AND PLASTIC POOLS**
		Underwater breathing apparatus and plastic pools or their equivalent shall not be used around keelboats between the preparatory signal of the first race and the end of the regatta. [DP]

	18	**RADIO COMMUNICATION**
Insert any alternative text that applies. Describe any radio communication bands or frequencies that will be used or allowed.		Except in an emergency, a boat that is racing shall not make voice or data transmissions and shall not receive voice or data communication that is not available to all boats. [DP]

	19	**PRIZES**
If perpetual trophies will be awarded state their complete names.		Prizes will be given as follows: _____.
	20	**DISCLAIMER OF LIABILITY**
The laws applicable to the venue in which the event is held may limit disclaimers. Any disclaimer should be drafted to comply with those laws.		Competitors participate in the regatta entirely at their own risk. See RRS 4, Decision to Race. The organizing authority will not accept any liability for material damage or personal injury or death sustained in conjunction with or prior to, during, or after the regatta.
	21	**INSURANCE**
Insert the currency and amount.		Each participating boat shall be insured with valid third-party liability insurance with a minimum cover of _____ per incident or the equivalent.
	22	**FURTHER INFORMATION**
Insert necessary contact information.		For further information please contact _____.

APPENDIX L
SAILING INSTRUCTIONS GUIDE

This guide provides a set of tested sailing instructions designed primarily for major championship regattas for one or more classes. It therefore will be particularly useful for world, continental and national championships and other events of similar importance. The guide can also be useful for other events; however, for such events some of these instructions will be unnecessary or undesirable. Race officers should therefore be careful in making their choices.

An expanded version of the guide, Appendix LE, is available on the World Sailing website. It contains provisions applicable to the largest and most complicated multi-class events, as well as variations on several of the sailing instructions recommended in this appendix. It will be revised from time to time, to reflect advances in race management techniques as they develop, and can be downloaded as a basic text for producing the sailing instructions for any particular event. Appendix L can also be downloaded from the World Sailing website.

The principles on which all sailing instructions should be based are as follows:

1   They should include only two types of statement: the intentions of the race committee and protest committee and the obligations of competitors.

2   They should be concerned only with racing. Information about social events, assignment of moorings, etc., should be provided separately.

3   They should not change the racing rules except when clearly desirable. (When they do so, they must follow rule 86 by referring specifically to the rule being changed and stating the change.)

4   They should not repeat or restate any of the racing rules.

5   They should not repeat themselves.

6   They should be in chronological order; that is, the order in which the competitor will use them.

7   They should, when possible, use words or phrases from the racing rules.

Rule references within the sailing instructions use RRS, SI and NoR to denote the source of the rule. 'RRS x' is a rule in The Racing Rules of Sailing. 'SI x' is a rule in the sailing instructions, and 'NoR x' is a rule in the notice of race.

To use this guide, first review rule J2 and decide which instructions will be needed. Instructions that are required by rule J2.1 are marked with an asterisk (*). Delete all inapplicable or unnecessary instructions. Select the version preferred where there is a choice. Follow the directions in the left margin to fill in the spaces where a solid line (_____) appears and select the preferred wording if a choice or option is shown in brackets ([. . .]).

After deleting unused instructions, renumber all instructions in sequential order. Be sure that instruction numbers are correct where one instruction refers to another.

Care should be taken to ensure that there is no conflict between a rule in the notice of race and a rule in the sailing instructions.

If the sailing instructions are made available electronically, printed copies should be provided on request.

On separate lines, insert the full name of the regatta, the inclusive dates from equipment inspection, event measurement or the practice race until the final race or closing ceremony, the name of the organizing authority, and the city and country.	_____ _____ _____ _____

SAILING INSTRUCTIONS

The notation '[DP]' in a rule in the SI means that the penalty for a breach of that rule may, at the discretion of the protest committee, be less than disqualification.

1   RULES

1.1* The regatta will be governed by the rules as defined in *The Racing Rules of Sailing.*

Use the first sentence if appropriate. Insert the name. List by number and title the prescriptions that will not apply (see RRS 88.2). Use the second sentence if it applies and if entries from other national authorities are expected, and state the prescriptions in full. Include the prescriptions in English when appropriate (see RRS 90.2(b)).

1.2 [The following prescriptions of the _____ national authority will not apply: _____.] [The prescriptions that will apply are stated in full below.]

(OR)

Use if appropriate, but only if the national authority for the venue of the event has not adopted a prescription to RRS 88.

1.2 No national prescriptions will apply.

List by name any other documents that govern the event; for example, The Equipment Rules of Sailing, to the extent that they apply.

1.3* _____ will apply.

See RRS 86. Either insert here the rule number(s) and state the changes, or, if not using this instruction, do the same in each instruction that changes a racing rule.

1.4 Racing rule(s) _____ will be changed as follows: _____.

Insert the rule number(s) and class name. Make a separate statement for the rules of each class.

1.5 Under RRS 87, rule(s) _____ of the _____ class rules [will not apply] [is (are) changed as follows: _____].

1.6 If there is a conflict between languages the English text will take precedence.

2* **NOTICES TO COMPETITORS**

Insert the location(s). If notices are online, state how and where they may be found.

Notices to competitors will be posted on the official notice board(s) located at _____.

3 **CHANGES TO SAILING INSTRUCTIONS**

Change the times if different.

Any change to the sailing instructions will be posted before 0900 on the day it will take effect, except that any change to the schedule of races will be posted by 2000 on the day before it will take effect.

	4	**SIGNALS MADE ASHORE**
Insert the location.	4.1	Signals made ashore will be displayed at _____.
Insert the number of minutes.	4.2	When flag AP is displayed ashore, '1 minute' is replaced with 'not less than _____ minutes' in the race signal AP.
	(OR)	
Insert the number of minutes.	4.2	Flag D with one sound means 'The warning signal will be made not less than _____ minutes after flag D is displayed. [Boats are requested not to leave the harbour until this signal is made.] [Boats shall not leave the harbour until this signal is made. [DP]]'

	5	**SCHEDULE OF RACES**

Revise as desired and insert the dates and classes. Include a practice race if any. When the series consists of qualifying races and final races, specify them. The schedule can also be given in an attachment.

5.1* Dates of racing:

Date	Class _____	Class_____
_____	racing	racing
_____	racing	reserve day
_____	reserve day	racing
_____	racing	racing
_____	racing	racing

Insert the classes and numbers.

5.2* Number of races:

Class	Number	Races per day
_____	_____	_____
_____	_____	_____

One extra race per day may be sailed, provided that no class becomes more than one race ahead of schedule and the change is made according to SI 3.

Insert the time.	**5.3***	The scheduled time of the warning signal for the first race each day is _____.
	5.4	To alert boats that a race or sequence of races will begin soon, the orange starting line flag will be displayed with one sound at least five minutes before a warning signal is made.
Insert the time.	**5.5**	On the last scheduled day of racing no warning signal will be made after _____.

	6*	**CLASS FLAGS**

Insert the classes and names or descriptions of the flags.

Class flags will be:

Class	Flag
_____	_____
_____	_____
_____	_____

	7	**RACING AREAS**
Insert a number or letter.		Attachment _____ shows the location of racing areas.

	8	**THE COURSES**
Insert a number or letter. A method of illustrating various courses is shown in Addendum A. Insert the course length if applicable.	**8.1***	The diagrams in Attachment _____ show the courses, including the approximate angles between legs, the order in which marks are to be passed, and the side on which each mark is to be left. [The approximate course length will be _____.]
	8.2	No later than the warning signal, the race committee signal vessel will display the approximate compass bearing of the first leg.
	8.3	Courses will not be shortened. This changes RRS 32.
Include only when changing positions of marks is impracticable.	**8.4**	Legs of the course will not be changed after the preparatory signal. This changes RRS 33.
	9	**MARKS**
Change the mark numbers as needed and insert the descriptions of the marks.	**9.1***	Marks 1, 2, 3 and 4 will be _____.
Use the second alternative when Marks 4S and 4P form a gate, with Mark 4S to be left to starboard and Mark 4P to port.	**(OR)**	
	9.1*	Marks 1, 2, 3, 4S and 4P will be _____.
	(OR)	
Insert the number or letter used in SI 8.1.	**9.1***	Marks are described in Attachment _____.
Unless it is clear from the course diagrams, list the marks that are rounding marks.	**9.2**	The following marks are rounding marks: _____.
Insert the descriptions of the marks.	**9.3**	New marks, as provided in SI 12.1, will be _____.
Describe the starting and finishing marks: for example, the race committee signal vessel at the starboard end and a buoy at the port end. SI 11.2 will describe the starting line and SI 13 the finishing line.	**9.4***	The starting and finishing marks will be _____.
Include if SI 12.2 is included.	**9.5**	A race committee vessel signalling a change of a leg of the course is a mark as provided in SI 12.2.
	10	**AREAS THAT ARE OBSTRUCTIONS**
Describe each area by its location and any easily recognized details of appearance.		The following areas are designated as obstructions: _____.
	11	**THE START**
Include only if the asterisked option in RRS 26 will be used. Insert the number of minutes.	**11.1**	Races will be started by using RRS 26 with the warning signal made _____ minutes before the starting signal.
	(OR)	
Describe any starting system other than that stated in RRS 26.	**11.1**	Races will be started as follows: _____. This changes RRS 26.
	11.2*	The starting line will be between staffs displaying orange flags on the starting marks.

(OR)

11.2* The starting line will be between a staff displaying an orange flag on the starting mark at the starboard end and the course side of the port-end starting mark.

(OR)

Insert the description.   **11.2*** The starting line will be _____.

11.3 Boats whose warning signal has not been made shall avoid the starting area during the starting sequence for other races. [DP]

Insert the number of minutes.   **11.4** A boat that does not start within _____ minutes after her starting signal will be scored Did Not Start without a hearing. This changes RRS A4 and A5.

Insert the channel number.   **11.5** If any part of a boat's hull, crew or equipment is on the course side of the starting line during the two minutes before her starting signal and she is identified, the race committee will attempt to broadcast her sail number on VHF channel _____. Failure to make a broadcast or to time it accurately will not be grounds for a request for redress. This changes RRS 62.1(a).

12   CHANGE OF THE NEXT LEG OF THE COURSE

12.1 To change the next leg of the course, the race committee will move the original mark (or the finishing line) to a new position.

(OR)

12.1 To change the next leg of the course, the race committee will lay a new mark (or move the finishing line) and remove the original mark as soon as practicable. When in a subsequent change a new mark is replaced, it will be replaced by an original mark.

When SI 12.2 is included, SI 9.5 must also be included. Reverse 'port' and 'starboard' when the mark is to be left to starboard.   **12.2** Except at a gate, boats shall pass between the race committee vessel signalling the change of the next leg and the nearby mark, leaving the mark to port and the race committee vessel to starboard. This changes RRS 28.

13   THE FINISH

13.1* The finishing line will be between staffs displaying orange flags on the finishing marks.

(OR)

13.1* The finishing line will be between a staff displaying an orange flag on the finishing mark at the starboard end and the course side of the port-end finishing mark.

(OR)

Insert the description.   **13.1*** The finishing line will be _____.

13.2 If the race committee is absent when a boat finishes, she should report her finishing time, and her position in relation to nearby boats, to the race committee at the first reasonable opportunity.

	14	**PENALTY SYSTEM**
Include SI 14.1 only when the Two-Turns Penalty will not be used. Insert the number of places or describe the penalties.	**14.1** **(OR)**	The Scoring Penalty, RRS 44.3, will apply. The penalty will be _____ places.
	14.1	The penalties are as follows: _____ .
Insert the class(es).	**14.2**	For the _____ class(es) RRS 44.1 is changed so that the Two-Turns Penalty is replaced by the One-Turn Penalty.
Unless all of Appendix P applies, state any restrictions.	**14.3**	Appendix P will apply [as changed by SI(s) [14.2] [and] [14.4]].
Recommended only for junior events.	**14.4**	RRS P2.3 will not apply and RRS P2.2 is changed so that it will apply to any penalty after the first one.

	15	**TIME LIMITS AND TARGET TIMES**
Insert the classes and times. Omit the Mark 1 time limit and target time if inapplicable.	**15.1***	Time limits and target times are as follows:

Class	Time limit	Mark 1 time limit	Target time
_____	_____	_____	_____
_____	_____	_____	_____
_____	_____	_____	_____

If no boat has passed Mark 1 within the Mark 1 time limit the race will be abandoned. Failure to meet the target time will not be grounds for redress. This changes RRS 62.1(a).

	15.2	Boats failing to finish within _____ after the first boat sails the course and finishes will be scored Did Not Finish without a hearing. This changes RRS 35, A4 and A5.
Insert the time (or different times for different classes).		

	16	**PROTESTS AND REQUESTS FOR REDRESS**
State the location if necessary.	**16.1**	Protest forms are available at the race office[, located at _____]. Protests and requests for redress or reopening shall be delivered there within the appropriate time limit.
Change the time if different.	**16.2**	For each class, the protest time limit is 90 minutes after the last boat has finished the last race of the day or the race committee signals no more racing today, whichever is later.
Change the posting time if different. Insert the protest room location and, if applicable, the time for the first hearing.	**16.3**	Notices will be posted no later than 30 minutes after the protest time limit to inform competitors of hearings in which they are parties or named as witnesses. Hearings will be held in the protest room, located at _____, beginning at [the time posted] [_____].
	16.4	Notices of protests by the race committee, technical committee or protest committee will be posted to inform boats under RRS 61.1(b).
	16.5	A list of boats that, under SI 14.3, have been penalized for breaking RRS 42 will be posted.
	16.6	Breaches of SIs 11.3, 18, 21, 23, 25, 26 and 27 will not be grounds for a protest by a boat. This changes RRS 60.1(a).

	16.7	On the last scheduled day of racing a request for redress based on a protest committee decision shall be delivered no later than 30 minutes after the decision was posted. This changes RRS 62.2.
Include only if RRS 70.5 applies.	**16.8**	Decisions of the [protest committee] [international jury] will be final as provided in RRS 70.5.

17   SCORING

Include only if the Low Point System of Appendix A will not be used. Describe the system.	**17.1**	The scoring system is as follows: _____.
Insert the number.	**17.2**	_____ races are required to be completed to constitute a series.
Insert the numbers throughout.	**17.3**	(a) When fewer than _____ races have been completed, a boat's series score will be the total of her race scores.
		(b) When from _____ to _____ races have been completed, a boat's series score will be the total of her race scores excluding her worst score.
		(c) When _____ or more races have been completed, a boat's series score will be the total of her race scores excluding her two worst scores.

18   SAFETY REGULATIONS

Insert the procedure for check-out and check-in.	**18.1**	Check-Out and Check-In: _____. [DP]
	18.2	A boat that retires from a race shall notify the race committee as soon as possible. [DP]

19   REPLACEMENT OF CREW OR EQUIPMENT

	19.1	Substitution of competitors will not be allowed without prior written approval of the [race committee] [protest committee]. [DP]
	19.2	Substitution of damaged or lost equipment will not be allowed unless authorized by the [race committee] [protest committee]. Requests for substitution shall be made to the committee at the first reasonable opportunity. [DP]

20   EQUIPMENT AND MEASUREMENT CHECKS

Insert the time(s).	On the water, a boat can be instructed by a member of the race committee or the technical committee to proceed immediately to a designated area for inspection. Ashore, equipment may be inspected or measured at times specified in the class rules, the notice of race, and at the following time(s) _____.

21   EVENT ADVERTISING

See World Sailing Regulation 20.4. Insert necessary information on the display of event advertising material.	Boats shall display event advertising supplied by the organizing authority as follows: _____. If this rule is broken, World Sailing Regulation 20.9.2 applies. [DP]

22   OFFICIAL BOATS

Insert the descriptions. If appropriate, use different identification markings for boats performing different duties.	Official boats will be marked as follows: _____.

23   SUPPORT BOATS

23.1 Team leaders, coaches and other support persons shall stay outside areas where boats are racing from the time of the preparatory signal for the first class to start until all boats have finished or retired or the race committee signals a postponement, general recall or abandonment. [DP]

Insert the identification markings. National   **23.2** Support boats shall be marked with _____. [DP]
letters are suggested for international events.

24   TRASH DISPOSAL

Trash may be placed aboard support or official boats.

25   HAUL-OUT RESTRICTIONS

Keelboats shall not be hauled out during the regatta except with and according to the terms of prior written permission of the race committee. [DP]

26   DIVING EQUIPMENT AND PLASTIC POOLS

Underwater breathing apparatus and plastic pools or their equivalent shall not be used around keelboats between the preparatory signal of the first race and the end of the regatta. [DP]

27   RADIO COMMUNICATION

Insert any alternative text that applies.   Except in an emergency, a boat that is racing shall not make voice or data
Describe any radio communication bands or   transmissions and shall not receive voice or data communication that is not
frequencies that will be used or allowed.   available to all boats. [DP]

28   PRIZES

If perpetual trophies will be awarded state their   Prizes will be given as follows: _____.
complete names.

29   DISCLAIMER OF LIABILITY

The laws applicable to the venue in which   Competitors participate in the regatta entirely at their own risk. See RRS 4,
the event is held may limit disclaimers. Any   Decision to Race. The organizing authority will not accept any liability for material
disclaimer should be drafted to comply with   damage or personal injury or death sustained in conjunction with or prior to,
those laws.   during, or after the regatta.

30   INSURANCE

Insert the currency and amount.   Each participating boat shall be insured with valid third-party liability insurance with
                                                  a minimum cover of _____ per incident or the equivalent.

ADDENDUM A

ILLUSTRATING THE COURSE

Shown here are diagrams of course shapes. The boat's track is represented by a discontinuous line so that each diagram can describe courses with different numbers of laps. If more than one course may be used for a class, state how each particular course will be signalled.

A Windward-Leeward Course

Start – 1 – 2 – 1 – 2 – Finish

Options for this course include

(1)   increasing or decreasing the number of laps,

(2)   deleting the last windward leg,

(3)   using a gate instead of a leeward mark,

(4)   using an offset mark at the windward mark, and

(5)   using the leeward and windward marks as starting and finishing marks.

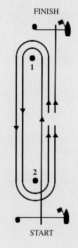

A Triangle-Windward-Leeward Course

Start – 1 – 2 – 3 – 1 – 3 – Finish

Options for this course include

(1)   increasing or decreasing the number of laps,

(2)   deleting the last windward leg,

(3)   varying the interior angles of the triangle (45°–90°– 45° and 60°–60°–60° are common),

(4)   using a gate instead of a leeward mark for downwind legs,

(5)   using an offset mark at the beginning of downwind legs, and

(6)   using the leeward and windward marks as starting and finishing marks.

Be sure to specify the interior angle at each mark.

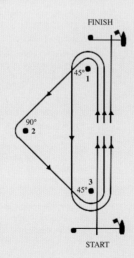

Trapezoid Courses

Start – 1 – 2 – 3 – 2 – 3 – Finish

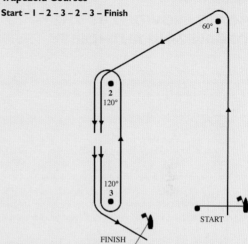

Start – 1 – 4 – 1 – 2 – 3 – Finish

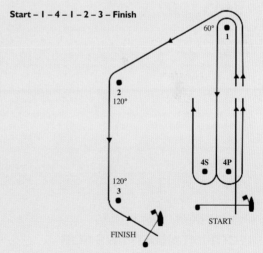

Options for these courses include

(1)   adding additional legs,

(2)   replacing the gate shown by a single mark, or using a gate also in the outer loop,

(3)   varying the interior angles of the reaching legs,

(4)   using an offset mark at the beginning of downwind legs, and

(5)   finishing boats upwind rather than on a reach.

Be sure to specify the interior angle of each reaching leg.

ADDENDUM B

BOATS PROVIDED BY THE ORGANIZING AUTHORITY

The following sailing instruction is recommended when all boats will be provided by the organizing authority. It can be changed to suit the circumstances. When used, it should be inserted after SI 3.

4   BOATS

4.1   Boats will be provided for all competitors, who shall not modify them or cause them to be modified in any way except that

(a)   a compass may be tied or taped to the hull or spars;

(b)   wind indicators, including yarn or thread, may be tied or taped anywhere on the boat;

(c)   hulls, centreboards and rudders may be cleaned, but only with water;

(d)   adhesive tape may be used anywhere above the water line; and

(e)   all fittings or equipment designed to be adjusted may be adjusted, provided that the class rules are complied with.

4.2   All equipment provided with the boat for sailing purposes shall be in the boat while afloat.

4.3   The penalty for not complying with one of the above instructions will be disqualification from all races sailed in which the instruction was broken.

4.4   Competitors shall report any damage or loss of equipment, however slight, to the organizing authority's representative immediately after securing the boat ashore. The penalty for breaking this instruction, unless the protest committee is satisfied that the competitor made a determined effort to comply, will be disqualification from the race most recently sailed.

4.5   Class rules requiring competitors to be members of the class association will not apply.

APPENDIX M

RECOMMENDATIONS FOR PROTEST COMMITTEES

This appendix is advisory only; in some circumstances changing these procedures may be advisable. It is addressed primarily to protest committee chairmen but may also help judges, protest committee secretaries, race committees and others connected with protest and redress hearings.

In a protest or redress hearing, the protest committee should weigh all testimony with equal care; should recognize that honest testimony can vary, and even be in conflict, as a result of different observations and recollections; should resolve such differences as best it can; should recognize that no boat or competitor is guilty until a breach of a *rule* has been established to the satisfaction of the protest committee; and should keep an open mind until all the evidence has been heard as to whether a boat or competitor has broken a *rule*.

M1   PRELIMINARIES (may be performed by race office staff)

•   Receive the *protest* or request for redress.

•   Note on the form the time the *protest* or request is delivered and the protest time limit.

•   Inform each *party*, and the race committee when necessary, when and where the hearing will be held.

M2   BEFORE THE HEARING

M2.1 Make sure that

•   each *party* has a copy of or the opportunity to read the *protest* or request for redress and has had reasonable time to prepare for the hearing.

•   only one person from each boat (or *party*) is present unless an interpreter is needed.

•   all boats and people involved are represented. If they are not, however, the committee may proceed under rule 63.3(b).

•   boats' representatives were on board when required (rule 63.3(a)). When the *parties* were in different races, both organizing authorities must accept the composition of the protest committee (rule 63.8). In a *protest* concerning class rules, obtain the current class rules and identify the authority responsible for interpreting them (rule 64.3(b)).

M2.2 Determine if any members of the protest committee saw the incident. If so, require each of them to state that fact in the presence of the *parties* (rule 63.6).

M2.3 Assess *conflicts of interest*.

•   Ensure that all protest committee members declare any possible *conflicts of interest*. At major events this will often be a formal written declaration made before the event starts that will be kept with the protest committee records.

•   At the start of any hearing, ensure that the *parties* are aware of any *conflicts of interest* of protest committee members. Ask the *parties* if they consent to the members. If a *party* does not object as soon as possible after a *conflict of interest* has been declared, the protest committee may take this as consent to proceed and should record it.

•   If a *party* objects to a member, the remainder of the protest committee members need to assess whether the *conflict of interest* is significant. The assessment will consider the level of the event, the level of the conflict and the perception of fairness. It may be acceptable to balance conflicts between protest committee members. Guidance may be found on the World Sailing website.

Record the decision and the grounds for that decision.

- In cases of doubt it may be preferable to proceed with a smaller protest committee. Except for hearings under rule 69, there is no minimum number of protest committee members required.

- When a request for redress is made under rule 62.1(a) and is based on an improper action or omission of a body other than the protest committee, a member of that body should not be a member of the protest committee.

M3   THE HEARING

M3.1 Check the validity of the *protest* or request for redress.

- Are the contents adequate (rule 61.2 or 62)?

- Was it delivered in time? If not, is there good reason to extend the time limit (rule 61.3 or 62.2)?

- When required, was the protestor involved in or a witness to the incident (rule 60.1(a))?

- When necessary, was 'Protest' hailed and, if required, a red flag displayed correctly (rule 61.1(a))?

- When the flag or hail was not necessary, was the protestee informed?

- Decide whether the *protest* or request for redress is valid (rule 63.5).

- Once the validity of the *protest* or request has been determined, do not let the subject be introduced again unless truly new evidence is available.

M3.2 Take the evidence (rule 63.6).

- Ask the protestor and then the protestee to tell their stories. Then allow them to question one another. In a redress matter, ask the *party* to state the request.

- Invite questions from protest committee members.

- Make sure you know what facts each *party* is alleging before calling any witnesses. Their stories may be different.

- Allow anyone, including a boat's crew, to give evidence. It is the *party* who normally decides which witnesses to call, although the protest committee may also call witnesses (rule 63.6). The question asked by a *party* 'Would you like to hear N?' is best answered by 'It is your choice.'

- Call each *party*'s witnesses (and the protest committee's if any) one by one. Limit *parties* to questioning the witness(es) (they may wander into general statements).

- Invite the protestee to question the protestor's witness first (and vice versa). This prevents the protestor from leading his witness from the beginning.

- Allow members of the protest committee who saw the incident to give evidence (rule 63.6), but only while the *parties* are present. Members who give evidence may be questioned, should take care to relate all they know about the incident that could affect the decision, and may remain on the protest committee (rule 63.3(a)).

- Try to prevent leading questions or hearsay evidence, but if that is impossible discount the evidence so obtained.

- Accept written evidence from a witness who is not available to be questioned only if all *parties* agree. In doing so they forego their rights to question that witness (rule 63.6).

- Ask one member of the committee to note down evidence, particularly times, distances, speeds, etc.

- Invite first the protestor and then the protestee to make a final statement of her case, particularly on any application or interpretation of the *rules*.

M3.3 Find the facts (rule 63.6).

- Write down the facts; resolve doubts one way or the other.

- Call back *parties* for more questions if necessary.

- When appropriate, draw a diagram of the incident using the facts you have found.

M3.4 Decide the *protest* or request for redress (rule 64).

- Base the decision on the facts found (if you cannot, find some more facts).

- In redress cases, make sure that no further evidence is needed from boats that will be affected by the decision.

M3.5 Inform the *parties* (rule 65).

- Recall the *parties* and read them the facts found, conclusions and *rules* that apply, and the decision. When time presses it is permissible to read the decision and give the details later.

- Give any *party* a copy of the decision on request. File the *protest* or request for redress with the committee records.

M4   REOPENING A HEARING (rule 66)

M4.1 When a *party*, within the time limit, has asked for a hearing to be reopened, hear the *party* making the request, look at any video, etc., and decide whether there is any significant new evidence that might lead you to change your decision. Decide whether your interpretation of the *rules* may have been wrong; be open-minded as to whether you have made a mistake. If none of these applies refuse to reopen; otherwise schedule a hearing.

M4.2 Evidence is 'new'

- if it was not reasonably possible for the *party* asking for the reopening to have discovered the evidence before the original hearing,

- if the protest committee is satisfied that before the original hearing the evidence was diligently but unsuccessfully sought by the *party* asking for the reopening, or

- if the protest committee learns from any source that the evidence was not available to the *parties* at the time of the original hearing.

M5   MISCONDUCT (rule 69)

M5.1 An action under this rule is not a *protest*, but the protest committee gives its allegations in writing to the competitor before the hearing. The hearing is conducted under rules similar to those governing a protest hearing but the protest committee must have at least three members (rule 69.2(a)). Use the greatest care to protect the competitor's rights.

M5.2 A competitor or a boat cannot protest under rule 69, but the protest form of a competitor who tries to do so may be accepted as a report to the protest committee, which can then decide whether or not to call a hearing.

M5.3 Unless World Sailing has appointed a person for the role, the protest committee may appoint a person to present the allegation. This person might be a race official, the person making the allegation or other appropriate person. When no reasonable alternative person is available, a person who was appointed as a member of the protest committee may present the allegation.

M5.4 When it is desirable to call a hearing under rule 69 as a result of a Part 2 incident, it is important to hear any boat-vs.-boat *protest* in the normal way, deciding which boat, if any, broke which *rule*, before proceeding against the competitor under rule 69.

M5.5 Although action under rule 69 is taken against a competitor, boat owner or *support person*, and not a boat, a boat may also be penalized (rules 69.2(h)(2) and 64.4).

M5.6 When a protest committee upholds a rule 69 allegation it will need to consider if it is appropriate to report to either a national authority or World Sailing. Guidance on when to report may be found in the World Sailing Case Book. When the protest committee does make a report it may recommend whether or not further action should be taken.

M5.7 Unless the right of appeal is denied in accordance with rule 70.5, a *party* to a rule 69 hearing may appeal the decision of the protest committee.

M5.8 Further guidance for protest committees about misconduct may be found on the World Sailing website.

M6   APPEALS (rule 70 and Appendix R)

When decisions can be appealed,

- retain the papers relevant to the hearing so that the information can easily be used for an appeal. Is there a diagram endorsed or prepared by the protest committee? Are the facts found sufficient? (Example: Was there an *overlap*? Yes or No. 'Perhaps' is not a fact found.) Are the names of the protest committee members and other important information on the form?

- comments by the protest committee on any appeal should enable the appeals committee to picture the whole incident clearly; the appeals committee knows nothing about the situation.

M7   PHOTOGRAPHIC EVIDENCE

Photographs and videos can sometimes provide useful evidence but protest committees should recognize their limitations and note the following points:

- The *party* producing the photographic evidence is responsible for arranging the viewing.

- View the video several times to extract all the information from it.

- The depth perception of any single-lens camera is very poor; with a telephoto lens it is non-existent. When the camera views two *overlapped* boats at right angles to their course, it is impossible to assess the distance between them. When the camera views them head on, it is impossible to see whether an *overlap* exists unless it is substantial.

- Ask the following questions:

  - Where was the camera in relation to the boats?

  - Was the camera's platform moving? If so in what direction and how fast?

  - Is the angle changing as the boats approach the critical point? Fast panning causes radical change.

  - Did the camera have an unrestricted view throughout?

APPENDIX N

INTERNATIONAL JURIES

See rules 70.5 and 91(b). This appendix shall not be changed by the notice of race, sailing instructions or national prescriptions.

N1   COMPOSITION, APPOINTMENT AND ORGANIZATION

N1.1 An international jury shall be composed of experienced sailors with excellent knowledge of the racing rules and extensive protest committee experience. It shall be independent of and have no members from the race committee, and be appointed by the organizing authority, subject to approval by the national authority if required (see rule 91(b)), or by World Sailing under rule 89.2(c).

N1.2 The jury shall consist of a chairman, a vice chairman if desired, and other members for a total of at least five. A majority shall be International Judges.

N1.3 No more than two members (three, in Groups M, N and Q) shall be from the same national authority.

N1.4 (a)   The chairman of a jury may appoint one or more panels composed in compliance with rules N1.1, N1.2 and N1.3. This can be done even if the full jury is not composed in compliance with these rules.

(b)   The chairman of a jury may appoint panels of at least three members each, of which the majority shall be International Judges. Members of each panel shall be from at least three different national authorities except in Groups M, N and Q, where they shall be from at least two different national authorities. If dissatisfied with a panel's decision, a *party* is entitled to a hearing by a panel composed in compliance with rules N1.1, N1.2 and N1.3, except concerning the facts found, if requested within the time limit specified in the sailing instructions.

N1.5 When a full jury, or a panel, has fewer than five members, because of illness or emergency, and no qualified replacements are available, it remains properly constituted if it consists of at least three members and if at least two of them are International Judges. When there are three or four members they shall be from at least three different national authorities except in Groups M, N and Q, where they shall be from at least two different national authorities.

N1.6 When it is considered desirable that some members not participate in discussing and deciding a *protest* or request for redress, and no qualified replacements are available, the jury or panel remains properly constituted if at least three members remain and at least two of them are International Judges.

N1.7 In exception to rules N1.1 and N1.2, World Sailing may in limited circumstances (see World Sailing Regulation 25.8.13) authorize an international jury consisting of a total of only three members. All members shall be International Judges. The members shall be from three different national authorities (two, in Groups M, N and Q). The authorization shall be stated in a letter of approval to the organizing authority and in the notice of race and sailing instructions, and the letter shall be posted on the event's official notice board.

N1.8 When the national authority's approval is required for the appointment of an international jury (see rule 91(b)), notice of its approval shall be included in the sailing instructions or be posted on the official notice board.

N1.9 If the jury or a panel acts while not properly constituted, its decisions may be appealed.

N2 RESPONSIBILITIES

N2.1 An international jury is responsible for hearing and deciding all *protests*, requests for redress and other matters arising under the rules of Part 5. When asked by the organizing authority or the race committee, it shall advise and assist them on any matter directly affecting the fairness of the competition.

N2.2 Unless the organizing authority directs otherwise, the jury shall decide

(a) questions of eligibility, measurement or rating certificates; and

(b) whether to authorize the substitution of competitors, boats or equipment when a *rule* requires such a decision.

N2.3 The jury shall also decide matters referred to it by the organizing authority or the race committee.

N3 PROCEDURES

N3.1 Decisions of the jury, or of a panel, shall be made by a simple majority vote of all members. When there is an equal division of votes cast, the chairman of the meeting may cast an additional vote.

N3.2 Members shall not be regarded as having a significant *conflict of interest* (see rule 63.4) by reason of their nationality, club membership or similar. When otherwise considering a significant *conflict of interest* as required by rule 63.4, considerable weight must be given to the fact that decisions of an international jury cannot be appealed and this may affect the perception of fairness and lower the level of conflict that is significant. In case of doubt, the hearing should proceed as permitted by rule N1.6.

N3.3 If a panel fails to agree on a decision it may adjourn, in which case the chairman shall refer the matter to a properly constituted panel with as many members as possible, which may be the full jury.

N4 MISCONDUCT (Rule 69)

N4.1 World Sailing Regulation 35, Disciplinary Code, contains procedures that apply to specific international events with regard to the appointment of a person to conduct any investigation. These procedures override any conflicting provision of this appendix.

N4.2 A person shall be responsible for presenting to the hearing panel any allegations of misconduct under rule 69. This person shall not be a member of the hearing panel but may be a member of the jury. Such a person shall be required to make full disclosure of all material that may come into his possession in the course of his investigation to the person subject to allegations of a breach of rule 69.

N4.3 Prior to a hearing, the hearing panel, to the extent practically possible, shall not act as an investigator of any allegations made under rule 69. However, during the hearing the panel shall be entitled to ask any investigative questions it may see fit.

N4.4 If the panel decides to call a hearing, all material disclosed to the panel in order for them to make that decision must be disclosed to the person subject to the allegations before the hearing begins.

APPENDIX P

SPECIAL PROCEDURES FOR RULE 42

All or part of this appendix applies only if the notice of race or sailing instructions so state.

P1 OBSERVERS AND PROCEDURE

P1.1 The protest committee may appoint observers, including protest committee members, to act in accordance with rule P1.2. A person with a significant *conflict of interest* shall not be appointed as an observer.

P1.2 An observer appointed under rule P1.1 who sees a boat breaking rule 42 may penalize her by, as soon as reasonably possible, making a sound signal, pointing a yellow flag at her and hailing her sail number, even if she is no longer *racing*. A boat so penalized shall not be penalized a second time under rule 42 for the same incident.

P2   PENALTIES

P2.1 First Penalty

When a boat is first penalized under rule P1.2 her penalty shall be a Two-Turns Penalty under rule 44.2. If she fails to take it she shall be disqualified without a hearing.

P2.2 Second Penalty

When a boat is penalized a second time during the regatta, she shall promptly retire. If she fails to do so she shall be disqualified without a hearing and her score shall not be excluded.

P2.3 Third and Subsequent Penalties

When a boat is penalized a third or subsequent time during the regatta, she shall promptly retire. If she does so her penalty shall be disqualification without a hearing and her score shall not be excluded. If she fails to do so her penalty shall be disqualification without a hearing from all races in the regatta, with no score excluded, and the protest committee shall consider calling a hearing under rule 69.2.

P2.4 Penalties Near the Finishing Line

If a boat is penalized under rule P2.2 or P2.3 and it was not reasonably possible for her to retire before *finishing*, she shall be scored as if she had retired promptly.

P3   POSTPONEMENT, GENERAL RECALL OR ABANDONMENT

If a boat has been penalized under rule P1.2 and the race committee signals a *postponement*, general recall or *abandonment*, the penalty is cancelled, but it is still counted to determine the number of times she has been penalized during the regatta.

P4   REDRESS LIMITATION

A boat shall not be given redress for an action by a member of the protest committee or its designated observer under rule P1.2 unless the action was improper due to a failure to take into account a race committee signal or a class rule.

P5   FLAGS O AND R

P5.1 When Rule P5 Applies

Rule P5 applies if the class rules permit pumping, rocking and ooching when the wind speed exceeds a specified limit.

P5.2 Before the Starting Signal

(a) The race committee may signal that pumping, rocking and ooching are permitted, as specified in the class rules, by displaying flag O before or with the warning signal.

(b) If the wind speed becomes less than the specified limit after flag O has been displayed, the race committee may *postpone* the race. Then, before or with a new warning signal, the committee shall display either flag R, to signal that rule 42 as changed by the class rules applies, or flag O, as provided in rule P5.2(a).

(c) If flag O or flag R is displayed before or with the warning signal, it shall be displayed until the starting signal.

P5.3 After the Starting Signal

After the starting signal,

(a) if the wind speed exceeds the specified limit, the race committee may display flag O with repetitive sounds at a *mark* to signal that pumping, rocking and ooching are permitted, as specified in the class rules, after passing the *mark*;

(b) if flag O has been displayed and the wind speed becomes less than the specified limit, the race committee may display flag R with repetitive sounds at a *mark* to signal that rule 42, as changed by the class rules, applies after passing the *mark*.

APPENDIX R

PROCEDURES FOR APPEALS AND REQUESTS

See rule 70. A national authority may change this appendix by prescription but it shall not be changed by sailing instructions.

R1   APPEALS AND REQUESTS

Appeals, requests by protest committees for confirmation or correction of their decisions, and requests for interpretations of the *rules* shall be made in compliance with this appendix.

R2   SUBMISSION OF DOCUMENTS

R2.1 To make an appeal,

(a) no later than 15 days after receiving the protest committee's written decision or its decision not to reopen a hearing, the appellant shall send an appeal and a copy of the protest committee's decision to the national authority. The appeal shall state why the appellant believes the protest committee's decision or its procedures were incorrect;

(b) when the hearing required by rule 63.1 has not been held within 30 days after a *protest* or request for redress was delivered, the appellant shall, within a further 15 days, send an appeal with a copy of the *protest* or request and any relevant correspondence. The national authority shall extend the time if there is good reason to do so;

(c) when the protest committee fails to comply with rule 65, the appellant shall, within a reasonable time after the hearing, send an appeal with a copy of the *protest* or request and any relevant correspondence.

If a copy of the *protest* or request is not available, the appellant shall instead send a statement of its substance.

R2.2 The appellant shall also send, with the appeal or as soon as possible thereafter, all of the following documents that are available to her:

(a) the written *protest(s)* or request(s) for redress;

(b) a diagram, prepared or endorsed by the protest committee, showing the positions and tracks of all boats involved, the course to the next *mark* and the required side, the force and direction of the wind, and, if relevant, the depth of water and direction and speed of any current;

(c) the notice of race, the sailing instructions, any other conditions governing the event, and any changes to them;

(d) any additional relevant documents; and

(e) the names, postal and email addresses, and telephone numbers of all *parties* to the hearing and the protest committee chairman.

R2.3 A request from a protest committee for confirmation or correction of its decision shall be sent no later than 15 days after the decision and shall include the decision and the documents listed in rule R2.2. A request for an interpretation of the *rules* shall include assumed facts.

R3   RESPONSIBILITIES OF NATIONAL AUTHORITY AND PROTEST COMMITTEE

Upon receipt of an appeal or a request for confirmation or correction, the national authority shall send to the *parties* and protest committee copies of the appeal or request and the protest committee's decision. It shall ask the protest committee for any relevant documents listed in rule R2.2 not sent by the appellant or the protest committee, and the protest committee shall promptly send them to the national authority. When the national authority has received them it shall send copies to the *parties*.

R4   COMMENTS AND CLARIFICATIONS

R4.1 The *parties* and protest committee may make comments on the appeal or request or on any of the documents listed in rule R2.2 by sending them in writing to the national authority.

R4.2 The national authority may seek clarifications of *rules* governing the event from organizations that are not *parties* to the hearing.

R4.3 The national authority shall send copies of comments and clarifications received to the *parties* and protest committee as appropriate.

R4.4 Comments on any document shall be made no later than 15 days after receiving it from the national authority.

R5   INADEQUATE FACTS; REOPENING

The national authority shall accept the protest committee's finding of facts except when it decides they are inadequate. In that case it shall require the committee to provide additional facts or other information, or to reopen the hearing and report any new finding of facts, and the committee shall promptly do so.

R6   WITHDRAWING AN APPEAL

An appellant may withdraw an appeal before it is decided by accepting the protest committee's decision.

APPENDIX S
STANDARD SAILING INSTRUCTIONS

This appendix applies only if the notice of race so states.

These Standard Sailing Instructions may be used at an event in place of printed sailing instructions made available to each boat. To use them, state in the notice of race that 'The sailing instructions will consist of the instructions in RRS Appendix S, Standard Sailing Instructions, and supplementary sailing instructions that will be on the official notice board located at _____.'

The supplementary sailing instructions will include:

1. A table showing the schedule of races, including the day and date of each scheduled day of racing, the number of races scheduled each day, the scheduled time of the first warning signal each day, and the latest time for a warning signal on the last scheduled day of racing (see SI 5 below).

2. The location of the race office and of the flag pole on which signals made ashore will be displayed (SI 4.1).

3. A list of the marks that will be used and a description of each one (SI 8). How new marks will differ from original marks (SI 10).

4. The time limits, if any, that are listed in SI 12.

5. Any changes or additions to the instructions in this appendix.

A copy of the supplementary sailing instructions will be available to competitors on request.

SAILING INSTRUCTIONS

1   RULES

1.1 The regatta will be governed by the rules as defined in *The Racing Rules of Sailing*.

2   NOTICES TO COMPETITORS

2.1 Notices to competitors will be posted on the official notice board.

2.2 Supplementary sailing instructions (called 'the supplement' below) will be posted on the official notice board.

3   CHANGES TO SAILING INSTRUCTIONS

3.1 Any change to the sailing instructions will be posted before 0800 on the day it will take effect, except that any change to the schedule of races will be posted by 2000 on the day before it will take effect.

4   SIGNALS MADE ASHORE

4.1 Signals made ashore will be displayed from the flag pole. The supplement will state its location.

4.2 When flag AP is displayed ashore, '1 minute' is replaced with 'not less than 60 minutes' in the race signal AP.

5   SCHEDULE OF RACES

5.1 The supplement will include a table showing the days, dates, number of races scheduled, the scheduled times of the first warning signal each day, and the latest time for a warning signal on the last scheduled day of racing.

6   CLASS FLAGS

6.1 Each class flag will be the class insignia on a white background or as stated in the supplement.

7   THE COURSES

7.1 No later than the warning signal, the race committee will designate the course by displaying one or two letters followed by a number, and it may also display the approximate compass bearing of the first leg.

7.2 The course diagrams are on the pages following SI 13. They show the courses, the order in which marks are to be passed, and the side on which each mark is to be left. The supplement may include additional courses.

8   MARKS

8.1 A list of the marks that will be used, including a description of each one, will be included in the supplement.

9   THE START

9.1 Races will be started by using RRS 26.

9.2 The starting line will be between a staff displaying an orange flag on the race committee vessel and the course side of the starting mark.

10   CHANGE OF THE NEXT LEG OF THE COURSE

10.1 To change the next leg of the course, the race committee will lay a new mark (or move the finishing line) and remove the original mark as soon as practicable. When in a subsequent change a new mark is replaced, it will be replaced by an original mark.

11   THE FINISH

11.1 The finishing line will be between a staff displaying an orange flag on the race committee vessel and the course side of the finishing mark.

12   TIME LIMITS

12.1 The supplement will state which of the following time limits, if any, will apply and, for each, the time limit.

- Mark 1 Time Limit   Time limit for the first boat to pass Mark 1.

- Race Time Limit   Time limit for the first boat to sail the course and finish.

- Finishing Window   Time limit for boats to finish after the first boat sails the course and finishes.

12.2 If no boat has passed Mark 1 within the Mark 1 Time Limit, the race shall be abandoned.

12.3 Boats failing to finish within the Finishing Window shall be scored Did Not Finish without a hearing. This changes RRS 35, A4 and A5.

13   PROTESTS AND REQUESTS FOR REDRESS

13.1 Protest forms are available at the race office. Protests and requests for redress or reopening shall be delivered there within the appropriate time limit.

13.2 For each class, the protest time limit is 60 minutes after the last boat has finished the last race of the day or the race committee signals no more racing today, which ever is later.

13.3 Notices will be posted no later than 30 minutes after the protest time limit to inform competitors of hearings in which they are parties or named as witnesses and where the hearings will be held.

13.4 Notices of protests by the race committee, technical committee or protest committee will be posted to inform boats under RRS 61.1(b).

13.5 On the last scheduled day of racing a request for redress based on a protest committee decision shall be delivered no later than 30 minutes after the decision was posted. This changes RRS 62.2.

COURSE DIAGRAMS

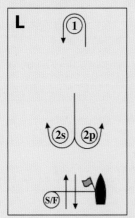

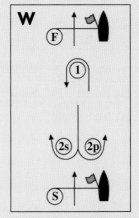

Course L – Windward/Leeward, Leeward Finish	
Signal	*Mark Rounding Order*
L2	Start – 1 – 2s/2p – 1 – Finish
L3	Start – 1 – 2s/2p – 1 – 2s/2p – 1 – Finish
L4	Start – 1 – 2s/2p – 1 – 2s/2p – 1 – 2s/2p – 1 – Finish

Course W – Windward/Leeward, Windward Finish	
Signal	*Mark Rounding Order*
W2	Start – 1 – 2s/2p – Finish
W3	Start – 1 – 2s/2p – 1 – 2s/2p – Finish
W4	Start – 1 – 2s/2p – 1 – 2s/2p – 1 – 2s/2p – Finish

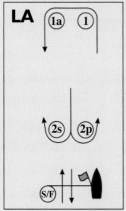

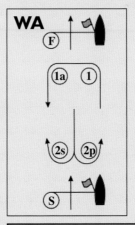

Course LA – Windward/Leeward with Offset Mark, Leeward Finish	
Signal	*Mark Rounding Order*
LA2	Start – 1 – 1a – 2s/2p – 1 – 1a – Finish
LA3	Start – 1 – 1a – 2s/2p – 1 – 1a – 2s/2p – 1 – 1a – Finish
LA4	Start – 1 – 1a – 2s/2p – 1 – 1a – 2s/2p – 1 – 1a – 2s/2p – 1 – 1a – Finish

Course WA – Windward/Leeward with Offset Mark, Windward Finish	
Signal	*Mark Rounding Order*
WA2	Start – 1 – 1a – 2s/2p – Finish
WA3	Start – 1 – 1a – 2s/2p – 1 – 1a – 2s/2p – Finish
WA4	Start – 1 – 1a – 2s/2p – 1 – 1a – 2s/2p – 1 – 1a – 2s/2p – Finish

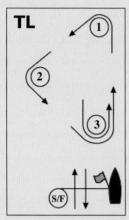

Course TL – Triangle, Leeward Finish	
Signal	*Mark Rounding Order*
TL2	Start – 1 – 2 – 3 – 1 – Finish
TL3	Start – 1 – 2 – 3 – 1 – 3 – 1 – Finish
TL4	Start – 1 – 2 – 3 – 1 – 3 – 1 – 3 – 1 – Finish

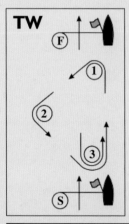

Course TW – Triangle, Windward Finish	
Signal	*Mark Rounding Order*
TW2	Start – 1 – 2 – 3 – Finish
TW3	Start – 1 – 2 – 3 – 1 – 3 – Finish
TW4	Start – 1 – 2 – 3 – 1 – 3 – 1 – 3 – Finish

APPENDIX T

ARBITRATION

This appendix applies only if the notice of race or sailing instructions so state.

Arbitration adds an extra step to the protest resolution process but can eliminate the need for some protest hearings, thus speeding up the process for events in which many protests are expected. Arbitration may not be appropriate for all events as it requires an additional knowledgeable person to act as the arbitrator. Further guidance on arbitration can be found in the World Sailing International Judges Manual, which can be downloaded from the World Sailing website.

T1   POST-RACE PENALTIES

(a)   Provided that rule 44.1(b) does not apply, a boat that may have broken one or more rules of Part 2 or rule 31 in an incident may take a Post-Race Penalty at any time after the race until the beginning of a protest hearing involving the incident.

(b)   A Post-Race Penalty is a 30% Scoring Penalty calculated as stated in rule 44.3(c). However, rule 44.1(a) applies.

(c)   A boat takes a Post-Race Penalty by delivering to the arbitrator or a member of the protest committee a written statement that she accepts the penalty and that identifies the race number and where and when the incident occurred.

T2   ARBITRATION MEETING

An arbitration meeting will be held prior to a protest hearing for each incident resulting in a *protest* by a boat involving one or more rules of Part 2 or rule 31, but only if each *party* is represented by a person who was on board at the time of the incident. No witnesses will be permitted. However, if the arbitrator decides that rule 44.1(b) may apply or that arbitration is not appropriate, the meeting will not be held, and if a meeting is in progress, it will be closed.

T3   ARBITRATOR'S OPINION

Based on the evidence given by the representatives, the arbitrator will offer an opinion as to what the protest committee is likely to decide:

(a)   the *protest* is invalid,

(b)   no boat will be penalized for breaking a rule, or

(c)   one or more boats will be penalized for breaking a rule, identifying the boats and the penalties.

T4   ARBITRATION MEETING OUTCOMES

After the arbitrator offers an opinion,

(a)   a boat may take a Post-Race Penalty, and

(b)   a boat may ask to withdraw her *protest*. The arbitrator may then act on behalf of the protest committee in accordance with rule 63.1 to allow the withdrawal.

Unless all *protests* involving the incident are withdrawn, a protest hearing will be held.